DK Pocket Genius

ANCIENT EGYPT

FACTS AT YOUR FINGERTIPS

LONDON, NEW YORK, MUNICH,
MELBOURNE, and DELHI

DK DELHI
Project editor Virien Chopra
Art editors Vikas Chauhan, Pooja Pawwar
Senior editor Samira Sood
Senior art editor Govind Mittal
Assistant editor Jubbi Francis
DTP designers Arvind Kumar,
Jaypal Singh Chauhan
Picture researcher Sumedha Chopra
Managing editor Saloni Talwar
Managing art editor Romi Chakraborty
CTS manager Balwant Singh
Production manager Pankaj Sharma

DK LONDON
Senior editor Rob Houston
Senior art editor Philip Letsu
US editor Margaret Parrish
Jacket editor Manisha Majithia
Jacket designer Laura Brim
Jacket manager Amanda Lunn
Production editor Rebekah Parsons-King
Production controller Mary Slater

Publisher Andrew Macintyre
Associate publishing director Liz Wheeler
Art director Phil Ormerod
Publishing director Jonathan Metcalf

Consultant John Haywood

TALL TREE LTD.
Editors Rob Colson, Joe Fullman, Jon Richards
Art editor Ed Simkins

First published in the United States in 2012
by DK Publishing
375 Hudson Street, New York, New York 10014

Copyright © 2012 Dorling Kindersley Limited

12 13 14 15 16 10 9 8 7 6 5 4 3 2 1
001–184270–Nov/12

A catalog record for this book
is available from the Library of Congress.

ISBN: 978-0-7566-9813-3

Printed and bound by South China
Printing Company, China

**Discover more at
www.dk.com**

CONTENTS

Scales and sizes
This book contains profiles of Egyptian buildings, monuments, and artifacts, with scale drawings to indicate their size.

1,000 ft
(304.8 m)

6 ft
(1.8 m)

6 in
(15 cm)

Geo-locator
The location of a temple is marked as a red dot on this map of Egypt.

Gold bracelet of Sheshonq II

The Nile River

For 5,000 years, the Nile River has been the focus of Egyptian life. The many cities and monuments of ancient Egypt, shown below, were all built along the banks of the river, the main source of water in this arid region.

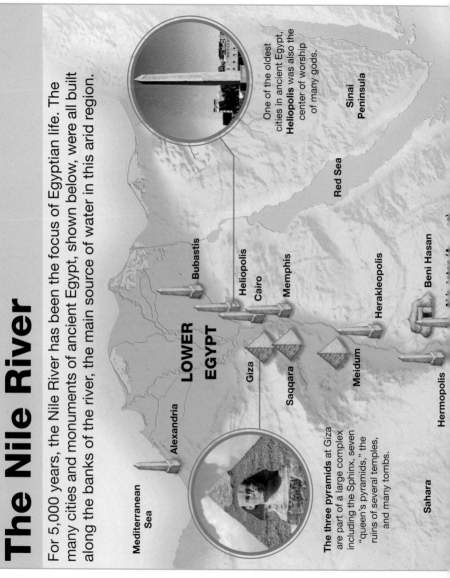

One of the oldest cities in ancient Egypt, **Heliopolis** was also the center of worship of many gods.

The three pyramids at Giza are part of a large complex including the Sphinx, seven "queen's pyramids," the ruins of several temples, and many tombs.

Mediterranean Sea

Alexandria

Bubastis

Heliopolis

Cairo

Memphis

LOWER EGYPT

Giza

Saqqara

Meidum

Herakleopolis

Beni Hasan

Hermopolis

Sahara

Red Sea

Sinai Peninsula

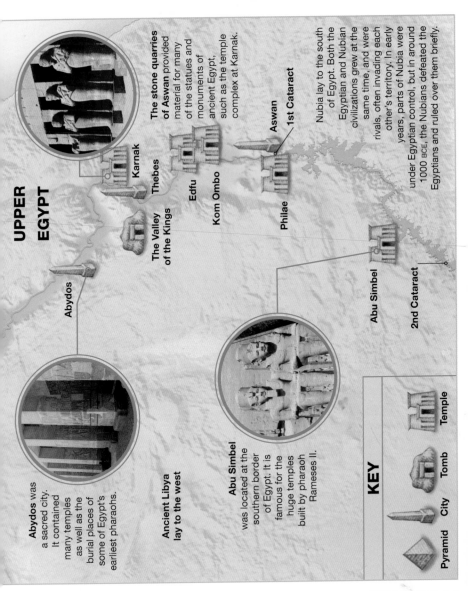

UPPER EGYPT

Abydos was a sacred city. It contained many temples as well as the burial places of some of Egypt's earliest pharaohs.

Ancient Libya lay to the west

Abu Simbel was located at the southern border of Egypt. It is famous for the huge temples built by pharaoh Rameses II.

The stone quarries of Aswan provided material for many of the statues and monuments of ancient Egypt, such as the temple complex at Karnak.

Nubia lay to the south of Egypt. Both the Egyptian and Nubian civilizations grew at the same time, and were rivals, often invading each other's territory. In early years, parts of Nubia were under Egyptian control, but in around 1000 BCE, the Nubians defeated the Egyptians and ruled over them briefly.

Abydos

Karnak

Thebes

The Valley of the Kings

Edfu

Kom Ombo

Aswan

1st Cataract

Philae

Abu Simbel

2nd Cataract

KEY

Pyramid   City   Tomb   Temple

History of ancient Egypt

"Ancient Egypt" is the period between about 3500 BCE and 30 BCE, when Egypt was ruled by dynasties of pharaohs. Historians divide this stretch of time into three main periods of prosperity—the Old, Middle, and New Kingdoms. The periods in between and after the kingdoms were times of unrest.

Pre-dynastic Period

People began farming in the Nile Valley in about 5000 BCE. They founded settlements next to their farms, which slowly grew into two kingdoms—Upper and Lower Egypt.

Ram-shaped palette used to grind cosmetic powders

3500 BCE	3250 BCE	3000 BCE	2750 BCE
Pre-dynastic Period		Early Dynastic Period	

Early Dynastic Period

Around 3100 BCE, Upper and Lower Egypt were unified under one rule. The first ruler of the I Dynasty was Hor-Aha. In this later painting the god Horus wears the Pschent, or double crown. It symbolized the unification of Egypt.

Tomb model of
beer-brewing,
c.2160 BCE

First Intermediate Period

During this period, power was divided between the 9th and 10th Dynasties, which ruled Lower Egypt from Herakleopolis, and the 11th Dynasty, which ruled Upper Egypt from Thebes.

Middle Kingdom

In 2055 BCE, Egypt was reunited by Mentuhotep, a pharaoh of the 11th Dynasty, who founded the Middle Kingdom. Pharaohs in this period were strong rulers who expanded the borders of Egypt into ancient Libya and Nubia. New art forms, representing common people instead of royalty, such as this statue, also developed.

2500 BCE	2250 BCE		2000 BCE	1750 BCE
Old Kingdom	First Intermediate Period		Middle Kingdom	

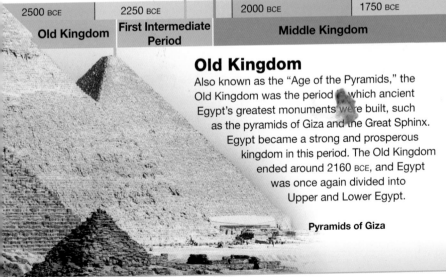

Old Kingdom

Also known as the "Age of the Pyramids," the Old Kingdom was the period in which ancient Egypt's greatest monuments were built, such as the pyramids of Giza and the Great Sphinx. Egypt became a strong and prosperous kingdom in this period. The Old Kingdom ended around 2160 BCE, and Egypt was once again divided into Upper and Lower Egypt.

Pyramids of Giza

Second Intermediate Period

During this period, Egypt was invaded by the Hyksos people from Asia who established the 15th and 16th Dynasties. They were defeated by the 17th Dynasty pharaoh, Seqenenra Taa, and his sons Ahmose and Kamose.

Nubian pyramid, built around 700–300 BCE

Boat-shaped offering to Kahmose, from around 1550 BCE

1750 BCE	1500 BCE	1250 BCE	1000 BCE
Second Intermediate Period	New Kingdom		Third Intermediate Period

New Kingdom

Lasting from 1550–1086 BCE, the New Kingdom is considered to be the greatest period in the history of ancient Egypt. Strong rulers, such as Ahmose I and Thutmose III, expanded the kingdom into Nubia, ancient Libya, and the Middle East. This time also saw the construction of numerous temples and monuments by pharaohs, most notably by Rameses II.

Pectoral of Rameses II, from around 1200 BCE

hird Intermediate Period

 this 400-year-long period, Egypt was
st conquered by the ancient Libyans, who
stablished the 22nd Dynasty, and later by
e Nubians, who began the 25th Dynasty.

Ptolemaic Period

With the death of Alexander, the rule of
Egypt passed to Ptolemy I Soter, who
established the Greek Ptolemaic Dynasty.
During this time, Egypt was under threat
from Rome, and its last
pharaoh, Cleopatra
VII, spent her
life trying to
make sure that
Egypt remained
independent.

**According to
ancient Egyptian
tradition, Cleopatra
VII was often
shown as a king**

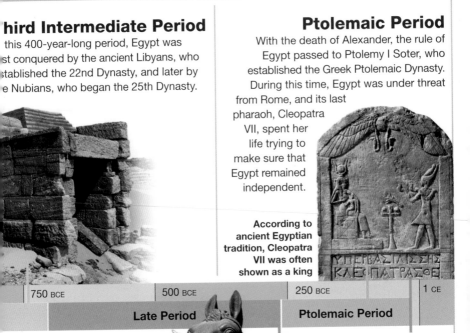

750 BCE	500 BCE	250 BCE	1 CE
	Late Period	**Ptolemaic Period**	

ate Period

he Late Period was the time
etween the Third Intermediate
eriod and Greek rule. The Nubian
haraohs were defeated by the
ssyrian Empire, which ruled Egypt
efore Egyptian pharaohs established
he 26th Dynasty. Egypt was then
vaded by the Persian Empire in
25 BCE, which began the 27th Dynasty.
our more dynasties ruled Egypt before
 was conquered by Alexander the
reat, king of Macedon in Greece.

**After Cleopatra's
death** in 30 BCE,
Egypt fell under
the rule of a number
of foreign powers
and did not gain
independence
until 1922, when
it became the
Republic of Egypt.

**Statue of Alexander
the Great**

Writing

Reading and writing were important skills in ancient Egypt. Scribes—official record-keepers—were among the few people who could read and write, and they held high positions in society. Royal scribes often advised pharaohs, helping them create laws.

Writing tools

Instead of paper, Egyptians used papyrus, which was made from a reedlike plant that grew on the banks of the Nile River. The plant's stem was cut into thin strips, which were pressed together to make sheets. Writing brushes were also made from reeds that grew on the banks of the river.

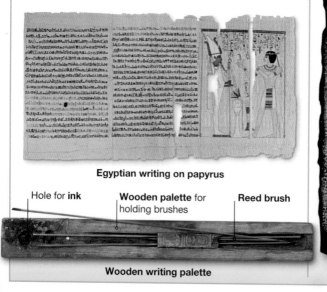

Egyptian writing on papyrus

Hole for **ink**   **Wooden palette** for holding brushes   **Reed brush**

Wooden writing palette

Hieroglyphics was a writing system in which sounds, objects, and ideas were represented by pictures called hieroglyphs. It was used on tombs and monuments, and in religious texts.

The demotic script was simpler and quicker to use than hieroglyphics. It was used for legal documents.

The Greek script became popular in the Ptolemaic Period. It is the source of many modern alphabets.

Rosetta Stone

The Egyptians wrote in different ways, using hieroglyphs in formal situations and the demotic script for daily use. However, the ability to read these scripts was lost for nearly 1,500 years. Then, in 1799, the Rosetta Stone was found, on which the same text was written in three different scripts—hieroglyphic, demotic, and Greek. By reading the Greek script, archeologists could translate the other two and so decipher these ancient writing symbols.

Warfare

Wars in ancient Egypt were fought mainly for territory. Some, such as Thutmose III's campaigns in Nubia, were fought to extend Egypt borders, while others were fought to protect Egyptian territory from invaders, such as the Hyksos and the Hittites.

Model of Egyptian spearmen from 11th–12th Dynasties, 2040–1780 BCE

Soldiers

In the Old Kingdom, the Egyptian army consisted of soldiers who were only recruited when a war started. By the time of the New Kingdom, however, the Egyptian armed forces were made up of full-time soldiers, including spearmen, archers, and charioteers.

Chariots

When the Hyksos invaded Egypt in the 15th century BCE, they used horse-drawn chariots that allowed them to move quickly in battle. The Egyptian pharaohs saw the advantages of these vehicles and added them to their armies.

Weapons

Egyptian soldiers used axes, swords, spears, and bows and arrows. Axes and swords were used in hand-to-hand combat, while spears and bows and arrows could be used by infantry—soldiers on foot—and by charioteers.

Small-bladed ax

Long-bladed ax

Short sword

Medals

A soldier who performed well in combat was awarded medals in the shape of flies. Worn around the neck, these medals meant that the soldier had repeatedly "stung" the enemy.

Tutankhamun riding a chariot into battle

The Nubians were first hired by Egyptian armies as temporary soldiers, but later became an

elite fighting force

MEDJAY

The word "Medjay" was first used to refer to people living in Medja, a part of Nubia. After they became part of the Egyptian armies, the Medjay were used as scouts for patrolling the desert. Over time, they became a policing force, in charge of protecting the royal palace and tombs. This model of Medjay soldiers was found in a tomb from the 11th–12th Dynasties.

Ancient Egyptians

Egyptian society was shaped like a pyramid. The pharaoh and his queen were at the top. Below them, the nobles, chief priests, head scribes, ministers, and army officers formed an upper class. Artisans and traders made up the middle layer, while laborers and farmers formed the base. The pharaoh made all the major decisions—in administrative and political matters, and in religious rituals. The image on the left shows Pharaoh Tutankhamun with his queen, Ankhesenamun.

CARTOUCHE
A cartouche is an oval border around hieroglyphs that spell out a pharaoh's name. The hieroglyphs inside this cartouche spell out the name of Ramesses II.

Royal life

The Egyptians believed their pharaoh was a living god and his queen was a goddess. Nobles and important officials of the court were called "friends of the pharaoh" and lived in the palace along with the royal family. They helped the pharaoh to rule the kingdom.

Social pyramid

At the top of Egyptian society was the pharaoh. He commanded the army and ruled the country through a network of nobles, officials, and scribes. Craftworkers were kept busy building and decorating tombs and temples, but most Egyptians were peasants who worked as farmers.

Nemes headdress represented the king as a sphinx or a falcon, both of which were symbols of the god Horus

The pharaoh was the most powerful person in the entire kingdom.

Flail and crook, symbols of the pharaoh's power

Tutankhamun's sarcophagus

Scribes, priests, and noblemen formed the upper class.

Skilled craftworkers, such as sculptors, belonged to the middle class.

Unskilled workers, such as farmers and fishermen, made up the lowest class.

Power of the pharaoh

A pharaoh had many names and titles, all of which indicated his status and power. The first was the *nomen*, the name given to him at birth. After he came to the throne, he took another name—the *praenomen*. For example, Thutmose III's *nomen* was Thutmose Neferkheperu, while his *praenomen* was Menkheperre. Other titles included the *Nebty* name, which signified that the pharaoh was lord of both Upper and Lower Egypt. A pharaoh's regalia—his ornaments and dress— were also symbols of his power.

Nefertiti, queen of Akhenaten

Queens

Pharaohs had many wives, but only the one who held the title of "great royal wife" ruled beside him as his queen.

Senites, Seneb's wife

Seneb

Noblemen

Important noblemen and officials had titles like "Fanbearer on the Right of the King" and "Master of the Horse." This is a statue of Seneb, an Egyptian nobleman who held 20 titles, including "Beloved of the King."

Radjedef-Ankh, Seneb's son

FOCUS ON...
REGALIA
Each object of a
pharaoh's regalia
had a special
significance.

▲ The uraeus represented
the goddess Wadjet as
well as the divine authority
of the pharaoh.

▲ The flail and crook
represented the pharaoh's
role as the provider and
shepherd of his people.

▲ The pschent, or the
double crown, meant
that the pharaoh had
power over all Egypt.

Royals and nobles

Pharaohs were the supreme rulers of ancient
Egypt. Their names, clothes, and regalia
were all symbolic of their power. Mayors,
tax collectors, and army generals helped
and advised the pharaoh on political and
administrative matters.

Djoser

Djoser is best known as the
first Egyptian ruler to have a
pyramid built for himself—the
Step Pyramid at Saqqara.
During his reign, he managed
to extend the boundaries of
his kingdom to the Sinai
Peninsula in the east and
Aswan in the south.

POSITION Pharaoh
PERIOD Old Kingdom
DYNASTY 3rd Dynasty
RULED 2667–2648 BCE

Imhotep

A leading scholar of his time, Imhotep held a number of positions under Djoser, including chief treasurer, chief scribe, and high priest of the Sun god. He designed and supervised the building of the Step Pyramid. He also wrote many books on architecture and medicine. Pictures and statues of Imhotep often show him seated with a papyrus spread across his knees.

POSITION	Treasurer
PERIOD	Old Kingdom
DYNASTY	3rd Dynasty
LIVED	2650–2600 BCE

After his death, Imhotep became associated with unlimited wisdom, and was worshiped as a god.

Khufu

The second pharaoh of the 4th Dynasty, Khufu came to the throne after the death of his father Sneferu. Khufu is remembered as the builder of the Great Pyramid of Giza, one of the wonders of the ancient world. The Greek historian Herodotus called him a wicked tyrant who built his pyramid using slave labor, but it is now known that the pyramid was built by craftworkers, who were well paid for their skills.

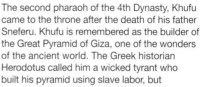

POSITION	Pharaoh
PERIOD	Old Kingdom
DYNASTY	4th Dynasty
RULED	2589–2566 BCE

Khafra

Khafra was the successor to Pharaoh Khufu. Egypt prospered under his reign, and there is evidence of trade with cities in other lands, such as Byblos in present-day Lebanon and Ebla in present-day Syria. This statue shows the god Horus as a falcon perched on Khafra's shoulders, protecting him.

POSITION	Pharaoh
PERIOD	Old Kingdom
DYNASTY	4th Dynasty
RULED	2558–2532 BCE

Userkaf

The founder of the 5th Dynasty, Userkaf began a tradition of building Sun temples at Abusir. This bust of Userkaf is the earliest statue of an Old Kingdom pharaoh wearing the deshret, or red crown, of Lower Egypt.

POSITION	Pharaoh
PERIOD	Old Kingdom
DYNASTY	5th Dynasty
RULED	2494–2487 BCE

Nyuserra

The name Nyuserra means "possessed of Ra's power." Nyuserra built the largest Sun temple for Ra, the Sun god, in Egypt, at Abusir. This twin statue shows him as a young and an old man.

Raneferef

Raneferef was in charge of all the artists and sculptors working for pharaohs Shepseskaf and Userkaf. He used his position to build a large tomb for himself at Saqqara, which contains two life-sized statues of him.

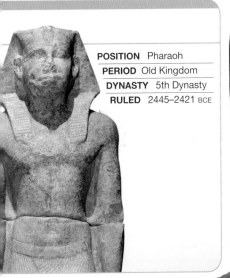

POSITION High Priest of Ptah

PERIOD Old Kingdom

DYNASTY 5th Dynasty

LIVED 2500–2465 BCE

POSITION Pharaoh

PERIOD Old Kingdom

DYNASTY 5th Dynasty

RULED 2445–2421 BCE

Menkaura

Khafra's son Menkaura was known as a fair ruler. He made it a law that the children of his officials would be taught along with the royal children. His officials' tombs have numerous inscriptions about his generosity.

POSITION Pharaoh

PERIOD Old Kingdom

DYNASTY 4th Dynasty

RULED 2532–2503 BCE

Mentuhotep II

During the First Intermediate Period, Egypt was divided into a number of different kingdoms. Mentuhotep II, the fifth pharaoh of the 11th Dynasty, brought Egypt under one rule and became the first pharaoh of the Middle Kingdom.

POSITION	Pharaoh
PERIOD	Middle Kingdom
DYNASTY	11th Dynasty
RULED	2055–2004 BCE

Painted limestone statue of Mentuhotep II

Amenemhat I

Double statue of Amenemhat I as a Nile god

Amenemhat I was the minister to Mentuhotep IV, the last ruler of the 11th Dynasty. After the pharaoh died, Amenemhat I took the throne and began the 12th Dynasty. To make sure that his dynasty continued to rule after he died, he made his son, Senusret I, his co-ruler. This system of co-regency was followed by all of his successors.

POSITION	Pharaoh
PERIOD	Middle Kingdom
DYNASTY	12th Dynasty
RULED	1985–1956 BCE

Senusret I

In 1971 BCE, Senusret I was made co-regent by his father, Amenemhat I. He took over the army, and fought to extend Egypt's control over Nubia. In 1962 BCE, his father was killed by his courtiers, who objected to his rule. Leaving his army, Senusret I rushed back to the capital to take the throne. Once crowned, he continued his father's work of expanding Egypt's borders by conquering Nubia.

POSITION	Pharaoh
PERIOD	Middle Kingdom
DYNASTY	12th Dynasty
RULED	1971–1926 BCE

Amenemhat II

For a brief period, Amenemhat II was a co-regent with his father Senusret I. During this time, he led a gold-mining expedition to Nubia. Treasures from his reign also include objects from Mesopotamia (in present-day Iraq) and Crete, suggesting that trade was well developed at this time.

POSITION	Pharaoh
PERIOD	Middle Kingdom
DYNASTY	12th Dynasty
RULED	1929–1895 BCE

Senusret III

Known for his military expeditions, Senusret III further expanded Egyptian rule over Nubia. He built a network of forts to keep watch along the southern border. He also built a canal through the Nile cataract at Elephantine, making it easier for ships to sail up the river.

POSITION	Pharaoh
PERIOD	Middle Kingdom
DYNASTY	12th Dynasty
RULED	1870–1831 BCE

Tetisheri

The wife of the 17th Dynasty pharaoh, Senakhtenre, Queen Tetisheri held an important place at the court. She was a valued adviser to her son Seqenenra Taa and her grandsons Kamose and Ahmose, who began the 18th Dynasty. After her death, a cenotaph—or monument—was erected at Abydos in her honor.

Because of her strong influence on her son and grandsons, modern scholars call Tetisheri the "Mother of the New Kingdom."

POSITION	Queen and Queen Mother
PERIOD	Second Intermediate Period
DYNASTY	17th–18th Dynasty
LIVED	1560–1525 BCE

Hatshepsut

One of the few women to rule Egypt, Hatshepsut was first appointed as regent for her stepson Thutmose III, who was too young to rule. In 1473 BCE, she declared herself pharaoh and began a prosperous reign that lasted 15 years.

POSITION	Pharaoh
PERIOD	New Kingdom
DYNASTY	18th Dynasty
RULED	1473–1458 BCE

Seqenenra Taa

When Seqenenra Taa came to the throne, most of Egypt was ruled by the Hyksos, warriors from Asia. Seqenenra Taa began fighting the Hyksos to free Egypt from their control. He was killed in battle, but his sons, Kamose and Ahmose, continued the war, defeating the Hyksos invaders and beginning the New Kingdom period.

POSITION	Pharaoh
PERIOD	Second Intermediate Period
DYNASTY	17th Dynasty
RULED	1558–1555 BCE

Senenmut

A powerful official during the reign of Hatshepsut, Senenmut took on many roles. He was the teacher of the pharaoh's children, the architect of Hatshepsut's temple, and her close adviser.

POSITION	Architect
PERIOD	New Kingdom
DYNASTY	18th Dynasty
IN OFFICE	1473–1458 BCE

Thutmose III

One of the greatest military rulers of ancient Egypt, Thutmose III conducted 17 military campaigns and conquered around 350 cities during his reign. He built a number of temples and monuments, such as the Temple of Amun at Karnak.

POSITION	Pharaoh
PERIOD	New Kingdom
DYNASTY	18th Dynasty
RULED	1479–1425 BCE

Stab wound on head of Seqenenra's mummy

URAEI
Part of a pharaoh's regalia, a uraeus was a cobra-shaped object associated with the snake-headed goddess, Wadjet. These uraei on Pharaoh Tutankhamun's throne have Sun disks on their heads. The Sun and uraeus represented the divine authority of the pharaoh.

According to Egyptian belief, the uraei protected the pharaoh by **spitting fire** at his enemies

Amenhotep II

The son of Thutmose III, Amenhotep II continued his father's campaigns. He was a skilled warrior and led his armies as far as the Sea of Galilee in present-day Israel.

POSITION Pharaoh
PERIOD New Kingdom
DYNASTY 18th Dynasty
RULED 1427–1400 BCE

Sennefer

The Mayor of Thebes, Sennefer served during the reign of Amenhotep II. He was a favorite of the pharaoh, and this helped him to become very wealthy.

POSITION Mayor of Thebes
PERIOD New Kingdom
DYNASTY 18th Dynasty
IN OFFICE 1427–1400 BCE

Akhenaten

For the first five years of his reign, Akhenaten was known as Amenhotep IV. He changed his name to Akhenaten, which means "living spirit of Aten," when he began worshiping the Sun god Aten. Akhenaten forbade the worship of all other gods, which made him very unpopular among the common people. He also began construction of a new capital city called Akhetaten at Amarna, an area that was not associated with any of the old gods. However, the city was abandoned soon after his death.

POSITION Pharaoh
PERIOD New Kingdom
DYNASTY 18th Dynasty
RULED 1352–1336 BCE

Nefertiti

Believed to have ruled Egypt along with her husband Akhenaten, Nefertiti vanished in the 14th year of his reign. No one knows what happened to her, but this bust, found at Akhetaten, gives an idea of the beauty for which she was famous. In fact, her name Nefertiti means "a beautiful woman has come."

Flat-topped crown decorated with ribbon

Instead of paintings of goddesses, Akhenaten had images of Nefertiti painted on the four sides of his sarcophagus.

POSITION	Great Royal Wife
PERIOD	New Kingdom
DYNASTY	18th Dynasty
LIVED	1370–1338 BCE

Tutankhamun

In his short nine-year reign, Tutankhamun ended Akhenaten's ban on worshiping gods other than Aten. He also moved the capital city back from Akhetaten to Thebes.

POSITION
Pharaoh

PERIOD
New Kingdom

DYNASTY
18th Dynasty

RULED
1336–1327 BCE

Maya

Maya held the important position of overseer of the treasury. It was his job to collect the taxes from the different parts of the kingdom.

POSITION Overseer of the treasury

PERIOD New Kingdom

DYNASTY 18th Dynasty

LIVED 1336–1295 BCE

Maya's wife Merit

Ramesses II

The third pharaoh of the 19th dynasty, Ramesses II was one of the greatest and most celebrated rulers of ancient Egypt. He fought the Hittites at Kadesh in 1274 BCE, and when there was no clear winner in the battle, he signed the world's earliest surviving peace treaty. A copy of this now hangs in New York City at the headquarters of the United Nations, the modern organization that deals with disputes between countries. Ramesses II ruled for more than 60 years, during which he built many monuments, such as the temples at Abu Simbel, to celebrate his achievements.

POSITION Pharaoh

PERIOD New Kingdom

DYNASTY 19th Dynasty

RULED 1279–1213 BCE

Maya

Nefertari

The chief wife of Ramesses II, Nefertari was from a noble family and married Ramesses II before he became the pharaoh. He built and dedicated the smaller temple at Abu Simbel to her. No other Egyptian queen was ever honored in this way.

POSITION Great Royal Wife

PERIOD New Kingdom

DYNASTY 19th Dynasty

LIVED 1279–1213 BCE

Psusennes I

The third king of the 21st Dynasty, Psusennes I was one of the few Egyptian pharaohs whose tomb was discovered intact. His burial mask, shown below, is made of gold and lapis lazuli, with black and white glass pieces for the eyes.

Eyebrows made of inlaid lapis lazuli

POSITION	Pharaoh
PERIOD	Third Intermediate Period
DYNASTY	21st Dynasty
RULED	1039–991 BCE

Sheshonq I

Before he became the pharaoh, Sheshonq I was a general under Psusennes II, the last king of the 21st Dynasty. He invaded the Israelite kingdom and carried off the treasures from Solomon's kingdom in Jerusalem.

POSITION	Pharaoh
PERIOD	Third Intermediate Period
DYNASTY	22nd Dynasty
RULED	945–924 BCE

Amasis

Also known as Ahmose II, Amasis was a general in the army of Apries, the fourth pharaoh of the 26th Dynasty. In 570 BCE, Apries launched an attack against Cyrene (in present-day Libya), but failed. The Egyptian soldiers believed that Apries had betrayed them and revolted. They chose Amasis as their new pharaoh and he established a long, prosperous reign.

POSITION	Pharaoh
PERIOD	Late Period
DYNASTY	26th Dynasty
RULED	570–526 BCE

Darius I the Great

Before he became the ruler of the Persian Empire, Darius I was a soldier in the Persian army led by Emperor Cambyses. After Cambyses invaded and conquered Egypt, Darius I overthrew him and became the pharaoh.

POSITION	Pharaoh
PERIOD	Late Period
DYNASTY	27th Dynasty
RULED	522–486 BCE

tatue of masis as Sphinx

Alexander the Great

One of the greatest military leaders in history, Alexander the Great was a Greek prince from Macedon. At the age of 21, he began his conquest of the known world. He defeated the Persian Empire and in 332 BCE, he came to Egypt, where he was made the pharaoh.

POSITION	Pharaoh
PERIOD	Ptolemaic Period
DYNASTY	Argead Dynasty
RULED	332–323 BCE

Ptolemy I

Founder of the Ptolemaic Dynasty, this Macedonian general succeeded Alexander the Great. Ptolemy I was a clever politician and his strategies helped him maintain peace after Alexander's death.

POSITION	Pharaoh
PERIOD	Ptolemaic Period
DYNASTY	Ptolemaic Dynasty
RULED	305–285 BCE

Ptolemy II

The successor to Ptolemy I, Ptolemy II was co-regent until he became the ruler in 285 BCE. He was married to Arsinoe I, but banished her after becoming pharaoh. He then married his sister, a custom common in ancient Egypt, but shocking to the Greeks.

POSITION	Pharaoh
PERIOD	Ptolemaic Period
DYNASTY	Ptolemaic Dynasty
RULED	285–246 BCE

Brooch showing
Ptolemy II with Arsinoe II

Arsinoe II

The sister of Ptolemy II, Arsinoe II was married to Lysimachus, the king of Thrace (in present-day Europe), but was forced to run away after his death. She came to Egypt, where she married her brother and became co-ruler. This brooch shows her with Ptolemy II.

POSITION	Queen
PERIOD	Ptolemaic Period
DYNASTY	Ptolemaic Dynasty
LIVED	316–270 BCE

Ptolemy III

Ptolemy III married a princess of Cyrene and united the kingdoms, establishing a peaceful reign. To keep the peace, he also arranged for his sister Berenice to marry Antiochus, the king of Syria. But after Antiochus's first wife Laodice murdered Antiochus and Berenice, Ptolemy III invaded Syria to avenge his sister's death.

POSITION	Pharaoh
PERIOD	Ptolemaic Period
DYNASTY	Ptolemaic Dynasty
RULED	246–221 BCE

Berenice II

A princess of Cyrene, Berenice II was the wife of Ptolemy III. According to legend, when Ptolemy III went to avenge the murder of his sister—also named Berenice—she cut off her hair and offered it to the gods for his safe return. The gods took her hair and turned it into a constellation called Coma Berenices.

POSITION Queen

PERIOD Ptolemaic Period

DYNASTY
Ptolemaic Dynasty

LIVED 269–221 BCE

Arsinoe III

Arsinoe III's husband, Ptolemy IV, was a weak ruler, who was controlled by his corrupt ministers. She disapproved of this corruption, but was powerless to prevent it. After her husband's death, the ministers were afraid that she would punish them, so they murdered her.

POSITION Queen

PERIOD
Ptolemaic Period

DYNASTY
Ptolemaic Dynasty

LIVED 246–204 BCE

Cleopatra VII

One of the few women to rule Egypt on her own, Cleopatra VII took many steps to prevent Rome from taking over her kingdom. She set up trade routes as far as India to keep Egypt's economy strong. She also began a romantic relationship with the Roman general Julius Caesar and, after Caesar's death, with Mark Antony. But when she and Antony were defeated by his rival Octavian, she killed herself, and Egypt became Roman territory.

POSITION Pharaoh

PERIOD Ptolemaic Period

DYNASTY
Ptolemaic Dynasty

RULED 51–30 BCE

Cleopatra VII was the last ruler of Egypt to be called Pharaoh, and was the only Ptolemaic pharaoh to speak Egyptian.

RAMESSES II
Crowned in his teens, Ramesses II ruled for around 60 years. He undertook a vast building program, expanding older temples and building new ones. During his reign, the Nile floods led to good harvests, helping him to maintain a stable kingdom. He is shown here at the annual harvest.

Ramesses II built a temple called the

Ramesseum

where only he, and no god,

was worshiped

Tombs and monuments

For the ancient Egyptians, death was only the beginning of a new life in the underworld. They built massive tombs for their dead, which were filled with treasures and objects to be used in the afterlife. The most well-known tombs are the pyramids—huge structures built for the earliest pharaohs. In the New Kingdom, tombs were dug in the Valley of the Kings near Thebes, and it is here that the greatest treasures of ancient Egypt have been found.

CANOPIC CHEST
The canopic chest of Tutankhamun contains four jars, which were carved to look like him. These jars were used to store his internal organs.

Building a pyramid

During the Old Kingdom, pharaohs built huge tombs, called pyramids. Pyramids were constructed on the western bank of the Nile River, because it was thought that the land of the dead lay to the west. A single pyramid could take up to 20 years, and around 100,000 workers, to build.

Evolution of pyramids

Early tombs were single-story buildings called mastabas. The Old Kingdom architect Imhotep designed a building made of six mastabas placed one on top of the other—the first pyramid. Later, builders began filling in the pyramid sides to create the first "true pyramids."

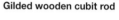
Gilded wooden cubit rod

Boning rods

A mastaba was made of mud bricks. Inside, a deep chamber was dug, in which the dead were buried.

The Great Pyramid of Giza is the world's largest true pyramid. It was built by placing large stone blocks together, which were then overlaid with polished limestone.

The Step Pyramid was designed as a stack of mastabas. It was made of small stone blocks laid like bricks.

Building tools

The sides of true pyramids were angled at 56 degrees, and all the stones were cut to the same size. Egyptian builders used tools such as the triangle to measure the angles, cubit rods to measure lengths, and boning rods to make sure that the stones were even.

Triangle

Pyramid builders

Laborers carried stones from quarries, sometimes over long distances, to build pyramids. At the construction site, they would lift the stones using ropes, or drag them up a ramp and lay them using cement or mortar.

Pyramids

The pyramids of Egypt have fascinated people for thousands of years. These massive stone structures were built as the final resting places for pharaohs and members of their families. There are more than 80 pyramids spread across Egypt.

FOCUS ON...
BUILDING MATERIALS
The Egyptians used many different types o stone to build pyramid

Great Pyramid of Giza

The largest pyramid ever built, the Great Pyramid of Giza took 20 years and about 2,300,000 blocks of limestone to complete. Each block weighs an average of 2.75 tons (2.5 metric tonnes). Inside, the pyramid has a huge network of passages, galleries, and hidden chambers, some of which have not been explored even to this day.

DEDICATED TO Khufu

BUILT IN 2589 BCE
(3rd Dynasty Old Kingdom)

SIZE 482 ft (147 m) tall

LOCATION Giza

Stone at top of pyramid is called the capstone

Shaft for workers

Burial chamber o Pharaoh Khufu

Rough, dark limestone blocks used for inner structure

Outer casing was made of smooth, white limestone slabs

◀ In the Old Kingdom, pyramids were made of limestone blocks. Sketches and plans of pyramids were also drawn on pieces of limestone.

◀ The statues, tablets, and sarcophagi that were placed inside the pyramids, were made of black basalt.

◀ Pyramids in the Middle Kingdom were made mostly of mud bricks. Limestone was used as an outer casing.

Pyramid of Khafra

Also known as the Pyramid of Chefren, this is the second largest of the pyramids of Giza. Pharaoh Khafra built this pyramid on higher ground, so that it would look like his pyramid was taller than Khufu's.

DEDICATED TO Khafra

BUILT IN 2520 BCE (3rd Dynasty Old Kingdom)

SIZE 472 ft (144 m) tall

LOCATION Giza

Pyramid of Menkaura

The last pyramid to be built at Giza, the Pyramid of Menkaura is much smaller than its neighbors. At its southern foot, three smaller pyramids were built for the wives of Pharaoh Menkaura.

DEDICATED TO Menkaura

BUILT IN 2490 BCE (3rd Dynasty Old Kingdom)

SIZE 213 ft (65 m) tall

LOCATION Giza

Pyramid of Menkaura's queen

Pyramid of Neferirkara

While the pyramid was being built, its intended user—Pharaoh Neferirkara—died, and so it was left unfinished. It was designed to be a step pyramid with six levels, but during its construction, the builders decided to fill in the steps to give it the shape of a true pyramid.

DEDICATED TO Neferirkara

BUILT IN 2475–2455 BCE
(5th Dynasty Old Kingdom)

SIZE 230 ft (70 m) tall

LOCATION Abusir

Pyramid of Sahura

Pyramid of Teti

Although its outer casing has broken down over the years, making it look like a pile of rubble, the Pyramid of Teti has well-preserved chambers and corridors inside. The walls of the burial chamber are inscribed with texts and the chamber ceiling is painted with stars.

DEDICATED TO Teti

BUILT IN 2323–2291 BCE (6th Dynasty Old Kingdom)

SIZE 170 ft (52.5 m) tall

LOCATION Saqqara

s pyramid was constructed of roughly limestone blocks held together with mud. was then cased with white limestone. To the east of the pyramid is the mortuary temple of the pharaoh who had it built, Sahura. Mortuary temples were built next to the pyramids of pharaohs to celebrate their reigns.

Ruins of Sahura's mortuary temple

DEDICATED TO Sahura

BUILT IN 2487–2475 BCE (5th Dynasty Old kingdom)

SIZE 154 ft (47 m) tall

LOCATION Abusir

Bent Pyramid

Also known as the Gleaming Pyramid of the South, the Bent Pyramid was originally designed to have a steep angle of 54 degrees. But this made the structure unstable. The builders then changed the angle of the remaining part to 43 degrees, giving the pyramid its unique shape.

DEDICATED TO Sneferu

BUILT IN 2613–2589 BCE
(4th Dynasty Old Kingdom)

SIZE 330 ft (100 m) tall

LOCATION Dashur

Red Pyramid

Pharaoh Sneferu tried three times to build a true pyramid. His first two attempts—the Meidum Pyramid and the Bent Pyramid—failed. It was only with the Red Pyramid that he succeeded. This pyramid gets its name from the red sandstone found at its base.

DEDICATED TO Sneferu

BUILT IN 2613–2589 BCE
(4th Dynasty Old Kingdom)

SIZE 345 ft (105 m) tall

LOCATION Dashur

Meidum Pyramid

The construction of the Meidum Pyramid was started by an earlier ruler but completed by Pharaoh Sneferu. It was first built as a step pyramid with eight steps. These steps were later filled in and an outer casing was added. Over the centuries, the outer casing has collapsed and only the central core now remains.

DEDICATED TO Sneferu

BUILT IN 2613-2589 BCE
(4th Dynasty Old Kingdom)

SIZE 213 ft (65 m) tall

LOCATION Fayum

Most of the limestone casing of this pyramid was removed and used to build the city of Cairo.

Pyramid of Unas

From the outside, this looks more like a small hill or rubble than a royal pyramid. What makes it so important is the presence of the earliest Egyptian religious texts, called pyramid texts, covering the walls of the burial chamber. They are a collection of spells meant to protect the dead in the afterlife.

DEDICATED TO Unas

BUILT IN 2375–2345 BCE
(5th Dynasty Old Kingdom)

SIZE 62 ft (18.5 m) tall

LOCATION Saqqara

Step Pyramid

Pyramid of Userkaf

The mortuary temple of this pyramid complex faces south instead of east, which was usually the case. This was probably because Userkaf worshiped the Sun, and this way, the temple would remain in sunlight all day long.

DEDICATED TO Userkaf

BUILT IN 2494–2487 BCE
(5th Dynasty Old Kingdom)

SIZE 160 ft (49 m) tall

LOCATION Abusir

The very first Egyptian pyramid, the Step Pyramid was built as a series of rectangular structures set one on top of the other. The burial chambers of the pharaoh and his family are cut deep into the underground rock below the pyramid. There are 15 doors set on the outer wall of the pyramid, but only one is real. The other 14 are fakes put there to fool tomb robbers.

DEDICATED TO Djoser

BUILT IN 2680 BCE
(3rd Dynasty Old Kingdom)

SIZE 200 ft (60 m) tall

LOCATION Saqqara

Black Pyramid

Also known as the Pyramid of Amenemhat III, the Black Pyramid was an architectural disaster. It was built on unstable ground very near to the Nile River. This allowed water to seep in and weaken the structure. Although the damage was repaired, the pharaoh chose not to use it and had another tomb built for himself at Hawara.

DEDICATED TO Amenemhat III

BUILT IN 1860–1814 BCE
(12th Dynasty Middle Kingdom)

SIZE 246 ft (75 m) tall

LOCATION Dashur

The entire outer casing of the Meidum Pyramid has crumbled away, giving it the nickname

"the collapsed pyramid"

BREAKING DOWN
There are several theories about the collapse of the Meidum Pyramid. Some people believe its shape put a lot of pressure on the structure. Others argue that an earthquake weakened the building.

Tombs

Instead of pyramids, pharaohs of the New Kingdom chose underground tombs cut deep into mountains as their burial sites in order to foil robbers. The largest site of such tombs is the Valley of the Kings near Thebes. By 2012, 63 tombs had been discovered here. Next to this site is the Valley of the Queens, where more than 70 tombs of queens and princesses have been found.

Tomb of Ramesses VII

Because of its location at the entrance of the Valley of the Kings, this tomb was given the name KV 1. It has only one burial chamber, with a small hollow beyond it, which is believed to be an unfinished room. A painting on the right wall shows the gods reviving the Sun disk in fire.

TOMB NUMBER KV 1

BUILT IN 1136–1129 BCE
(20th Dynasty New Kingdom)

LOCATION Valley of the Kings, Thebes

Tomb of Ramesses IV

Ancient Greek and Roman travelers often used the tombs in the Valley as shelters. KV 2 was one such tomb. It contains drawings and inscriptions by different travelers who stayed in the tomb. Visitors inscribed their name, profession, place of origin, and personal comments about the tomb.

TOMB NUMBER KV 2

BUILT IN 1155–1149 BCE
(20th Dynasty New Kingdom)

LOCATION Valley of the Kings, Thebes

Tomb of the sons of Ramesses II

This tomb was considered an unimportant hole in the ground until the remains of the sons of Ramesses II were discovered by a team of archeologists in 1995. It is the largest tomb in the Valley. Up to 121 chambers and corridors have been found so far and experts believe that the tomb may have 150 chambers in total.

Statue of Osiris is found in corridor number seven

TOMB NUMBER KV 5

BUILT IN 1279–1213 BCE (19th Dynasty New Kingdom)

LOCATION Valley of the Kings, Thebes

Tomb of Ramesses V and Ramesses VI

Ramesses V began building this tomb for himself, but it was completed by his brother and successor, Ramesses VI, who decorated the new sections with his own name and images. However, since no mummies have been found inside the tomb, it is not known if Ramesses VI was the only pharaoh to be buried in it, or if the two pharaohs were buried next to each other.

TOMB NUMBER KV 9

BUILT IN 1149–1137 BCE (20th Dynasty New Kingdom)

LOCATION Valley of the Kings, Thebes

Tomb of Amenhotep III

One of the oldest tombs in the Valley, KV 22 has been completely looted and every trace of gold or precious metal has been removed. The lid of the sarcophagus was broken into several pieces, but has now been restored.

TOMB NUMBER KV 22

BUILT IN 1390–1352 BCE (18th Dynasty New Kingdom)

LOCATION Valley of the Kings, Thebes

Tomb of Tutankhamun

The entrance to KV 62 was hidden under a pile of rock and debris during the construction of KV 9, keeping it safe from tomb robbers. This is why it was found almost completely intact and still containing most of its treasures.

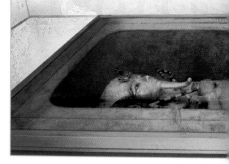

Tomb of Amenhotep II

This tomb is located in the southwestern part of the Valley of the Kings. It shows signs of having been looted repeatedly, but luckily, the mummy of Amenhotep II was found intact inside its sarcophagus. The tomb was also used to store other royal mummies, including those of Thutmose IV, Amenhotep III, Seti II, and Ramesses IV.

TOMB NUMBER KV 35

BUILT IN 1425–1400 BCE
(18th Dynasty New Kingdom)

LOCATION Valley of the Kings, Thebes

Sarcophagus of
Amenhotep II

OMB NUMBER KV 62

UILT IN 1333–1323 BCE
8th Dynasty New Kingdom)

OCATION Valley of Kings, Thebes

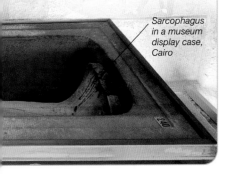

Sarcophagus
in a museum
display case,
Cairo

Tomb of Seti I

This is the longest and deepest tomb in the Valley. Its walls are covered with religious paintings in which the pharaoh is shown with different deities. This painting shows Nephthys, protector of the dead, holding him in her arms.

TOMB NUMBER KV 17

BUILT IN 1290–1279 BCE
(19th Dynasty New Kingdom)

LOCATION Valley of the Kings, Thebes

Tomb of Ay

Also called Southern Tomb 25, this is one of 25 tombs discovered near Akhetaten. It contains paintings of Ay, an Egyptian nobleman, and his family praying to the Sun god Aten. It has, painted on its walls, one of the longest hymns to Aten ever found.

TOMB NUMBER Amarna Tomb 25

BUILT IN 1352–1334 BCE
(18th Dynasty New Kingdom)

LOCATION Amarna

Tomb of Sennefer

Tombs of royal courtiers and nobles were built near the Valley of the Kings. This is the tomb of Sennefer, the mayor of Thebes. It is entered through a steep tunnel, which leads to a set of chambers. The ceiling of the tomb is decorated with grape vines, which has given the tomb its nickname of "tomb of vines."

TOMB NUMBER TT 95

BUILT IN 1425–1400 BCE
(18th Dynasty New Kingdom)

LOCATION Tombs of the Nobles, Thebes

Tomb of Menna

This tomb was built for Menna, a scribe and supervisor of the lands belonging to the pharaoh. The paintings inside the tomb show scenes from Menna's life. In this image, he can be seen sitting in front of a table laden with food. Other paintings show him supervising farmers and recording the harvest.

TOMB NUMBER TT 69

BUILT IN 1400–1352 BCE
(18th Dynasty New Kingdom)

LOCATION Sheikh Abd el-Qurna, Thebes

Tomb of Peshedu

The builders and artists who worked on royal tombs lived in a village near the Valley of the Kings, now called Deir el-Medina, or "workers' village." The site also contains the tombs of these craftworkers. TT 3 was built for Peshedu, who was an overseer of tomb artists. Its walls and ceiling are decorated with paintings of deities and religious symbols.

TOMB NUMBER TT 3

BUILT IN 1149–1137 BCE
(20th Dynasty New Kingdom)

LOCATION Deir el-Medina, Thebes

The god Ptah shown in the form of a falcon   *Wadjet eye*

Tomb of Nefertari

Built by Ramesses II for his wife Nefertari, QV 66 contains paintings of the queen being presented to the gods, as well as poetry written for her by her husband.

TOMB NUMBER
QV 66

BUILT IN
1279–1213 BCE
(19th Dynasty
New Kingdom)

LOCATION Valley
of the Queens,
Thebes

The paintings on the walls of Nefertari's tomb show the **journey of her soul** to the afterlife

NEFERTARI'S TOMB

Discovered in 1904, QV 66, the tomb of Nefertari, is famous for its beautiful paintings, which depict the queen being presented before the main gods of ancient Egypt. She is shown here with Khepri, the scarab god, Horus, the falcon god, and Osiris, ruler of the underworld.

Tomb treasures

Pyramids and other tombs contained many artifacts and treasures. These were meant to help the dead live comfortably in the afterlife. However, most tombs were robbed and their priceless contents stolen in ancient times. The tomb of Pharaoh Tutankhaum was discovered almost intact and filled with glittering treasures.

Throne

This throne was discovered among the treasures of Pharaoh Tutankhamun. It is carved out of wood and covered with gold and silver. It is also decorated with colored glass, semiprecious stones, and faïence—a type of glazed ceramic. The design shows Tutankhamun with his queen, Ankhesenamun. The Sun disk above the royal couple represents Aten.

The lion head is meant to turn away evil spirits

The feet are carved to look like a lion's paws

DEDICATED TO	Tutankhamun
MADE IN	18th Dynasty New Kingdom
SIZE	3⅓ ft (1.02 cm) high
TOMB LOCATION	Valley of the Kings

Sarcophagus

When the tomb of Thutmose III was discovered in 1898, all that remained was some broken furniture, as well as statues and this sarcophagus. Everything else had been taken by tomb robbers. The sarcophagus is decorated with carvings of Egyptian gods and goddesses, and hieroglyphs.

DEDICATED TO   Thutmose III

MADE IN   18th Dynasty New Kingdom

SIZE   7½ ft (2.35 m) long

TOMB LOCATION   Valley of the Kings

Solar boat

In 1950, archeologists discovered a ship at the base of the Great Pyramid of Giza. One of the world's oldest boats, it was built for Pharaoh Khufu and buried as part of his funeral treasure. Also known as a solar boat, the ship was meant to help Khufu travel to the underworld.

The entire ship was built and then separated into 1,224 pieces, which were buried under thick limestone slabs.

DEDICATED TO   Khufu

MADE IN   4th Dynasty Old Kingdom

SIZE   143 ft (43.6 m) long

TOMB LOCATION   Giza

Hapi canopic jar

Canopic jars were used to store a mummy's organs. They were made to resemble one of the four sons of the god Horus, representing north, south, east, and west. This jar has the baboon-shaped head of Hapi, who stood for the north. It was placed facing north and contained the lungs.

DEDICATED TO Unknown

MADE IN 25th Dynasty Third Intermediate Period

SIZE 11 in (28 cm) tall

TOMB LOCATION Unknown

Qebehsenuef canopic jar

Qebehsenuef, the falcon-headed son of Horus, represented the west, and protected the intestines of the mummy. This jar was made for the mummy of Paiduf, a priest of the god Amun.

DEDICATED TO Paiduf

MADE IN 22nd Dynasty Third Intermediate Period

SIZE 11¾ in (29.5 cm) tall

TOMB LOCATION Unknown

Canopic shrine

The word "canopic" comes from the town of Canopus, where Osiris was worshiped in the form of a vase with a human head.

Canopic jars were placed inside a chest, which was then put inside a shrine. This canopic shrine was found in the tomb of Tutankhamun. It has a statue of a different goddess on each side. The goddess seen here is Serqet, the scorpion goddess.

DEDICATED TO
Tutankhamun

MADE IN 18th Dynasty New Kingdom

SIZE 6½ ft (2 m)

TOMB LOCATION
Valley of the Kings, Thebes

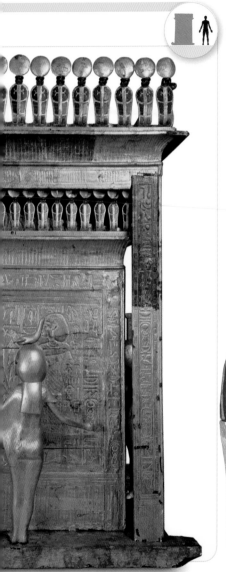

Duamutef canopic jar

Jackal-headed Duamutef stood for the east and protected the stomach in the afterlife. The jar was placed with the head facing east.

DEDICATED TO Paiduf

MADE IN 22nd Dynasty
Third Intermediate Period

SIZE 11¾ in
(29.5 cm) tall

TOMB LOCATION
Unknown

Imseti canopic jar

The only son of Horus and with the face of a human, Imseti was the protector of the liver. He represented the south and so the jar was placed with his head facing that direction.

DEDICATED TO Unknown

MADE IN 25th Dynasty
Third Intermediate Period

SIZE 12 in (31 cm) tall

TOMB LOCATION Unknown

Headrest

The Egyptians used headrests rather than pillows. This ivory headrest has been carved in the shape of Shu, the god of air. He is shown separating Earth from the sky. The lions on each side represent the eastern and western horizons.

DEDICATED TO
Tutankhamun

MADE IN 19th Dynasty
New Kingdom

SIZE 6¾ in (17.5 cm) long

TOMB LOCATION Valley of the Kings, Thebes

Earring

Earrings were brought to Egypt by the Hyksos—invaders from Asia. These earrings, made of gold and colored glass, were buried with Pharaoh Tutankhamun in his tomb.

DEDICATED TO Tutankhamun

MADE IN 19th Dynasty
New Kingdom

SIZE 3–4 in (8–10 cm) long

TOMB LOCATION Valley of the Kings, Thebes

Pendant

Designed in the shape of a winged scarab beetle holding the disk of the Sun, this pendant also spells out "Nebkheperure," which was the royal name of Tutankhamun. The basket shape at the bottom spells "neb," the beetle spells "kheperu," and the Sun disk spells out "re."

DEDICATED TO Tutankhamun

MADE IN 19th Dynasty
New Kingdom

SIZE 3½ in (9 cm) tall

TOMB LOCATION Valley of the Kings, Thebes

Mirror case

This mirror case is designed in the shape of an ankh, a hieroglyph that means "eternal life." The scarab decoration spells out Tutankhamun's name. There used to be a mirror inside the case, but it was stolen in ancient times.

DEDICATED TO Tutankhamun

MADE IN 19th Dynasty New Kingdom

SIZE 10½ in (27 cm) tall

TOMB LOCATION Valley of the Kings, Thebes

Pectoral

Found inside one of Tutankhamun's treasure boxes, this pectoral (jewelry worn on the chest) shows the pharaoh with the goddess Ma'at. He is wearing a war helmet and receiving an ankh from the goddess.

DEDICATED TO Tutankhamun

MADE IN 19th Dynasty New Kingdom

SIZE 3½ in (9 cm) wide

TOMB LOCATION Valley of the Kings, Thebes

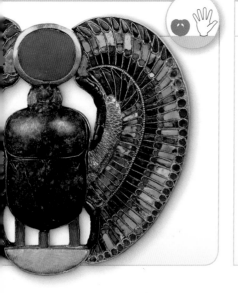

Gilt shrine

This tiny wooden shrine is covered with embossed sheets of gold, which show Queen Ankhesenamun with Tutankhamun. The shrine once contained a statue, but it was stolen by tomb robbers in ancient times.

DEDICATED TO Tutankhamun

MADE IN 19th Dynasty New Kingdom

SIZE 20¼ in (50.5 cm) tall

TOMB LOCATION Valley of the Kings, Thebes

Monuments

In addition to pyramids and tombs, the Egyptians also built monuments to honor their rulers and gods. They used limestone and granite for building, since these materials were readily available. From these, Egyptian artists created giant sculptures, such as the Great Sphinx and the Colossi of Memnon, which have lasted for centuries.

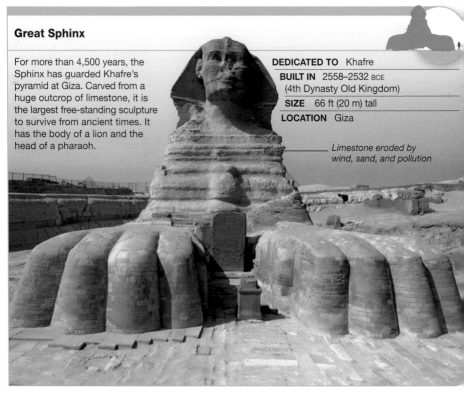

Great Sphinx

For more than 4,500 years, the Sphinx has guarded Khafre's pyramid at Giza. Carved from a huge outcrop of limestone, it is the largest free-standing sculpture to survive from ancient times. It has the body of a lion and the head of a pharaoh.

DEDICATED TO Khafre

BUILT IN 2558–2532 BCE
(4th Dynasty Old Kingdom)

SIZE 66 ft (20 m) tall

LOCATION Giza

Limestone eroded by wind, sand, and pollution

Alabaster sphinx of Memphis

Although smaller than the Great Sphinx in Giza, the alabaster sphinx of Memphis is an impressive example of Egyptian art. It is made of the mineral calcite and weighs about 88 tons (80 metric tonnes), making it the largest calcite statue ever found.

DEDICATED TO Hatshepsut

BUILT IN 1473–1458 BCE
(18th Dynasty New Kingdom)

SIZE 26 ft (8 m) tall

LOCATION Memphis

Colossi of Memnon

On the western bank of the Nile River stand the two Colossi of Memnon. These giants were originally built to guard the temple of Amenhotep III, which was looted by later pharaohs and eventually destroyed by floods. The statues show Amenhotep III seated, with his hands resting on his knees, looking east toward the rising Sun.

The faces of the statues have been destroyed over time

DEDICATED TO Amenhotep III

BUILT IN 1390–1352 BCE
(18th Dynasty New Kingdom)

SIZE 59 ft (18 m) tall

LOCATION Thebes

Seated colossus of Ramesses II

This statue of Pharaoh Ramesses II stands inside the Luxor Temple. It is made of granite and was built to celebrate the pharaoh's victory over the Hittites in the Battle of Kadesh in 1274 BCE.

DEDICATED TO Ramesses II

BUILT IN 1279–1213 BCE (18th Dynasty New Kingdom)

SIZE 26 ft (8 m) tall

LOCATION Luxor Temple

Baboon statue

Baboons were the sacred animals of Thoth, the god of wisdom. This baboon statue was erected by Amenhotep III. It is one of four baboon statues placed by the pharaoh at the Temple of Thoth in Hermopolis.

DEDICATED TO Thoth

BUILT IN 1390–1352 BCE (18th Dynasty New Kingdom)

SIZE 14¾ ft (4.5 m) tall

LOCATION Hermopolis

Criosphinx

Pyramidion

People who could not afford a full-sized pyramid for their dead often constructed a pyramid next to their tomb. Found in the workers' village of Deir el-Medina, this sandstone pyramidion was made for a workman named Hornefer. The hieroglyphs on each face form a prayer to the Sun god Ra and other gods.

DEDICATED TO Ra

BUILT IN 19th Dynasty New Kingdom

SIZE 16 in (40 cm) tall

LOCATION Deir el-Medina

The southern entrance to the Karnak Temple is an avenue that is lined with a row of structures called Criosphinxes. These have the body of a lion and the head of a ram. The figure between the paws of this criosphinx is that of a pharaoh, believed to be Amenhotep III.

DEDICATED TO Amun

BUILT IN Middle Kingdom to Ptolemaic Period

SIZE 4 ft (1.2 m) tall

LOCATION Karnak Temple

Cleopatra's Needle

Thutmose III constructed this 265-ton (240-metric-tonne) granite obelisk at Heliopolis. Nearly 200 years later, Ramesses II added the inscriptions to mark his military victories. In 1877, the Egyptian government gave the obelisk to the US as a gift, where it was nicknamed Cleopatra's Needle. Two other obelisks—in London and Paris, are also called this.

DEDICATED TO Horus

BUILT IN 1450 BCE (18th Dynasty Middle Kingdom)

SIZE 69 ft (21 m)

LOCATION Originally in Heliopolis; transported to New York City in 1877

Although the obelisk is now called Cleopatra's Needle, it was built more than 1,000 years before Cleopatra's birth.

According to legend, Thutmose IV dreamed that the Sphinx promised to make him

ruler of all Egypt

if he cleared away the sand covering it

GREAT SPHINX
The Great Sphinx is thought to be a form of the god Horus—protector of the pharaoh. When Thutmose IV came to the throne, he had a tablet, called the dream stela, built. This tablet, located between the paws of the Sphinx, tells the story of how the Sphinx made Thutmose IV the ruler of Egypt.

Religion

The Egyptians worshiped hundreds of gods and goddesses. Many deities were represented by animals, but the most powerful ones were always represented by the disk of the Sun. Temples were called the homes of the gods, and the priests who lived in them were known as the gods' servants. Here, the ram-headed god Khnum and the goddesses Hathor and Ma'at are wearing Sun disks on their heads.

KNOT OF ISIS
Amulets were worn to ward off evil. This knot-shaped amulet was associated with the goddess Isis and was placed on mummies to protect them in the afterlife.

Mythology

Ancient Egyptians worshiped hundreds of deities (gods and goddesses)—an ancient text lists as many as 740. Some were local, while others were worshiped throughout the kingdom. All the forces of nature, including the wind, rain, and Sun, were represented by deities

Sun gods

The Egyptians worshiped the Sun in many forms, such as Aten and Ra. Ra was merged with other gods to create powerful deities, such as Amun-Ra and Ra-Horakhty.

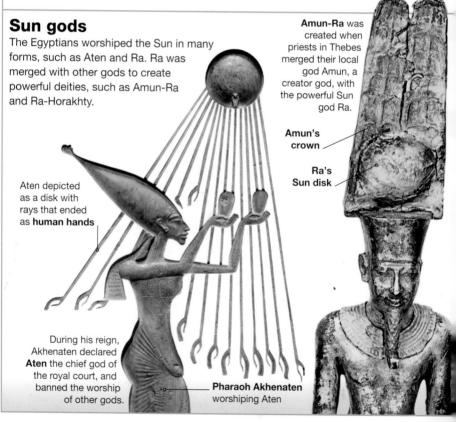

Amun-Ra was created when priests in Thebes merged their local god Amun, a creator god, with the powerful Sun god Ra.

Amun's crown

Ra's Sun disk

Aten depicted as a disk with rays that ended as **human hands**

During his reign, Akhenaten declared **Aten** the chief god of the royal court, and banned the worship of other gods.

Pharaoh Akhenaten worshiping Aten

roups of gods

fferent groups of deities were worshiped in different ties. In Memphis, the triad (group of three, shown the right) of Ptah, Sekhmet, and Nefertum was orshiped. In Heliopolis, the main deities were a oup of nine, called the Ennead, shown below. he arrows show how some gods were the parents others.

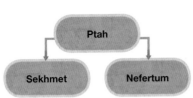

Memphis Triad

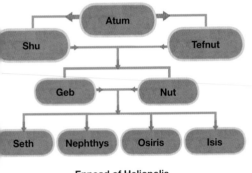

Ennead of Heliopolis

Ra-Horakhty was a falcon-headed Sun god and a version of the sky god Horus. He was the protector of the pharaohs.

Sun disk of Ra

Falcon head of Horus

Pharaoh as god

Egyptians believed that after a pharaoh died, he became a god. He was often shown in statues and paintings with other gods. Dead pharaohs were worshiped in buildings called mortuary temples.

Priests and rituals

Ancient Egyptians were deeply religious and believed that everything in their lives was controlled by gods and goddesses. In order to live a happy life and enter the afterlife, they performed rituals for the gods at important events, such as births, funerals, festivals, and royal coronations.

Role of priests

As the overseers of all religious rituals, priests led prayers and religious processions, and also made offerings to the gods. This painting shows Deniuenkhons, an Egyptian priestess, making offerings to the god Ra-Harakhty. The offerings include a plucked fowl, loaves of bread, lettuce, and a jar of beer. Priests also supervised the making of mummies, making sure that the appropriate spells were spoken and that protective amulets were placed correctly on the mummy.

Animal cults

Animal cults were an important part of Egyptian religion. The Apis Bull was a black calf with certain markings on its body, such as a diamond-shaped white patch on the forehead and a scarab-shaped mark under its tongue. It was worshiped as a form of Osiris. During religious festivals, it was dressed with colorful flowers and cloth and led through the streets by priests.

Oracles

Priests were also thought to be oracles—voices of the gods. People came to oracles when they needed advice. The oracles consulted the gods and gave their decisions. This mask of the jackal-headed god Anubis was worn by an oracle.

Mummies and the afterlife

Ka statue of Pharaoh Hor

The Egyptians believed in an afterlife where they would be reborn in their original bodies. For this to happen, the body had to be preserved in the form of a mummy. Before reaching the afterlife, the spirits of the dead were thought to journey through an underworld called *Duat*.

Forms of a soul

There were two important spirits that made up a person. The *ka*, which was the life-force, was symbolized by two raised hands. The *ba*, or soul, was symbolized by a bird with a human head.

Weighing the heart

In *Duat*, spirits were judged for their sins in the Hall of Judgment. The god Anubis weighed their hearts against a feather of Ma'at, the goddess of truth. If the heart was heavier than the feather, it meant that the person had committed many sins in life and was not allowed to be reborn—their heart was fed to the demon goddess Ammut. If the heart was lighter than the feather, the person lived forever.

The art of mummification

The mummification of a body was a complex process, involving numerous rituals and magic spells performed by priests. The main priest performed his duties wearing an Anubis mask, as seen below.

The body was cleaned using water and salt. The internal organs were taken out and placed in canopic jars.

The body was filled with bags of salt for 40 days, to dry it, after which it was stuffed with bandages and spices.

It was then coated with resin (a tree sap) and wrapped in linen strips over a period of 15 days, along with protective amulets.

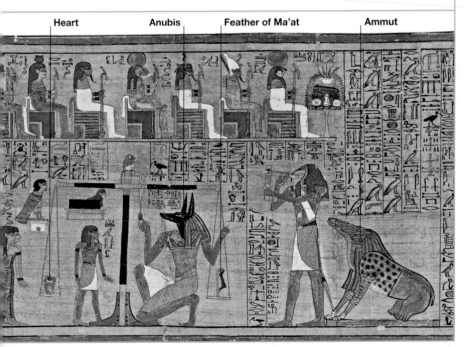

Heart · Anubis · Feather of Ma'at · Ammut

Gods and goddesses

The gods and goddesses of ancient Egypt were believed to control the movement of the Sun across the sky, the flooding of the Nile River, the afterlife, and childbirth. Each city and village had its patron god, and as the popularity of the god grew, he or she was given a higher status than other gods.

Ptah

The Egyptians had many myths about the creation of the world. In one such myth, the creator was the god Ptah. He formed all the other gods by imagining and naming them. Ptah was also the first sculptor and metalworker, using his skills to create the other beings of the universe. Ptah was often shown holding a staff that was decorated with the head of an animal. This staff was called the *was* scepter. He was worshiped as part of the Memphis Triad—a group of deities that included Nefertum and Sekhmet.

The *was scepter* symbolizes Ptah's power over chaos

RELATED SYMBOL Bull or Djed pillar
ALTERNATIVE NAMES Pteh, Peteh
PERIOD WORSHIPED Old Kingdom
CENTER OF WORSHIP Memphis

Nefertum

Headdress in shape of lotus flower

Ancient Egyptians believed that Nefertum was born from a blue lotus at the time of creation. He was worshiped in the Memphis Triad as the son of Ptah and Sekhmet. Amulets representing him were made in the shape of lotus flowers and were thought to bring good luck.

Nefertum was often shown with blue skin

RELATED SYMBOL
Lotus

ALTERNATIVE NAMES
Nefer-tum

PERIOD WORSHIPED
Old Kingdom

CENTER OF WORSHIP
Memphis

Sekhmet

The third deity in the Memphis Triad was Sekhmet. She was the companion of Ptah. A war goddess, Sekhmet fought and destroyed the enemies of Ra. She was also associated with medicine and healing.

RELATED SYMBOL	Lioness
ALTERNATIVE NAMES	Sakhmet
PERIOD WORSHIPED	Old Kingdom
CENTER OF WORSHIP	Memphis

Shu

The god of air, Shu was created by the breath of Atum. Shu was part of the Ennead of Heliopolis—a group of nine gods. He and his sister-companion Tefnut were the parents of Geb, the god of Earth, and Nut, the goddess of the sky.

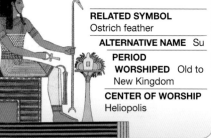

RELATED SYMBOL
Ostrich feather

ALTERNATIVE NAME Su

PERIOD WORSHIPED Old to New Kingdom

CENTER OF WORSHIP
Heliopolis

Tefnut

Tefnut was the goddess of moisture and rain. In 2200 BCE, a drought spread across Egypt. People believed that this was because she had argued with Shu and left the country, taking the rain with her.

RELATED SYMBOL
Lioness

ALTERNATIVE NAMES
Tefenet, Tefnet

PERIOD WORSHIPED
Old to New Kingdom

CENTER OF WORSHIP
Heliopolis

Atum

One of the oldest gods of Egypt, Atum was the chief god of the Ennead of Heliopolis. Over time, he merged with the god Ra. This new deity was worshiped as Atum-Ra, who was considered as the creator of the other gods of the Ennead.

RELATED SYMBOL Scarab beetle

ALTERNATIVE NAMES Tem or Temu

PERIOD WORSHIPED Old to New Kingdom

CENTER OF WORSHIP Heliopolis

Geb and Nut

Geb and Nut were the gods of Earth and the sky respectively. Geb's body was Earth, and his laughter caused earthquakes. Nut's body was the sky and was covered with stars.

RELATED SYMBOLS Man lying on ground (Geb) and woman arching over him (Nut)

ALTERNATIVE NAMES Seb, Keb, or Kebb (Geb) and Nuit or Nwt (Nut)

PERIOD WORSHIPED Old to Middle Kingdom

CENTER OF WORSHIP Heliopolis

Nephthys

The daughter of Geb and Nut, Nephthys was the goddess of assistance and protection. She accompanied the dead on their journey to the underworld and kept them safe.

RELATED SYMBOL Hieroglyph showing house and basket

ALTERNATIVE NAMES Nebhet

PERIOD WORSHIPED Old Kingdom

CENTER OF WORSHIP Heliopolis

Isis

The goddess of family life, Isis was part of the Ennead of Heliopolis as the wife of Osiris and the mother of Horus. After Osiris was killed by his brother Seth, she brought him back to life with a spell called the "Ritual of Life." This spell was later given to the Egyptians so that their dead could live forever in the afterlife.

RELATED SYMBOL   Cow horns

ALTERNATIVE NAMES   Aset, Ast, Iset, Uset

PERIOD WORSHIPED
Old Kingdom to Late Period

CENTER OF WORSHIP
Philae

Anubis

Ancient Egyptians often saw jackals scavenging in cemeteries, and so the jackal-headed god Anubis became closely linked with the dead. In paintings, Anubis is often shown preparing a body for mummification, as well as performing the "opening of the mouth" ritual.

RELATED SYMBOL   Jackal or wild dog

ALTERNATIVE NAMES   None

PERIOD WORSHIPED   Old to New Kingdom

CENTERS OF WORSHIP   Lycopolis (Modern-day Asyut) and Cynopolis

Seth

Seth was the god of the desert, violence, and thunderstorms. He had the body of a man, but the face of a strange, mythical creature. Although he was the chief rival of Horus—the patron god of pharaohs—Egyptians admired Seth for his strength and ferocity. This image from the throne of Sesostris I shows both Seth and Horus. Seth represents Lower Egypt, while Horus stands for Upper Egypt.

RELATED SYMBOL   Seth animal

ALTERNATIVE NAMES   Set

PERIOD WORSHIPED   Pre-dynastic to New Kingdom

CENTER OF WORSHIP   Ombos (near Naqada)

Anubis's fur was not reddish brown like a jackal's, but black. This was because the color black symbolized rebirth.

Osiris

According to an Egyptian myth, the god Osiris was the first ruler of Egypt. He was murdered by Seth, who wanted the kingdom for himself. After his wife Isis brought him back to life, he became a god and ruler of the underworld. Because he had been resurrected, or brought back to life, Osiris became the god of resurrection and a symbol of immortality.

RELATED SYMBOL
Crook and flail

ALTERNATIVE NAMES Asir

PERIOD WORSHIPED
Old Kingdom to Late Period

CENTER OF WORSHIP
Abydos

Horus

A sky god, Horus was the son of Osiris and Isis. He was born after Seth murdered Osiris. Horus fought Seth for 80 years, defeating him and becoming the ruler of Egypt.

Statue of Horus in the form of a falcon

RELATED SYMBOL
Falcon or hawk

ALTERNATIVE NAMES
Heru, Hor, Har

PERIOD WORSHIPED
Pre-dynastic to late Ptolemaic

CENTERS OF WORSHIP
Edfu and Heiraknopolis

Egyptians believed that if Ma'at didn't exist, the universe would sink into chaos

Ma'at

Ma'at was the goddess of truth, justice, and order. In Egyptian mythology, the hearts of the dead were weighed against one of Ma'at's feathers. If the heart was lighter than the feather, the dead would be reborn in the underworld.

RELATED SYMBOL Ostrich feather

ALTERNATIVE NAMES Maat, Mayet

PERIOD WORSHIPED Old Kingdom to Ptolemaic Period

CENTER OF WORSHIP All Egyptian cities

Hathor

Originally a fierce war goddess in Nubia, Hathor later took the form of a lioness. After Horus was born, she was brought to Egypt to look after him. Hathor then changed her character, becoming gentle and taking the form of a cow.

RELATED SYMBOL Cow

ALTERNATIVE NAMES None

PERIOD WORSHIPED Old Kingdom to Ptolemaic Period

CENTER OF WORSHIP Denderah

Khepri

Egyptians often saw scarabs, or dung beetles, rolling dung into a ball and pushing it across the ground. They associated this with Khepri, who rolled the Sun across the sky. This god was later merged with Ra and represented the rising Sun.

RELATED SYMBOL Scarab

ALTERNATIVE NAMES Kheper, Khepera, Chepri

PERIOD WORSHIPED New Kingdom

CENTER OF WORSHIP Heliopolis

Wadjet

In Pre-dynastic times, Wadjet was worshiped as the patron goddess of Lower Egypt. She later merged with the cat-goddess Bastet and was shown with the head of a lioness.

RELATED SYMBOL Cobra

ALTERNATIVE NAMES Wadjit, Buto

PERIOD WORSHIPED
Pre-dynastic to
Late Period

CENTER OF WORSHIP
Per-wadjet

Ra

The Sun-god Ra was one of the most popular gods of Egyptian religion. He was represented by the disk of the Sun, but in many places he was combined with local gods to make a powerful deity. One such deity was Ra-Harakhty, who was a combination of Ra and the sky-god Horus.

Ra-Harakhty holding an Ankh, the Egyptian symbol for eternal life

RELATED SYMBOL Sun

ALTERNATIVE NAMES Re

PERIOD WORSHIPED
Pre-dynastic to New Kingdom

CENTER OF WORSHIP Heliopolis

Isis once tricked Ra into revealing his secret name. This allowed her to become pregnant with Horus even after her husband's death.

Seshat

The goddess of writing and measurement, Seshat kept a record of the pharaoh's life. She noted down his achievements and triumphs, such as the temples he built and the wars he fought.

RELATED SYMBOL Seven-pointed star or flower on a pole

ALTERNATIVE NAMES
Sesha, Sesheta, Safekh-Aubi

PERIOD WORSHIPED
Pre-dynastic onward

CENTER OF WORSHIP None

Sobek

Crocodile-headed Sobek was the god of rivers and lakes. His temple at Faiyum had a live crocodile named Petsuchos. His followers believed that the crocodile was Sobek himself and was therefore sacred.

RELATED SYMBOL Crocodile

ALTERNATIVE NAMES Sebek, Sebek-Ra, Sobeq

PERIOD WORSHIPED
Old Kingdom to
Ptolemaic Period

CENTER OF WORSHIP
Kom Ombo

Thoth

The inventor of hieroglyphs, Thoth recorded the decision taken on the dead who were judged for rebirth. He also had a book containing all the wisdom in the world. Isis came to him when she needed a spell to bring Osiris back to life. This wall painting shows Queen Nefertari asking Thoth for a writing palette.

RELATED SYMBOL Ibis or baboon

ALTERNATIVE NAMES Tehuty, Djehuty, Tahuti

PERIOD WORSHIPED Late Period

CENTER OF WORSHIP Khnum (Hermopolis)

Amun

Amun was part of a group of eight gods called the Ogdoad of Hermopolis. Other members of this group were Heh and Hauhet, who represented eternity. The name Amun means "the hidden one." It was thought that he created himself and then the universe, while remaining distant and separate from it. This statue is from the New Kingdom, when Amun was merged with the Sun god Ra and adopted into the Ennead of Heliopolis as Amun-Ra.

RELATED SYMBOL
Ram or goose

ALTERNATIVE
NAMES Amen,
Ammon

PERIOD WORSHIPED
Middle to New Kingdom

CENTER OF WORSHIP
Thebes

Bastet

Originally taking the shape of a desert cat or a lioness, Bastet was a fierce deity. She was the daughter of Ra and represented the power of the Sun to ripen crops. Around 1500 BCE, Egyptians began domesticating cats. Bastet then came to be seen as kinder and was worshiped in the form of a cat or a woman with a cat's head.

RELATED SYMBOL Cat

ALTERNATIVE NAMES
Bast

PERIOD WORSHIPED
New Kingdom

CENTER OF WORSHIP
Bubastis

Taweret

With the head of a hippopotamus, the limbs of a lion, and the body of a human, Taweret had a strange appearance. She was also sometimes shown with the tail of a crocodile. She was worshiped as the goddess of childbirth.

RELATED SYMBOL Hippopotamus

ALTERNATIVE NAMES Taueret, Tawaret, Taurt

PERIOD WORSHIPED
Old Kingdom

CENTER OF WORSHIP
Jabal al-Silsila

Apep

Bes

A household god, Bes was the protector of women and newborn babies. It was said that if a baby smiled or laughed for no reason, it was because Bes was making funny faces.

RELATED SYMBOL
Dwarf god

ALTERNATIVE NAMES
Bisu, Aha

PERIOD WORSHIPED
Ptolemaic Period

CENTER OF WORSHIP
Homes

Aten

In Akhenaten's reign, only the Sun god Aten was worshiped. The god was depicted as the Sun's disk with rays that touched with human hands. Aten was probably the only Egyptian god who was not represented in a human or humanlike form.

RELATED SYMBOL Sun disk with rays ending as hands

ALTERNATIVE NAMES None

PERIOD WORSHIPED New Kingdom

CENTER OF WORSHIP Akhetaten (Amarna)

The serpent god of chaos, Apep was always locked away in the underworld. However, this did not stop him from waging a constant battle against the Sun god, Ra. He attacked Ra every day, but was defeated each time. This painting shows Ra, in the form of a cat, killing Apep.

RELATED SYMBOL Serpent

ALTERNATIVE NAMES Apophis

PERIOD WORSHIPED
New Kingdom

CENTER OF WORSHIP None

The "opening of the mouth" ceremony magically enabled the mummy to **breathe and speak**

Temples

Egyptian temples were designed to be imposing structures. They had massive stone walls and rows of columns carved with religious images and hieroglyphs. Since a temple was considered the home of a god, ordinary people could only enter the outer court. Priests performed sacred rituals in dark rooms at the heart of the temple.

Sun temple of Niuserre

This was one of the many Sun temples built during the 5th Dynasty. It was originally built using mud bricks, but was later rebuilt entirely with stone. A stone path connects the temple to the pyramid of Niuserre.

DEDICATED TO Ra

BUILT IN 5th Dynasty Old Kingdom

LOCATION Abu Gorab

The temple of Hathor at Abu Simbel was built by Ramesses II to honor Nefertari, his chief royal wife. The entire face of a stone hill was carved into giant statues of Ramesses II and Nefertari. Chambers inside the temple depict the royal couple making offerings to the gods.

DEDICATED TO Hathor

BUILT IN 1279–1213 BCE
(19th Dynasty New Kingdom)

LOCATION Abu Simbel, Nubia

Karnak temple complex

This temple complex began as a small set of buildings dedicated to local gods during the 11th Dynasty. By the 19th Dynasty, it was a huge complex with more than 80,000 people working in it as servants, guards, and priests.

DEDICATED TO Amun-Ra

BUILT IN 11th Dynasty onward

LOCATION Karnak

Statue of Amun

Temple of Dakka

A small structure, this temple was built by Arkamanian, an Ethiopian king, in 220 BCE. The Ptolemaic rulers later added more buildings, such as a gate and a columned porch.

DEDICATED TO Thoth

BUILT IN Ptolemaic Period

LOCATION New Wadi es-Sebua

Kom Ombo temple

Luxor temple

The Luxor temple is built on the eastern bank of the Nile River. It was completed by Amenhotep III. Pharaoh Ramesses II made many additions to the temple, building monuments such as this obelisk. Over the centuries, the temple was buried under sand and silt. This helped preserve its structures until it was excavated in 1881 CE.

DEDICATED TO Amun

BUILT IN c.1400 BCE
(18th–19th Dynasty
New Kingdom)

LOCATION Luxor

The obelisk is made of red granite and weighs more than 250 tons (227 metric tonnes)

The Kom Ombo temple is unique among the temples of ancient Egypt as it is dedicated to two gods—Sobek and Horus. The building has two entrances, two halls, and two sanctuaries. The left side of the temple is for Horus, while the right side is for Sobek.

DEDICATED TO Sobek and Horus

BUILT IN Ptolemaic Period

LOCATION Kom Ombo

Mortuary temple of Hatshepsut

Ancient Egyptians believed that the pharaohs became gods after death. To worship them, buildings called mortuary temples were built near their tombs. Designed by Pharaoh Hatshepsut's architect Senenmut, this temple is an extraordinary monument that rises from the desert plain in a series of grand terraces connected by long ramps.

DEDICATED TO Amun-Ra

BUILT IN 1470 BCE (18th Dynasty New Kingdom)

LOCATION Deir el-Bahari

Temple of Derr

Cut deep into rock, the Temple of Derr was built in the 30th year of Ramesses II's reign. Ancient Egyptians named it the "Temple of Ramesses–in-the-house-of-Ra." Early Christians converted it into a church and removed many of the decorations that covered the walls and roof.

DEDICATED TO Ra-Harakhty

BUILT IN 19th Dynasty New Kingdom

LOCATION Eastern bank of Nile in lower Nubia

Thutmose III, the pharaoh after Hatshepsut, erased all references to her in the temple, replacing them with his own name.

Temple of Amada

This is the oldest surviving Egyptian temple in Nubia and was constructed by Thutmosis III and Amenhotep II. Paintings and wall carvings inside the temple show the pharaohs making offerings to the gods.

DEDICATED TO Amun

BUILT IN 18th Dynasty New Kingdom

LOCATION Amada

Temple of Wadi es-Sebua

Wadi es-Sebua means "the valley of lions." The temple was so named because it had an avenue of sphinxes lining its approach. The temple is decorated with two colossi and many smaller statues of its builder, Ramesses II.

DEDICATED TO Amun-Ra

BUILT IN 1244–1229 BCE (19th Dynasty New Kingdom)

LOCATION Wadi es-Sebua, Lower Nubia

Temple of Hathor at Dendera

Dendera was the cult center of Hathor from Pre-dynastic times. The main hall of this temple has 18 columns, each decorated with the head of the goddess.

DEDICATED TO Hathor

BUILT IN 2250–343 BCE (6th–30th Dynasties Old Kingdom to Late Period)

LOCATION Dendera

Temple of Philae

As the center of the cult of Isis, the Temple of Philae was a place of pilgrimage for her worshipers. After the building of the Aswan Dam in the 1960s, parts of the temple were submerged under water. Between 1972 and 1980, the entire temple was moved to the island of Agilkia.

DEDICATED TO Isis

BUILT IN 380–362 BCE (30th Dynasty Late Period)

LOCATION Agilkia island, near Aswan

Deir el-Shelwit

This small structure was built while Egypt was ruled by the Roman Empire. The outer wall of the temple was constructed of material reused from New Kingdom buildings.

DEDICATED TO Isis

BUILT IN 1st century CE

LOCATION Luxor

Temple of Gerf Hussein

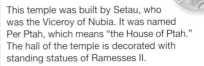

This temple was built by Setau, who was the Viceroy of Nubia. It was named Per Ptah, which means "the House of Ptah." The hall of the temple is decorated with standing statues of Ramesses II.

DEDICATED TO Ptah and Hathor

BUILT IN 1279–1213 BCE
(19th Dynasty New Kingdom)

LOCATION Built at lower Nubia, moved to a site near Aswan due to the construction of the Aswan Dam

Statue of Ramesses II holding crook and flail

Small Temple of Aten

The Small Temple of Aten was built by Akhenaten as part of his city of Akhetaten. Like much of the city, the temple was built using mudbricks, sandstone, and limestone plaster.

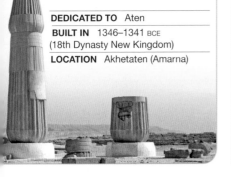

DEDICATED TO Aten

BUILT IN 1346–1341 BCE
(18th Dynasty New Kingdom)

LOCATION Akhetaten (Amarna)

Sacred artifacts

In ancient Egypt, only priests and royalty could enter the rooms and shrines inside a temple. Priests performed rituals to please the gods. The objects used in these rituals were sacred, often representing the gods themselves.

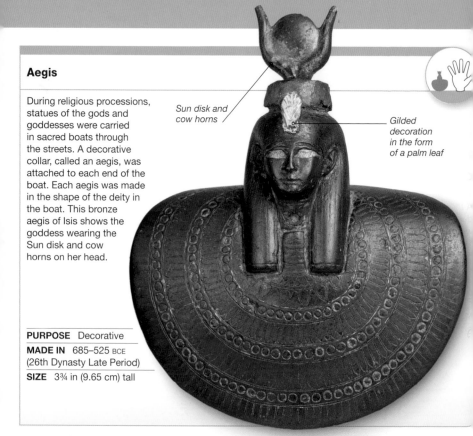

Aegis

During religious processions, statues of the gods and goddesses were carried in sacred boats through the streets. A decorative collar, called an aegis, was attached to each end of the boat. Each aegis was made in the shape of the deity in the boat. This bronze aegis of Isis shows the goddess wearing the Sun disk and cow horns on her head.

Sun disk and cow horns

Gilded decoration in the form of a palm leaf

PURPOSE Decorative

MADE IN 685–525 BCE (26th Dynasty Late Period)

SIZE 3¾ in (9.65 cm) tall

Copper standard

Egyptian priests carried standards, or poles, in their processions through temples. All that has survived of these are the emblems on top of the poles. This emblem shows Horus in the form of a falcon. He is wearing the combined crowns of Upper and Lower Egypt on his head.

PURPOSE Processions

MADE IN 685–525 BCE
(26th Dynasty Late Period)

SIZE 7¼ in (18.5 cm) tall

Situla

This bronze container held water from a sacred lake. Such lakes were a part of every temple complex. The situla was used to sprinkle holy water during religious rituals.

Bucket is decorated with images of gods and pharaohs

PURPOSE Carrying water

MADE IN Late Period

SIZE 10 in (25 cm) tall

Cult mirror

A temple was considered to be the home of a deity. So everyday objects, such as mirrors, were placed in temples for the deities to use. This is the cult mirror of the Moon god Khonsu. The face of the mirror is covered with different religious symbols.

PURPOSE Mirror for deity

MADE IN New Kingdom

SIZE 14½ in (37 cm) long

Eye of Horus

Mut, Khonsu's mother, receiving offerings from a priest

Head of Khonsu on top of handle

Corn mummy

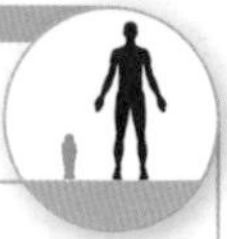

Egyptians saw the growth of a plant from a tiny seed as a symbol of rebirth, or resurrection. During the annual festival for Osiris, the god of resurrection, they made small mummies out of clay, sand, and corn seeds. These were then wrapped and put in coffins, which were placed in tombs as offerings to Osiris.

Coffin lid is decorated with images of deities

PURPOSE
Offering
MADE IN
Roman Period
SIZE 22 in (56 cm) tall

Ibis mummy case

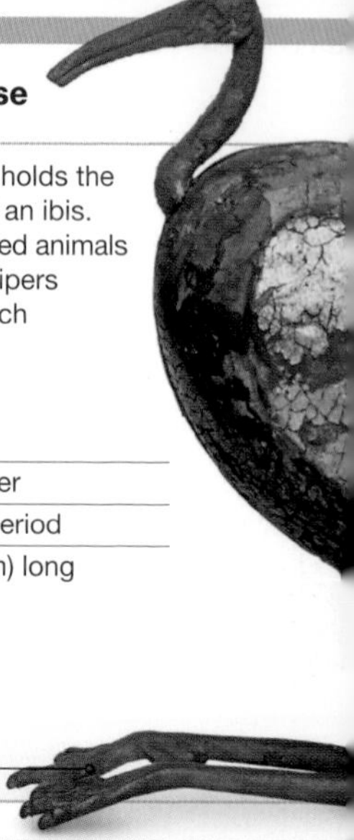

This gold container holds the mummified body of an ibis. Ibises were the sacred animals of Thoth. His worshipers often paid to get such mummies made as offerings to him.

PURPOSE Container
MADE IN Roman Period
SIZE 13½ in (34 cm) long

Feet are made of bronze

Crocodile mummy

The god of rivers and lakes, Sobek was represented by a crocodile. His priests even kept tame crocodiles in his temples. These reptiles were fed the best meats and wine. When a crocodile died, it was mummified and buried as an offering to Sobek.

Reeds used to pad out crocodile shape

Four million mummified ibises were discovered in an animal cemetery at Tuna El-gebel.

Cat mummy

Cats were sacred animals of the goddess Bastet and were kept in her temples. When these cats died, they were mummified, wrapped in linen cloth, and placed in cat-shaped coffins. It was considered a holy act for temple visitors to buy the coffins and have them buried.

PURPOSE Offering

MADE IN Roman Period

SIZE 18 in (46 cm) tall

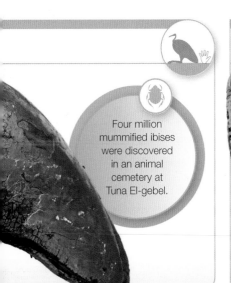

PURPOSE Offering

MADE IN Roman Period

SIZE 37 in (94 cm) long

Bulge of crocodile's eye can be seen through wrapping

Apis bull statuette

The Apis bull was worshiped as the living form of Osiris. When an Apis bull died, it was embalmed and buried in a massive stone sarcophagus in a temple called Serapeum. Worshipers often donated small sculptures, such as the one below, as offerings to the bull.

Sun disk between horns

PURPOSE Offering

MADE IN
Ptolemaic Period

SIZE 5½ in (14 cm) long

RESCUE EFFORT
To save the Temple of Philae from being submerged, a dam was built around the entire island, and the inside was pumped dry. Then the temple was taken apart and rebuilt on the island of Agilkia, which was completely reshaped to resemble Philae.

The Temple of Philae was dismantled into

40,000 blocks,

which, together, weighed
about 20,000 tons

Daily life

The lives of ancient Egyptians were closely linked to the Nile River. Farmers worked on the flood plain of the river, growing wheat, barley, fruits, and vegetables. Mud from the river was used to make household utensils, such as pots and spoons. Hunting wildlife around the river was a popular sport of the upper classes, as seen in the tomb painting on the left. It shows a nobleman and his family out on a bird hunt.

TERRA-COTTA BOTTLE
A type of hard-baked clay, terra-cotta was used widely in ancient Egypt. This terra-cotta bottle is shaped like a mother and her baby and was used to store milk.

Daily life

The common people of ancient Egypt worked as farmers or craftworkers, playing music and board games in their spare time. They usually wore linen clothes and makeup made from minerals.

Craftworkers

Using a variety of tools, such as drills, axes, and chisels, Egyptian craftworkers made many beautiful objects out of wood, gold, silver, and faïence.

Carpenters using tools such as saws, chisels, and hammer

Model of carpentry workshop found in tomb

Farming

The tomb painting on the left shows an Egyptian farmer cutting stalks of grain with a sickle. After cutting it, the farmer would clean the grain and store it in a large mud-brick granary.

Pond with ducks and fish

Painting of wealthy Egyptian's villa with garden

Living

Houses were made of mud bricks, with narrow windows to keep the Sun's heat out. Wealthy families lived in large villas with gardens and pools, while poorer people lived in simple homes.

Hunting

This shield shows Pharaoh Tutankhamun hunting and killing two lions. Hunting was popular with royalty and noblemen, as a way to show strength and courage.

Egyptians at home

Egyptians lived in houses made of mud bricks. Among the peasants, both men and women worked in the fields, while in wealthier families, the women stayed at home and the men worked as traders or officials.

Model of bread-making

Bread was an important part of the Egyptian diet. Bread-making was a tiring job, since it required kneeling down and grinding grain into flour for hours, as shown in the model below. Dirt or sand would get into the flour while it was being ground, making the bread hard and gritty. This caused damage to the teeth.

MADE IN
Middle Kingdom

SIZE 16¾ in (42.5 cm) wide

Model of Egyptian house

Models of houses were placed in tombs so that the dead could have a house in their next life. These were known as soul-houses. This model shows the house of a poor family. The house has a walled courtyard with models of food items, including meat and loaves of bread, placed in it.

MADE IN
12th Dynasty Middle Kingdom

SIZE 16¼ in (40.6 cm) long

◀ Egyptians ate bread with every meal. Bread was made of barley, wheat, and figs.

▲ The date palm tree was thought to be sacred and its fruit was placed as an offering in tombs.

▲ Figs were either eaten fresh or used to make fig wine.

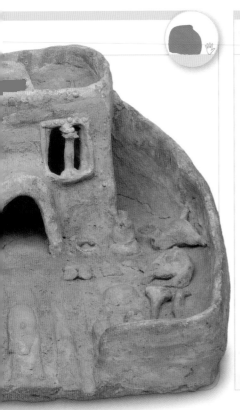

Wine jar

Wine and beer were two of the main drinks of ancient Egypt. Beer was drunk by everyone, but wine was usually used in religious ceremonies and drunk by the rich. This wine jar was probably used in the house of a wealthy family. Its narrow base shows that it would have been set on a stand or held by a servant.

MADE IN 21st Dynasty Third Intermediate Period

SIZE 9¼ in (23.5 cm) long

Clothes and cloth

Egyptians wore simple clothes made of linen. Men wore short skirts, called kilts, with a cloak around their shoulders. Women wore long, tight-fitting dresses. Both men and women wore wigs.

Wig

Wigs were used on public occasions and in religious ceremonies. This wig is made from 300 strands of actual human hair, each strand containing 400 hairs. The curly hair at the top has been strengthened with beeswax and resin.

MADE IN 18th Dynasty New Kingdom

SIZE 19¾ in (49.5 cm) long

Linen cloth

The types of linen available in Egypt ranged from coarse cloth worn by the poor, to fine gauze, which was worn by royalty. This piece of cloth has a pattern stitched on it in linen thread.

MADE IN Middle Kingdom

SIZE 4 in (10 cm) long

Spindle

Spindles were used to spin fiber into threads, which were then woven on a loom. This spindle was weighed down by a stone wheel or whorl.

MADE IN Middle Kingdom

SIZE 14½ in (37 cm) long

Fiber strands were twisted around spindle

Stone whorl

Leather sandals

Egyptians usually walked barefoot and wore footwear only on special occasions. The sandals worn by the poor were made of woven papyrus reeds, while those worn by the rich were made of leather or wood. These sandals were recovered from the tomb of Pharaoh Tutankhamun. They are made of wood and decorated with leather and gold leaf.

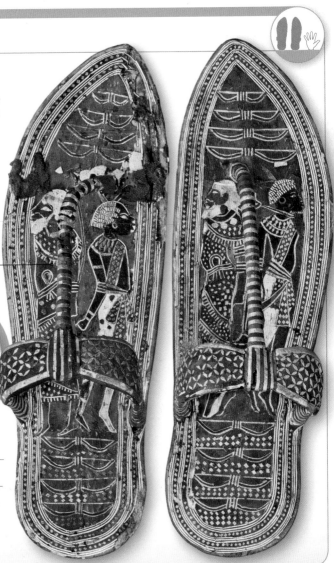

Figure of enemy soldier painted on sandal

Every time a pharaoh wore his sandals, he would symbolically trample on his enemies, who were depicted on the shoes.

MADE IN 18th Dynasty New Kingdom

SIZE 11 in (28 cm) long

Toys and games

Egyptian children played with balls, dolls, and toy animals, just as children do today. Adults preferred to play board games, such as senet and mehen. In fact, Tutankhamun liked senet so much that he was buried with four complete sets of the game to play in the afterlife.

Mehen (snake game)

This was one of the earliest known multiplayer board games played in Egypt. The board was in the shape of a coiled snake, which represented the god Mehen, who protected the Sun god Ra from his enemies. Players started at the tip of the snake's tail and moved their counters around the squares on the snake's body to the middle. The counters were sometimes carved with the names of Egypt's earliest pharaohs.

MADE IN Early Dynastic Old Kingdom

SIZE 14½ in (37 cm) wide

Hieroglyph of pharaoh's name

The first player to reach this point would win the game

Toy mouse

Ancient Egyptians used a variety of materials to make toys, including wood, bone, ivory, ceramics, and stone. Toys were modeled on objects, people, and animals that were common in everyday life. This wooden mouse had a string attached to its tail, which could be pulled to make the tail go up and down.

MADE IN New Kingdom

SIZE 3 in (7.5 cm) long (including tail)

Throwsticks

Throwsticks were used in Egypt in much the same way dice are used today. These sticks could be made of reed, wood, bone, or ivory, and were painted with different colors to tell the sides apart.

MADE IN 1500–1069 BCE (18th–20th Dynasty New Kingdom)

SIZE 7 in (18 cm) long

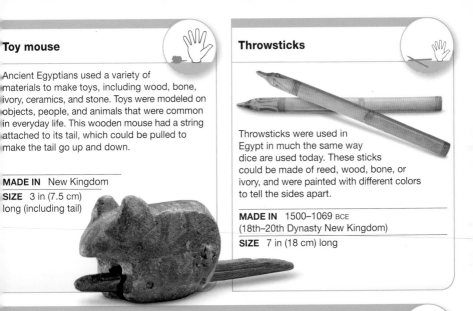

Senet

The game of senet symbolized a person's struggle against the forces of evil, which tried to prevent him or her from reaching the kingdom of Osiris. The game board had 30 squares. Some squares were dangerous to land on, others were lucky. The winner was believed to be protected by the gods.

MADE IN 1400–1200 BCE (18th–19th Dynasty New Kingdom)

SIZE 11 in (28 cm) long

Game counter

Painted toy horse

Only the wealthy owned horses in ancient Egypt. The animals were considered status symbols and were often given as gifts to the rulers of other kingdoms. This wooden horse was pulled along by a rope that was threaded through its muzzle.

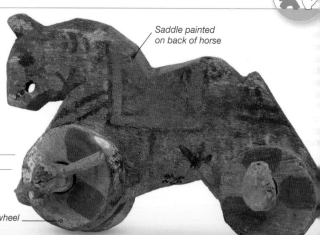

Saddle painted on back of horse

MADE IN Roman Period

SIZE 4½ in (11 cm) long

Wooden wheel

Dogs and jackals

In addition to mehen and senet, another popular board game was the game of dogs and jackals. The goal was to complete a circuit of the board before the other player. This board is shaped like a hippopotamus.

MADE IN 525–332 BCE (27th–30th Dynasty Late Period)

SIZE 8¾ in (21.5 cm) long

Wooden cat

This wooden toy is carved roughly into the shape of a cat. Pulling the string makes its lower jaw move up and down. It has bronze teeth and pieces of rock crystal for eyes.

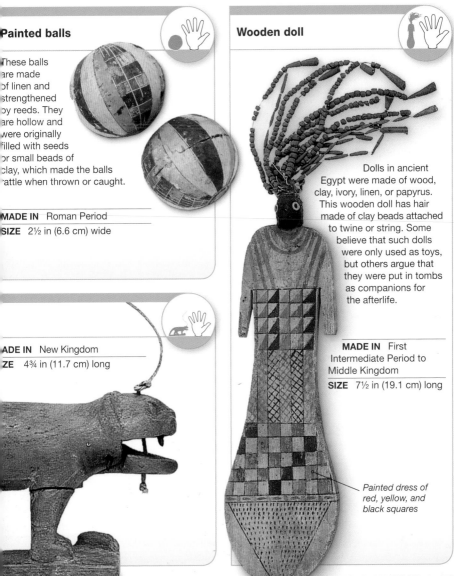

Painted balls

These balls are made of linen and strengthened by reeds. They are hollow and were originally filled with seeds or small beads of clay, which made the balls rattle when thrown or caught.

MADE IN Roman Period
SIZE 2½ in (6.6 cm) wide

ADE IN New Kingdom
ZE 4¾ in (11.7 cm) long

Wooden doll

Dolls in ancient Egypt were made of wood, clay, ivory, linen, or papyrus. This wooden doll has hair made of clay beads attached to twine or string. Some believe that such dolls were only used as toys, but others argue that they were put in tombs as companions for the afterlife.

MADE IN First Intermediate Period to Middle Kingdom
SIZE 7½ in (19.1 cm) long

Painted dress of red, yellow, and black squares

Music

Vital to Egyptian life, music was played during celebrations, religious festivals, and even during everyday work. Noblewomen would play the harp to help their husbands relax, while farmers would sing to their oxen to make them work better.

Sistrum

The sistrum was mainly associated with the goddess Hathor. Noblewomen and priestesses carried it at religious ceremonies. Small metal rings on the crossbars would move when the sistrum shook, producing a rattling sound.

Metal rings

Handle decorated with the head of Hathor

MADE IN Late Period
SIZE 16¼ in (41.7 cm) long

Harp

The harps played in ancient Egypt varied greatly in size, shape, and the number of strings. This five-stringed harp was found in the tomb of an Egyptian named Ani. The design of the pharaoh head on it suggests that it belonged to a court musician.

Head of Horus

Peg for tuning string

MADE IN New Kingdom
SIZE 38 in (97 cm) total length

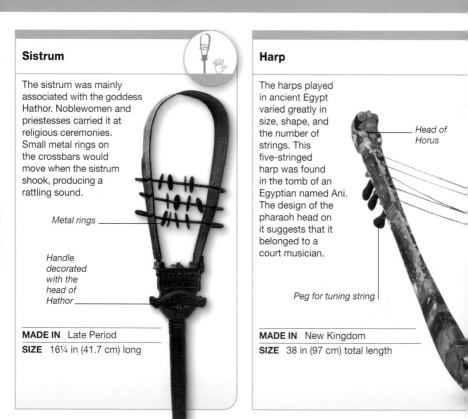

◀ This painting shows Egyptian musicians playing harps, lyres, and flutes. Among musicians, the ones who played in temples had the highest status. Mainly women, they were given the title *Shemayet,* meaning "musician." Next came the musicians of the royal court, who included gifted singers and harp players. There were also groups of musicians who traveled from place to place as troupes, playing at banquets and festivals.

End of harp is carved in the shape of a pharaoh wearing a Nemes headdress

Clappers

Clappers were used in Egyptian music in the same way as modern castanets. Musicians held the clappers in one hand and banged them together. Made of ivory and bone, these clappers were held together by a piece of string.

MADE IN 1991–1902 BCE (12th Dynasty Middle Kingdom)

SIZE 6½ in (17 cm) long

Clapper is carved to look like a hand

Hunting and fishing

Farming and livestock provided people with enough food, so hunting was mainly done as a sport. Egyptians hunted wild bulls, gazelles, lions, crocodiles, and hippopotamuses. Bird hunting was also popular among noblemen. Fishing, on the other hand, was done both for food and for fun.

Model of Tutankhamun with harpoon

This statue was found among the many treasures of Pharaoh Tutankhamun when his tomb was discovered in 1922. The statue shows Tutankhamun riding a papyrus-reed raft while hunting a hippopotamus. He has a spear or harpoon in one hand and a coiled bronze rope in the other. In the Middle Kingdom, the hippopotamus was associated with the god Seth, who spread chaos. By hunting it, Tutankhamun is shown as restoring order to the universe.

MADE IN 1340 BCE (18th Dynasty Middle Kingdom)

SIZE 29¾ in (75.5 cm) tall

Pleated skirt

Rafts were made by tying bundles of papyrus reed together

Arrow

Ancient Egyptians were skilled archers. They made arrows from the reeds that grew on the banks of the Nile River. The arrowheads were made of ivory, bone, flint, obsidian, or metal. The sharp tip of this bronze arrowhead could pierce through an animal's skin, injuring it severely.

MADE IN Late Period

SIZE 4¼ in (10.6 cm) long

Barb at end of arrow prevented it from being pulled out easily

Fishing hook

During the Old Kingdom, fish were usually caught in nets or by using spears. Later, fishermen began using bronze hooks, such as this one, to catch fish. These hooks were attached by a string to a pole. When a fish caught a hook in its mouth, it would tug the string and the fisherman would pull it out of the water.

MADE IN New Kingdom

SIZE 1¼ in (3 cm) long

Throwing stick

Shaped like boomerangs, these wooden throwing sticks were used to hunt wildfowl. The hunter would use a boat to approach the reeds where the birds were resting. When they emerged, he would hurl a stick at them in the hope of breaking their necks or wings, or at least stunning them.

MADE IN New Kingdom

SIZE 23 in (59 cm) long

Throwing sticks were also used in battle as weapons for hitting enemy soldiers from far away.

Farming

The Nile River flooded between July and September. When the floods ended, the banks of the river were covered with rich fertile soil. Farmers planted their crops in October and harvested them between March and May. The main crops were wheat, barley, and flax, but farmers also grew beans, lentils, onions, leeks, cucumbers, and lettuce.

Granary model

Ancient Egyptians used granaries to store grain. These buildings were made of mud bricks, which protected the grain from rodents and insects. This model shows workers storing grain inside the building, while a scribe is recording the amount being stored.

MADE IN Middle Kingdom
SIZE 17 in (43 cm) long

People often placed models of granaries in tombs, hoping to provide an unlimited supply of food in the afterlife.

Farmer model

In this model, the figure of the farmer is guiding the oxen as they drag a simple wooden plow behind them. The soil on the Nile flood plain was soft, allowing the farmers to plow it easily.

MADE IN 1985–1795 BCE
(12th Dynasty Middle Kingdom)

SIZE 17 in (43 cm) long

Wooden blade cuts through the soil

Winnowing fan

After the grain was harvested, it was winnowed, or separated, from its husk. The workers would gather up the grain in wooden, winnowing fans and throw it into the air. The lighter husks would blow away, leaving the grain to fall to the floor.

MADE IN New Kingdom

SIZE 19 in (48 cm) long

Raised edge of winnowing fan prevented grain from spilling out

Sickle

This simple sickle is made of wood and flint. The sharp pieces of flint attached to the blade allowed farmers to cut the stalks of grain during harvest. The stalks left behind were later gathered to make mats and baskets.

MADE IN 18th Dynasty New Kingdom

SIZE 11¼ in (28.5 cm) long

Cutting edge made of flint

When herding cattle across rivers, Egyptians **chanted spells** to protect their herd from crocodiles

Boats

The Nile River was the main highway of Egypt. Everything, from grain and cattle to coffins and building blocks, was transported by water. The earliest boats were made of bundles of papyrus reeds and propelled using oars. By 3000 BCE, Egyptians began building timber boats and using the wind to sail on the river.

Model of fishing skiffs

This is a model of two Egyptian boats called fishing skiffs. Such boats were made of papyrus, which made them easy to carry as well as to repair. In this model, the skiffs have a net stretched between them. As the boats move forward, fish are caught in the net and then pulled out.

MADE IN 12th Dynasty Middle Kingdom
SIZE 24½ in (62 cm) long

The Egyptians believed that the Sun god Ra himself traveled across the sky in a papyrus skiff.

Model of funeral boat

The Egyptians placed boats or models of boats in tombs because they believed that the dead were taken to the Underworld by boat. This model boat has two female mourners to accompany the mummy. The green color of the boat symbolizes rebirth in the afterlife.

MADE IN 12th Dynasty Middle Kingdom

SIZE 26 in (66.7 cm) long

Small statue of a mummy

Model of sailboat

Mostly used for transportation, sailboats were bigger than fishing boats. They had one square sail and were steered by two oars. This model sailboat was found in a tomb at Beni-Hasan, a cemetery on the eastern bank of the Nile. The sail and mast were missing and replacements were added based on other boats found at Thebes.

Square sail

Oar for changing boat's direction

MADE IN Around 2000 BCE (12th Dynasty Middle Kingdom)

SIZE 4 ft (1.2 m) long

Magic and medicine

Ancient Egyptians had great faith in magic and medicine. It was a common belief that wearing magical amulets could ward off any dangers that might threaten people or their families. Egyptian doctors wrote many manuals that described how to treat a variety of ailments, such as fevers, tumors, and eye disorders.

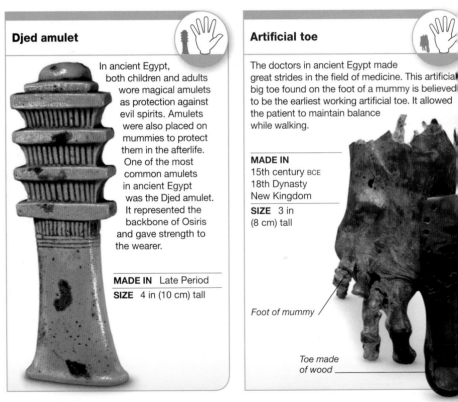

Djed amulet

In ancient Egypt, both children and adults wore magical amulets as protection against evil spirits. Amulets were also placed on mummies to protect them in the afterlife. One of the most common amulets in ancient Egypt was the Djed amulet. It represented the backbone of Osiris and gave strength to the wearer.

MADE IN Late Period

SIZE 4 in (10 cm) tall

Artificial toe

The doctors in ancient Egypt made great strides in the field of medicine. This artificial big toe found on the foot of a mummy is believed to be the earliest working artificial toe. It allowed the patient to maintain balance while walking.

MADE IN
15th century BCE
18th Dynasty
New Kingdom

SIZE 3 in (8 cm) tall

Foot of mummy

Toe made of wood

Prayer stela

Placed in houses as a protection against dangers, stelae were stone tablets with prayers on them addressed to the gods. This stela shows a prayer to Horus to protect the family from danger. Pictured in human form as a child, Horus is shown trampling two crocodiles, while gripping snakes, lions, and scorpions in his hand. These animals were not only signs of ill omens, but also real threats that were present in the desert.

Magic spells cover the stela's sides

MADE IN Ptolemaic Period

SIZE 10 in (26 cm) tall

Amuletic wand

Serpent armed with knife

Lion

Eye of Horus

Each individual design drawn on this wand was thought to have great power. The combination of all these designs made the wand even more powerful. Such wands were used to draw magical protective barriers around parts of a house.

MADE IN Middle Kingdom

SIZE 13 in (33 cm) long

Tools

Egyptian workers built giant structures using the simplest of tools. At first, tools were made of copper, which is a soft metal, so they would get blunt quickly. Later, Egyptians began using bronze, which is stronger than copper and stayed sharper.

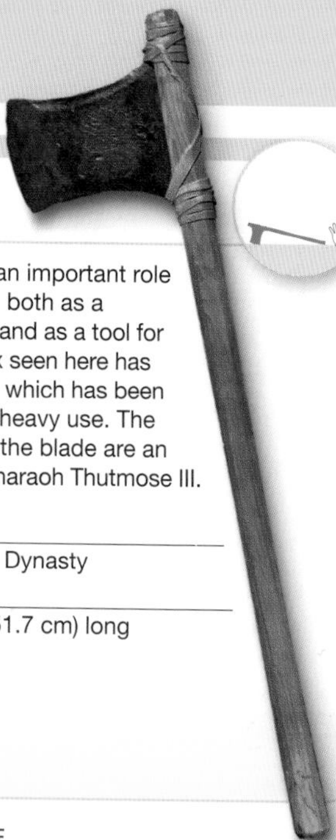

Adze

Adzes are tools used to cut and trim rough planks of wood and to shape and level wooden surfaces. Egyptian carpenters used them to build ships and make intricate wooden objects, such as chests, chairs, and even figurines. This adze was found in the tomb of Ani in Thebes.

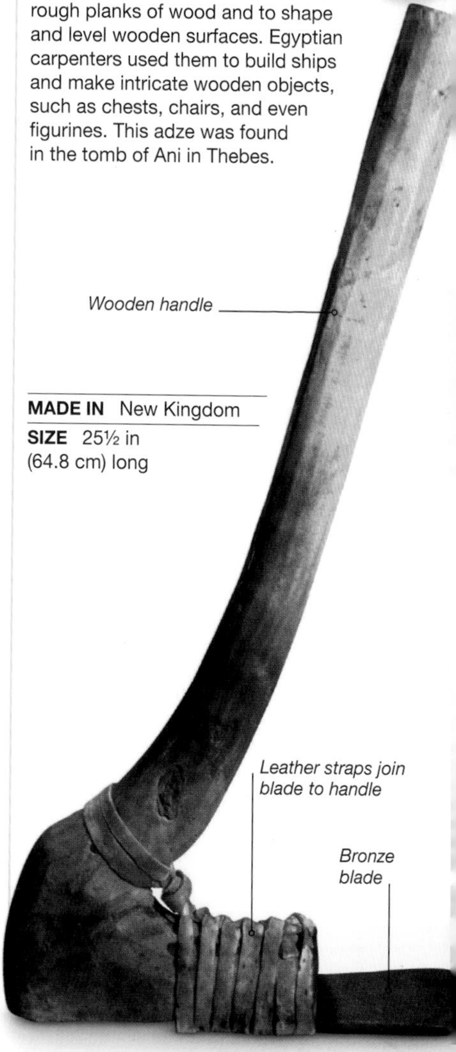

Wooden handle

MADE IN New Kingdom

SIZE 25½ in (64.8 cm) long

Leather straps join blade to handle

Bronze blade

Ax

The ax played an important role in Egyptian life, both as a weapon of war and as a tool for building. The ax seen here has a bronze blade, which has been blunted due to heavy use. The hieroglyphs on the blade are an inscription to Pharaoh Thutmose III.

MADE IN 18th Dynasty New Kingdom

SIZE 20¾ in (51.7 cm) long

Smoother

Once built, the walls of houses and tombs in ancient Egypt were coated with plaster. A smoother, such as the one shown below, flattened the plaster, creating a plain surface on which paintings could be made.

MADE IN New Kingdom

SIZE 6½ in (17 cm) long

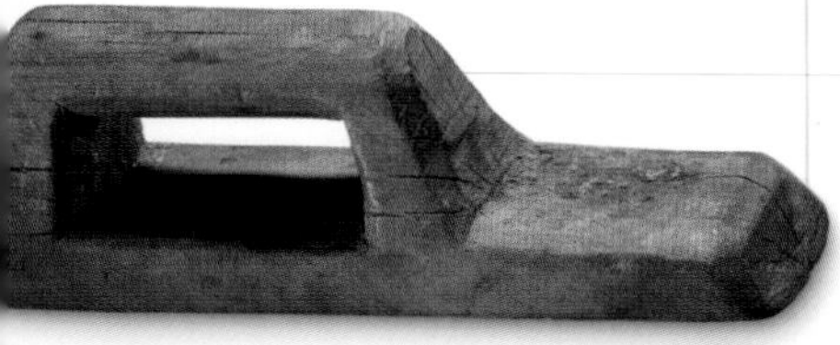

Chisel

Masons use chisels to work on stone. In ancient Egypt, fine details in reliefs, sculptures, and monuments were carved out using copper and bronze chisels. The tips of the chisels were sometimes heated to make it easier to cut the stone.

MADE IN Late Period

SIZE 6¾ in (17.5 cm) long

Bow drill

Egyptian workers used bow drills to make holes in wood and stone. A worker would wrap the the string of the bow around the drill holder, and move the bow back and forth to turn the metal drill fast enough to bore holes. The holder of this drill is well-worn, suggesting that the owner had used it a lot.

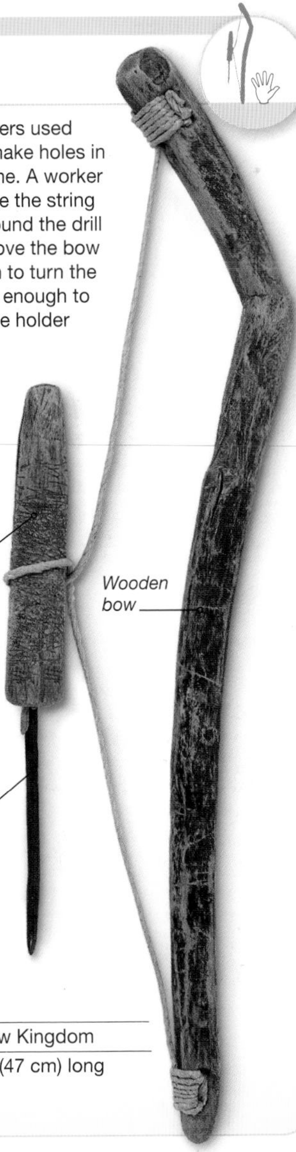

Drill holder

Wooden bow

Metal drill

MADE IN New Kingdom

SIZE 18½ in (47 cm) long

Jewelry

The craftworkers of ancient Egypt used many different materials to create beautiful pieces of jewelry. These materials included gold, silver, ivory, glass, and faïence. Egyptian jewelry was not only used for simple decoration, but also in official seals and to make lucky charms.

Bracelet of Nimlot

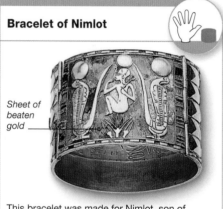

Sheet of beaten gold

This bracelet was made for Nimlot, son of Pharaoh Sheshonq I. The central design shows the god Horus as a child sitting on a lotus flower. Like many children in Egyptian art, the god is shown sucking his thumb. The hieroglyphs on the inside of the bracelet spell the owner's name. The bracelet was found at Sais, an important city during the Third Intermediate Period.

MADE IN 940 BCE (22nd Dynasty Third Intermediate Period)

SIZE 2½ in (6.3 cm) across

Falcon pectoral

A pectoral was a type of jewelry worn on the chest. This falcon pectoral was designed using a framework of metal cells that were filled with segments of faïence, glass, and gems. This technique is called cloisonné.

MADE IN 1370 BCE (18th Dynasty New Kingdom)

SIZE 6½ in (16 cm) wide

Metal plate shaped as wing

Traces of original inlay

Lucky girdle

Egyptian jewelers used an alloy called electrum—a mixture of gold and silver—in jewelry. The lucky charms on this girdle, or belt, were made of electrum and strung on papyrus twine, along with beads of amethyst, coral, lapis lazuli, and turquoise.

MADE IN 2055–1650 BCE
(11th–14th Dynasty Middle Kingdom)

SIZE 18½ in (47 cm) long

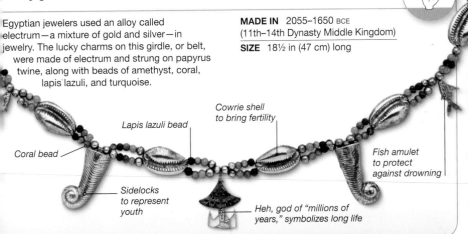

Cowrie shell
to bring fertility

Lapis lazuli bead

Coral bead

Fish amulet
to protect
against drowning

Sidelocks
to represent
youth

Heh, god of "millions of
years," symbolizes long life

Glass earring

Glass was also used to make jewelry, such as this earring. The purple and white edge of the earring was made by twisting strands of white and purple glass together. The ends of the earring are in the form of two loops, which held the wire that passed through the earlobe.

MADE IN 1550–1292 BCE
(18th Dynasty
New Kingdom)

SIZE ¾ in (2 cm)
diameter

Ring of Horemheb

Not all jewelry was made for display only. This ring bears the seal of Pharaoh Horemheb. It was probably used to stamp his official documents. The ring bears a cartouche with the hieroglyphs of Horemheb's name.

MADE IN 1323–1295 BCE
(19th Dynasty New Kingdom)

SIZE 1½ in (3.85 cm) diameter

Grooming

Personal appearance was very important to the Egyptians, and they went to great lengths to look beautiful. Many of the objects they used, such as combs, mirrors, and makeup, survive today.

FOCUS ON...
MAKEUP
Egyptians used pigments made from minerals for makeup.

Mirror

Most Egyptian men and women used mirrors made of copper or bronze. However, mirrors for royalty were made of polished silver. The owner of this silver mirror was Princess Sat-Hathor Yunet, daughter of Senusret II. The handle of the mirror is made of obsidian, a type of natural glass.

Handle is decorated with the face of the goddess Hathor, who was linked with beauty

MADE IN 1991–1802 BCE
(12th Dynasty Middle Kingdom)
SIZE 11 in (28 cm) long

Cosmetic jar

Men and women wore creams and perfumed oils not only to look beautiful, but also to prevent sunburn and damage from the sandy winds that blew in from the desert. These cosmetics were stored in this duck-shaped container.

MADE IN 1350–1300 BCE
(18th Dynasty New Kingdom)
SIZE 7 in
(17.5 cm) long

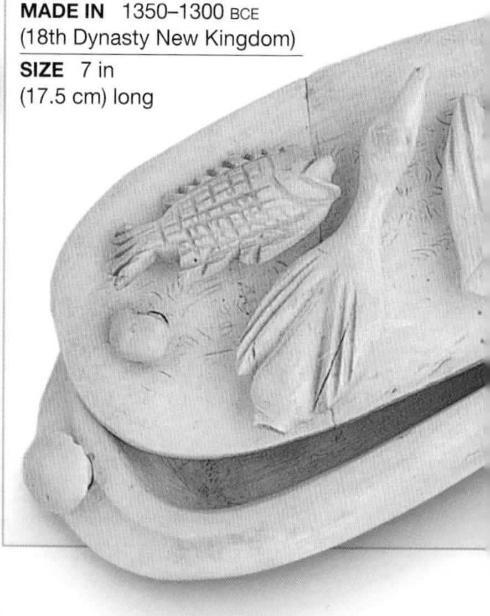

▲ They used the mineral galena to make kohl, a black eye paint.

▲ They ground malachite, a mineral of copper, to make green eye paint.

▲ They made a pigment called red ocher out of a mineral of iron.

Kohl tube

The ancient Egyptians believed that using kohl protected the eye against diseases and the harsh rays of the Sun. They made kohl by grinding galena into a powder and mixing it with water to make a fine paste. This paste was stored inside narrow tubes, and applied to eyebrows, eyelashes, and eyelids using a thin stick.

Glass tube

MADE IN 1375–1275 BCE
(19th Dynasty New Kingdom)

SIZE 3½ in (8.7 cm) long

Knob holds cover in place

Wing of duck forms cover for container

EGYPTIAN FEAST
The Egyptians held feasts to celebrate birth, marriage, and religious festivals, or even just to entertain their friends. The cooks prepared huge meals consisting of cakes sweetened with honey and different kinds of meat, such as ibis, goose, and antelope, flavored with herbs and spices.

The African American Experience
during World War II

The African American History Series

Series Editors:
Jacqueline M. Moore, Austin College
Nina Mjagkij, Ball State University

Traditionally, history books tend to fall into two categories: books academics write for each other, and books written for popular audiences. Historians often claim that many of the popular authors do not have the proper training to interpret and evaluate the historical evidence. Yet, popular audiences complain that most historical monographs are inaccessible because they are too narrow in scope or lack an engaging style. This series, which will take both chronological and thematic approaches to topics and individuals crucial to an understanding of the African American experience, is an attempt to address that problem. The books in this series, written in lively prose by established scholars, are aimed primarily at nonspecialists. They focus on topics in African American history that have broad significance and place them in their historical context. While presenting sophisticated interpretations based on primary sources and the latest scholarship, the authors tell their stories in a succinct manner, avoiding jargon and obscure language. They include selected documents that allow readers to judge the evidence for themselves and to evaluate the authors' conclusions. Bridging the gap between popular and academic history, these books bring the African American story to life.

Volumes Published
Booker T. Washington, W.E.B. Du Bois, and the Struggle for Racial Uplift
   Jacqueline M. Moore
Slavery in Colonial America, 1619–1776
   Betty Wood
African Americans in the Jazz Age: A Decade of Struggle and Promise
   Mark Robert Schneider
A. Philip Randolph: A Life in the Vanguard
   Andrew E. Kersten
The African American Experience in Vietnam: Brothers in Arms
   James Westheider
Bayard Rustin: American Dreamer
   Jerald Podair
African Americans Confront Lynching: Strategies of Resistance
   Christopher Waldrep
Lift Every Voice: The History of African-American Music
   Burton W. Peretti
To Ask for an Equal Chance: African Americans in the Great Depression
   Cheryl Lynn Greenberg
The African American Experience during World War II
   Neil A. Wynn

Joe Louis

The African American Experience during World War II

Neil A. Wynn

ROWMAN & LITTLEFIELD PUBLISHERS, INC.
Lanham • Boulder • New York • Toronto • Plymouth, UK

Published by Rowman & Littlefield Publishers, Inc.
A wholly owned subsidiary of The Rowman & Littlefield Publishing Group, Inc.
4501 Forbes Boulevard, Suite 200, Lanham, Maryland 20706
http://www.rowmanlittlefield.com

Estover Road, Plymouth PL6 7PY, United Kingdom

British Library Cataloguing in Publication Information Available

Library of Congress Cataloging-in-Publication Data

Wynn, Neil A.
  The African American experience during World War II / Neil A. Wynn.
    p. cm.—(The African American history series)
  Includes bibliographical references.
  ISBN 978-1-4422-0016-6 (cloth : alk. paper)—ISBN 978-1-4422-0017-3 (electronic)
  1. World War, 1939-1945—African Americans. 2. World War, 1939-1945—Social aspects—United States. 3. African Americans—History—1877-1964. 4. United States—Race relations—History—20th century. 5. World War, 1939-1945—Participation, African American. 6. African American soldiers—History—20th century. 7. United States—Armed Forces—African Americans—History—20th century. I. Title.
  D810.N4W89 2010
  940.53089'96073—dc22
                                                                          2009050243

♾ ™ The paper used in this publication meets the minimum requirements of American National Standard for Information Sciences—Permanence of Paper for Printed Library Materials, ANSI/NISO Z39.48-1992.

Printed in the United States of America

Contents

~

Acknowledgments

I would like to thank the editors of the series, Nina Mjagkij and Jacqueline Moore, for asking me to write this book in the first place, for their patience given the length of time it took to produce, and for their assistance and advice in completing it. The editor at Rowman & Littlefield, Niels Aaboe, and his assistant Elisa Weeks, production editor Elaine McGarraugh, and copyeditor Jennifer Kelland Fagan were also supportive above and beyond the call of duty. I am very grateful for the support of colleagues at the University of Gloucestershire during increasingly hard financial times that impacted on all staff! Pam Jerrard and Lois Oldham (assisted by Sophie Murphy) provided a great deal of help and encouragement in their own different ways, and I could not have managed without the help of Jill Roebuck and other colleagues in the Inter-Library Loan Service in Learning Information Service. My fellow historians (Neil Armstrong, Melanie Ilic, and Iain Robertson) have always been encouraging, as have other friends and workmates in the Department of Humanities.

I was asked to write this book at about the same time I was working with Gregory Cooke on the film *Choc'late Soldier from the USA*. Working with Greg rekindled interest in a subject I had not written about for a while, so his involvement was most timely. Through researching on the British aspect of black service in the war for this film, I not only became a "local" historian but met some wonderful people, especially Mrs. Pat Edmead and others who had lived through the war and become involved in the black experience themselves.

Most of all I must thank my wife, Regina, who has always been a great help and tolerated the many lonely evenings and weekends required to complete this book. However, I dedicate this volume to my granddaughters, Claudia, Freya, and Rosa Tilly, in the hope they might learn something from it one day.

~

Overview

The symbolism of President Barack Obama's presence in Normandy on June 6, 2009, to deliver remarks commemorating the sixty-fifth anniversary of the D-day landings in France was enormous. As the president acknowledged, the landings carried special significance in a war against an ideology that "sought to subjugate and humiliate and exterminate. It perpetrated murder on a massive scale, fuelled by a hatred of those who were deemed different and therefore inferior."[1] Although it was undoubtedly recognized at the time, many Americans were themselves denied equality and suffered hatred simply because of the color of their skin; discrimination ensured that only a few African Americans participated in the Normandy landings. President Obama's 2008 election indicated how far the United States had progressed toward a more equal and fair society since 1944.

When the Japanese attacked Pearl Harbor on December 7, 1941, one of the heroes on that day of "infamy" was a black sailor from Waco, Texas, Dorie Miller. A mess man on the USS *West Virginia*, Miller carried his wounded captain to safety and then manned a machine gun, downing a number of Japanese aircraft before leaving the sinking vessel. Initially denied any official recognition, after protest in the black press Miller received the Navy Cross on May 27, 1942. He died in November 1943 when the escort carrier *Liscombe Bay* was sunk in the Pacific. In many ways Miller represented the often contradictory experience of the African American in World War II. Limited by his race to a menial role in the navy, he nonetheless responded as a loyal American and acted above and beyond the call of duty. He died still

in the service of his country, and while the navy continued with the policy of segregation throughout the war, it used Miller's image in a recruiting poster. Like another famous African American, boxing world champion and army veteran Joe Louis, Dorie Miller transcended the restrictions placed upon him by the racial policies of the day and went from being simply a black hero to becoming a symbol of America itself. In doing so, he and Lewis represented the impact that the war was to have on American race relations as well as its

"Above and Beyond the Call of Duty." Dorie Miller with his Navy Cross at Pearl Harbor, May 27, 1942. LC-USZC4-2328 (8-10).

limitations. While both served, they did so in segregated armed forces, and Miller, like all African Americans in the navy, could only serve in a limited role. Louis too served in a segregated army, but because of his status he had slightly more opportunity than most other black soldiers. Given these racial policies, it is indeed ironic that both men were in advertising campaigns to sell the war, an irony not lost on many African Americans.

Yet, despite the barriers they faced, World War II was enormously significant in the African American experience. Much has now been written on the war's impact on black America, both from a national and local perspective, since Richard M. Dalfiume's groundbreaking article in 1968 on "The Forgotten Years of the Negro Revolution" or my own *The Afro-American and the Second World War* first published in 1973. It is now widely accepted that the war years were crucial in the development of the emerging civil rights movement in terms of the effects on, and of, military service, as well as the social and economic impact of the war. Indeed, some historians write of the war as a "turning point" or "watershed" in civil rights history. However, it is important to locate the war years in a broader context and to show the elements of continuity as well as change between the New Deal era of the 1930s and the Cold War years that followed World War II in the development of American race relations. More than sixty years on, we can now incorporate the existing scholarship to locate the war years within the long-term developments of the twentieth century and add to our understanding of the civil rights movement in the United States.

Chronology

1938   February   Robert Vann, publisher of the *Pittsburgh Courier*, establishes the Committee for the Participation of Negroes in National Defense.

1939   September 1   German armies invade Poland, starting World War II.

1940   September 16   The Selective Service Act is introduced, with clauses prohibiting discrimination but not segregation.

Officer training programs are opened for African Americans in the army.

September 27   A. Philip Randolph, T. Arnold Hill, and Walter White meet President Franklin Roosevelt and government officials in the White House to call for action to end discrimination in the defense industries and segregation in the armed forces.

October   After announcing that the policy of segregation will continue in the armed forces, the government announces that Benjamin O. Davis Sr. has been appointed the first ever African American general, Judge William H. Hastie becomes civilian aide to the secretary of war, Col. Campbell C. Johnson becomes Negro adviser to the director of Selective Service, and an air-training school is to be established.

1941   January   Randolph calls for a march on Washington of ten thousand African Americans to protest discrimination in the defense industries and subsequently publishes this call in *Black Worker* in March.

March   The air-training program for black pilots begins at Tuskegee Institute in Alabama.

June 18   President Roosevelt meets with Randolph and White in the White House to try to prevent the march on Washington from taking place.

June 25   President Roosevelt issues Executive Order 8802 establishing a Fair Employment Practices Committee (FEPC) to ensure an end to discrimination in employment in the defense industries, thereby averting the march on Washington called by Randolph and scheduled for July 1.

October   The first FEPC hearings on job discrimination are held in Los Angeles, California. Subsequent hearings are held in Chicago, New York City, and Birmingham, Alabama.

December 7   Japanese aircraft attack the American fleet in Pearl Harbor, and the United States officially enters World War II the following day.

1942   February 14   The *Pittsburgh Courier* launches the "Double V" campaign for victory at home and abroad.

April   African Americans are admitted to the U.S. Marine Corps and for general service in the navy.

The Congress of Racial Equality (CORE) is established in Chicago.

June   The March on Washington Movement holds a rally in New York, followed by a similar rally in Chicago and one in St. Louis in August. Plans for further rallies are shelved.

The first African American troops arrive in Northern Ireland and Great Britain.

1943   January 31   Hastie resigns as civilian aide to the secretary of war.

The war effort is disrupted by more than 240 riots and racial incidents across the country in towns and cities and in and around military camps.

May   Strikes and rioting occur at Alabama Drydock & Shipping Company in Mobile.

May 27   President Roosevelt issues Executive Order 9346 establishing a reconstituted FEPC.

June 3   White servicemen and civilians attack Mexican and African American youths in the Los Angeles "zoot suit" riot.

June 15   Shipyard workers in Beaumont, Texas, strike and then attack African Americans during a riot.

June 20–24   Thirty-four people (twenty-five black) are killed in a race riot in Detroit.

August 1–2   An incident involving a white policeman and black soldier sparks a riot in Harlem, New York City, in which five people are killed.

September   The FEPC finally holds hearings into discrimination in southern railroad companies and unions.

1944   April 3   In *Smith v. Allwright*, the Supreme Court rules the all-white Democratic Party primary in Texas unconstitutional.

June 6   The all-black 320th Anti-Aircraft Barrage Balloon Battalion takes part in the D-day landings in Normandy, launching the Allied attack on Nazi-occupied Europe.

July 17   More than three hundred people, many of them African American stevedores, are killed in an explosion in the harbor of Port Chicago, California. Black seamen subsequently refuse to return to unload ships, and fifty are convicted of mutiny.

August   A Philadelphia Transit strike protesting the upgrading of black workers paralyzes the city and requires that troops be sent in before the dispute is settled.

December   Following a German offensive in the Ardennes, volunteers are called up from black noncombat troops to serve in integrated units.

1945   April 12 President Roosevelt dies in office and is succeeded by Harry S. Truman.

May 8   V-E Day (Victory in Europe Day) ends the war in Europe.

August 15   V-J Day (Victory in Japan Day) ends the war against Japan.

September   The Gillem Committee under Gen. Alvan C. Gillem is appointed to investigate the army's use of African American troops. It reports in April 1946.

1946   February   Policemen in Aiken, South Carolina, attack and blind African American World War II veteran Isaac Woodward.

June 3   In *Morgan v. Virginia* the Supreme Court rules segregation in interstate transport unconstitutional.

July 2   African American veterans and their wives are taken from their car near Monroe, Georgia, by a white mob and shot to death.

December 6   President Truman appoints the President's Committee on Civil Rights.

1947   April   Jackie Robinson becomes the first African American in sixty years to play for a professional baseball team when he makes his appearance for the Brooklyn Dodgers.

            Members of CORE, including Bayard Rustin, organize the Journey of Reconciliation, from Washington, D.C., into the upper South, to test the Supreme Court decision against segregated interstate transport. The campaigners are subsequently arrested, and several serve prison sentences in North Carolina.

            June 29   President Truman addresses the National Association for the Advancement of Colored People from the steps of the Lincoln Memorial.

            October 29   The President's Committee on Civil Rights issues its landmark report *To Secure These Rights*.

            November   Randolph and Grant Reynolds organize the Committee against Jim Crow in Military Service and Training.

1948   January 12   In *Sipuel v. Board of Regents of Oklahoma University*, the Supreme Court rules that the Oklahoma University Law School may not deny entry to students simply on the grounds of race or provide separate facilities that are inadequate.

            February 2   President Truman presents his civil rights message to Congress.

            March 22   African American leaders, including Randolph, meet with President Truman and urge him to insist on antisegregation amendments to the legislation to reinstitute the draft.

            March 30   Randolph, representing the Committee against Jim Crow in Military Service and Training, testifies to the Senate Armed Services Committee.

            May 3   In *Shelley v. Kraemer*, the Supreme Court declares that restrictive housing covenants on grounds of race cannot be enforced.

            June 26   Randolph announces the formation of the League for Non-Violent Civil Disobedience against Military Segregation. He informs President Truman on June 29, 1948, that unless the president issues an executive order ending segregation in the armed forces, African American youth will resist the draft law.

            July 14   The Democratic National Convention adopts a liberal civil rights plank, calling for, among other things, the desegregation of the armed forces.

            July 26   President Truman signs Executive Order 9980, prohibiting discrimination in the federal government and requiring employment

on merit only, and Executive Order 9981, declaring that "there shall be equality of treatment and opportunity for all persons in the armed services without regard to race, color, religion, or national origin." Shortly afterward, Randolph calls off the threatened civil disobedience campaign.

~

Introduction

The African American and
War in Historical Context

Once let the black man get upon his person the brass letters US, let him
get an eagle on his button, and a musket on his shoulder, and bullets in
his pocket, and there is no power on earth or under the earth which can
deny that he has earned the right of citizenship in the United States.

—Frederick Douglass, "Should the Negro Enlist in the Union Army?"
National Hall, Philadelphia, July 6, 1863.[1]

As this quotation from the former slave and leading black spokesman of the
mid-nineteenth century, Frederick Douglass, indicates, African Americans
had always realized the importance of military service in furthering their
demands for equality; white Americans, too, had been aware that military
participation carried implications regarding claims for equal citizenship.
While black Americans hoped to serve as equals in order to press their claims
for full citizenship, white Americans often opposed black military service for
exactly the same reason. The struggle over this previously contested issue
reached new levels during World War II.

More than five thousand African Americans fought in the War of Independence, and individuals like Crispus Attucks, the runaway slave who
died in the 1770 Boston Massacre, or Peter Salem, another slave who fought
at Bunker Hill in 1775, are often seen as representatives of the American
revolutionary principles of freedom and equality. However, this would be
a real oversimplification. The victory of the American colonists was also a
victory for slave owners: as Douglass later remarked famously, July Fourth

was a white celebration, not one shared by African Americans. Not only did several of the signatories of the Declaration of Independence own slaves, but when George Washington, also a slave owner, took command of the Continental army, he specifically excluded blacks from serving as soldiers. It was the British, led by former governor of Virginia Lord Dunmore, who offered freedom to slaves who took up arms against the American rebels. Only then did the colonists accept free blacks and slaves as soldiers, promising them their freedom in return. As a result, African Americans fought in almost every campaign of the war; yet, slavery was still written into the Constitution and continued as a crucial element of life in the South. The revolutionary ideology did, however, weaken the institution in northern states, and the first antislavery societies began to emerge at approximately the same time as the Revolution.

African Americans fought with their countrymen against the British again in 1812, and although several units served with Andrew Jackson at the battle of New Orleans, this did little to deter the spread of slavery in the South. As was the case in the War of Independence, many African Americans escaped slavery by joining the British rather than remaining with the Americans. However, ultimately it was another war and the contribution of African Americans in it that brought the institution of slavery to an end. The issue of black military service arose at the very start of the Civil War in 1861, but initially determined not to make the conflict one about slavery, President Abraham Lincoln ordered black volunteers turned away. Many Northerners supported the president's position not on strategic grounds for fear of alienating the border slave states but on racial grounds and the belief that African Americans would make bad soldiers. Additionally, black military service would imply an equality few whites were prepared to recognize. Only as the war dragged on did such attitudes change, and in the preliminary Emancipation Proclamation of 1862, President Lincoln not only indicated that slavery would end in those parts of the South that continued to resist but also called for black volunteers to fight. The enactment of the proclamation in 1863 meant that the war begun to save the Union had become one to end slavery; black military participation ensured that this would be the case. Slavery ended with the Thirteenth Amendment in 1865, and African Americans gained the rights of equal citizenship and suffrage with the Fourteenth and Fifteenth amendments in 1868 and 1870, respectively.

During the Civil War, 186,097 African Americans served in 167 all-black army regiments, and almost 40,000 died; another 29,000 served in the navy. However, they did not serve as equals. Until 1864 black soldiers earned half the amount paid to whites and served predominantly in noncombat roles.

There were few black officers, and other white troops often viewed the white officers of black regiments with contempt. However, many black soldiers did see combat in several theaters, and they fought courageously in a number of important battles, most famously at Fort Wagner in July 1863, when the Fifty-fourth Massachusetts Regiment led the assault on the Confederate positions. African Americans suffered high casualties during the war, at least in part because the Confederate troops adopted a policy of no quarter where black soldiers were concerned. Black men, women, and children were massacred at Fort Pillow, Tennessee, in April 1864, and rebel forces killed wounded black prisoners at Poison Springs, Arkansas, the same month.

Twenty-three African Americans received the Medal of Honor for their bravery in the Civil War, among them six seamen. In recognition of African Americans' military contribution, in 1866 Congress established four segregated, black, regular army units on a permanent basis: the Ninth and Tenth cavalries and the Twenty-fourth and Twenty-fifth infantries. All four regiments served in Texas and Kansas and saw action against various Native American tribes. It was Native Americans who nicknamed the black fighters "Buffalo Soldiers," a label that persisted through to World War II. The black regiments saw action in Cuba in 1898 during the war with Spain. Five members of the Tenth Cavalry earned the Medal of Honor, and several received citations for their bravery during the battle of San Juan Hill in which they fought beside future president Theodore Roosevelt's "Rough Riders." Initially, Roosevelt and others recognized the contribution of the so-called Smoked Yankees in positive terms, but later in his career Roosevelt suggested that the black soldiers' accomplishments stemmed simply from determined white leadership and that they had to be prevented from deserting the battlefield.

After the Spanish-American War, the African American units served in the Philippines and took part in suppressing a local uprising there. Despite their contribution to an essentially imperialist war, when the black troops returned to their bases in Texas and the Southwest to serve once again, they met with contempt and often faced discrimination and violence. In 1906 the first battalion of the Twenty-fifth Infantry was transferred from Nebraska to Brownsville, Texas, to serve beside the Texas National Guard. The local white population and white soldiers resented the black soldiers' presence equally, and black soldiers were attacked or mistreated on several occasions. During the night of August 14, 1906, several shots were fired in the town by a group of about twelve unidentified people. A local inhabitant was killed, one was wounded, and a policeman was also injured. It was assumed that black soldiers had shot up the town, but when no one confessed or indicated

who was responsible, all 167 men in three battalions were given dishonorable discharges and barred from further military or federal service. Senator Joseph B. Foraker of Ohio protested this decision and insisted on an investigation, which discovered that the evidence against the black soldiers was weak. In 1909 Foraker persuaded Congress to allow the discharged men to reenlist, but the initial decision was not overturned until 1972, when the one surviving black soldier was paid $25,000 in compensation.

The Brownsville affair points to the generally deteriorating racial climate in the United States at the start of the twentieth century. Between 1900 and 1917, over one thousand black Americans were lynched, and white communities attacked their black neighbors in several race riots. The worst of these occurred in Atlanta, Georgia, in September 1906 when at least twenty-five blacks and two whites died during three days of violence after the local press reported four supposed assaults by black men on white women. Two years later, a riot broke out in Springfield, Illinois, again after two black men were alleged to have sexually assaulted white women. When the two accused were removed from the town for their own protection, mobs of white people attacked the black community, destroying property and causing at least two African American deaths. Five white people were killed, some by blacks defending their property or their lives.

Some white Americans caught the significance of Springfield being the home of Abraham Lincoln, and appalled by the rising tide of violence, a group of progressive reformers and journalists met in 1909 to establish the National Association for the Advancement of Colored People (NAACP), today the longest-existing civil rights organization. Initially a largely white-led organization, the NAACP included a leading black educator and activist, W. E. B. Du Bois, who became the editor of the association's monthly journal, *The Crisis*. The emergence of the NAACP was, however, very much an exceptional development. In the years before World War I, the systematic economic discrimination, political exclusion, and racial segregation known as Jim Crow in the South were at their height and, together with the widespread acceptance of racist ideologies elsewhere in the country, had undermined the gains made in the period of Reconstruction after the Civil War. On the eve of World War I, race relations in the United States were at their lowest ebb.

The events in Houston, Texas, in 1917 highlighted the situation of black soldiers. Posted to the city in July, units of the Twenty-fourth Infantry experienced a constant barrage of harassment and insult from white civilians. The soldiers, some of whom had seen service in the Philippines, also demonstrated a reluctance to follow the Jim Crow laws on public transport

and became involved in several clashes with motormen when they refused to use segregated seating. After Houston police had beaten and arrested two soldiers, more than one hundred men from the Twenty-fourth armed themselves, marched into town, and began to shoot police officers. In total seventeen whites died in the riot, and four of the black soldiers were also shot. Afterward sixty-three men were charged with mutiny in time of war, and a speedy court-martial found fifty-four men guilty; thirteen were sentenced to death, and the executions were quickly carried out. Another thirteen received death sentences in subsequent trials, but of these only the six convicted of murder were executed.

With American entry into World War I on April 6, 1917, many African Americans rushed to volunteer to serve in the army. They were generally turned away. Black Americans soon discovered that their participation in the war "to make the world safe for democracy," in President Woodrow Wilson's phrase, would be resisted and therefore limited. The debates over the introduction of the first draft in the United States with the passage of the Selective Service Act revealed only too well how little had changed since the time of the Civil War. Many Americans, some in the military, claimed that African Americans made poor soldiers or that their service would harm military unity. Some southern politicians argued that arming African Americans would lead to violence at home. However, when passed in May 1917, the act made no mention of race, and 3 million African Americans were registered for service. Ironically, nearly 31 percent, approximately 370,000, were drafted as compared to 26 percent of white registrants due to the discriminatory composition and attitude of draft boards.

Most of the African Americans who served in the army during World War I were confined to noncombat roles. The four established regular army regiments were not included among those sent to Europe but remained either in the United States, Hawaii, or the Philippines. Instead, the vast majority of the new black recruits were assigned to specially created service units as quartermasters, cooks, bakers, drivers, stevedores, or laborers. The forty thousand or so African American soldiers who did see combat duty served in the Ninety-second Division or the Ninety-third, which primarily comprised National Guard units from Connecticut, Illinois, Massachusetts, New York, and Ohio. The regiments of the Ninety-third Division were assigned to serve with the French troops because, it was said, the French had experience with their own colonial troops. However, the assignment was probably due as much to the French forces' desperate need of manpower. Known as *les enfants perdus* ("the lost children"), the various units served with some distinction. The 369th Infantry Regiment, known to the Germans as "Hell Fighters,"

803rd Pioneer Infantry Band, No. 16, on the USS Philippines *(troop ship) from Brest, France, July 18, 1919. Gladstone Collection, Prints and Photographs Division. Reproduction Number: LC_USZC4-6163 (7-5).*

remained at the front for over 190 days, longer than any other American regiment. The entire 371st and 372nd infantries were awarded the Croix de Guerre by the French for their service.

The Ninety-second Division was not committed to action until September 1918, when it took part in the Meuse-Argonne offensive. Poorly prepared, poorly equipped, and poorly led, the black troops were asked to perform a series of difficult maneuvers. In the midst of the action, confusion about the orders received caused the operation to fail. Rather than address the root causes, the command structure blamed the soldiers themselves, and they did not see action again until near the end of the war. This episode highlighted the lack of good officers among the black regiments. Most of the officers were white, and many were southerners chosen because they supposedly understood the African American temperament; in reality many of them had a poor view of their own men, and many had been assigned to the regiment because they themselves had poor standing in the military. Only after strong protest from black spokesmen and civil rights organizations was a segregated officer-training camp for blacks established at Camp Des Moines, Iowa; the first 639 black soldiers received their commissions in October 1917. By the

end of the war, twelve hundred black officers had been commissioned, but they could only serve in black regiments.

The African American soldiers who did see service in France often found a warm welcome. The French, much more liberal in their racial attitudes, were glad to see anyone who came to help defeat the invading German armies. This applied to French women, too, and white Americans found this particularly offensive. American officials became so concerned about the likely effects of fraternization between African Americans and their French allies that the liaison officer working with the French circulated a secret memorandum warning them against dealing with African Americans in the same way as white Americans or praising them too highly. Relations between white women and black soldiers were to be discouraged. Similarly, at the end of the war, black soldiers were congratulated on their service but warned not to expect things to be different when they got home. Thus, despite the 750 battle deaths and 5,000 wounded among African American soldiers, it appeared that little had changed.

Many things had changed at home, however. Even before 1917 the demand for food, munitions, and other war materials from the warring nations created a war boom in the United States. This increased after American entry into the conflict, and as the normal supplies of immigrant labor dwindled, northern industries turned to the southern black population as an alternative. Pushed by the deteriorating social and economic situation in the South, attracted by the high wages and better conditions in the North, and encouraged by previous migrants and the black press, especially the *Chicago Defender* and *The Crisis*, thousands of black sharecroppers made their way north in what became known as the "Great Migration." Between 1870 and 1910 approximately sixty-seven thousand black Americans left the South per decade; between 1910 and 1920 the number was probably around four hundred thousand, mostly concentrated after 1915. The majority of the migrants headed for the major centers of war production in Chicago, Detroit, Philadelphia, and New York. Many found industrial work for the first time, and a new black working class emerged. The benefits of the move included new opportunities and higher earnings—the disadvantage was that the additional population crowded into existing black neighborhoods that increasingly took on the characteristics of ghettos. Attempts to move into white areas met with resistance, and there was considerable conflict in the workplace and on public transport.

White resentment of the black newcomers spilled over into violence, and in 1917 a major race riot broke out in East St. Louis in which white mobs killed more than forty African Americans. In the South, too, the migration

of black workers threatened the economic relationships between white landowners and black tenants, destabilizing the racial status quo. Lynchings increased during the war, rising from thirty-eight in 1917 to sixty-four in 1918. Even more horrendous levels of violence were reached in the immediate aftermath of the war.

The increasing bloodshed at home forced African Americans to question their role in the war. Many had initially rushed to serve, and W. E. B. Du Bois, now emerging as one of the leading black spokesmen, had famously—perhaps infamously as evidence suggests that Du Bois had been offered a commission in return for his support—urged African Americans to "close ranks" with their white countrymen. However, by the summer of 1918 the poor treatment of black soldiers and the discrimination and conflict at home forced many black leaders and newspaper editors to question this approach. On July 28, 1917, the NAACP staged a silent march of about ten thousand people in New York City to protest lynching and the attacks in East St. Louis with banners asking, "Why not make America safe for Democracy?" A few African Americans expressed a general opposition to fighting in a white man's war, and some, among them the young socialists A. Philip Randolph and Chandler Owen, also urged blacks not to support the war—not because of race but on class grounds. They did, however, point out that previous military service by African Americans had brought few rewards.

In an attempt to overcome any doubts African Americans might have about the war, the Wilson administration appointed Emmett J. Scott, the former private secretary to Booker T. Washington, as special assistant to the secretary of war, and George Haynes of the National Urban League was appointed director of Negro economics in the Department of Labor. Neither post, however, was much more than a public relations effort. In truth there was little recognition of the contribution that African Americans made to the war effort—rather the reverse. The war seemed to strengthen white prejudice and brought new levels of violence to the North as well as the South: black military service was disparaged, and returning black servicemen were seen as a threat. African Americans did not accept such slights quietly. Increasingly, a new mood could be detected as a "new Negro" emerged, one prepared to fight back, to insist on rights, and no longer to simply turn the other cheek. The NAACP grew in membership, and by the end of the war its leadership was primarily black. James Weldon Johnson became the national secretary, and Walter White became assistant secretary, then field secretary in 1918, then executive secretary in 1929. White later became a significant figure in civil rights during the Great Depression and World War II years. Writing in 1942, he said, "Few Negro families fail to have at least one member old

enough to remember the glowing promises made to them during the last war and the sickening disillusion of postwar days when the Ku Klux Klan instead of democracy was the Negro's reward."[2] The memories of World War I would help to shape the efforts to achieve equal citizenship in World War II, but by then the civil rights movement also had greater strength and experience to draw upon as a result of developments in the interwar period.

CHAPTER ONE

~

African Americans
on the Eve of War
From New Negro to New Deal, 1920–1939

I'd rather be in the army than outside where I was so raggedy and didn't have no jobs. I was glad to put on a United States Army uniform and get some food. I didn't care about the rifle what scared me. In the army, I wasn't gettin' killed on a train, I wasn't gonna starve. I felt proud to salute and look around and see all the good soldiers of the United States. I was a good soldier and got five battle stars. I'd rather be in the army now than see another Depression.

—Louis Banks, reflecting on the Depression years, 1971.[1]

The twenty years or so between the end of World War I and the start of World War II represent a period of enormous change for African Americans. While dramatic economic, social, and cultural forces affected black Americans, like other Americans, as the country went from postwar readjustment to economic boom and then collapse, the underlying continuity in American racial attitudes and beliefs shaped their experience. More than 85 percent of the 10.5 million Africans in the United States in 1920 still lived in the South, with almost 70 percent of those living in rural areas and mostly as tenant farmers. By 1920 the pattern of segregated life was well established, and Jim Crow laws ensured a separate existence for the races in most aspects of their lives. At the same time, a variety of laws effectively disfranchising the black population had undermined the political rights established after the Civil War. Should any doubt arise about their "place," violence and lynching remained a constant threat. However, World War I had generated

a huge movement of the black population to the North where new industrial jobs opened up and new communities and organizations were formed, albeit in the growing urban ghettos. During the interwar period, an articulate black leadership rejected pre–World War I accommodationism and sought different ways to challenge the discrimination and prejudice inherent in the everyday lives of African Americans. Through a growing literary movement and expanding press, these leaders found a voice that increasingly expressed a sense of racial identity and could respond when new international forces challenged basic liberal ideologies and notions of freedom and equality. Thus, by 1939, though much remained the same, much had also changed, and African Americans found themselves in a better position to advance their claims to equal citizenship.

In 1919, an outbreak of violence across the country rudely dashed any hopes that African Americans might have held that their participation in the war to "make the world safe for democracy" would win them some recognition and reward. More than eighty African Americans, some of them still in uniform, died at the hands of lynch mobs, and others died in the more than twenty-five riots that broke out as rioting white Americans took to the streets in towns and cities ranging from Charleston, South Carolina, and Longview, Texas, to Omaha, Nebraska, and Elaine, Arkansas. The most serious in size and consequences took place in July in Chicago, the city that had been the magnet for many wartime black migrants but turned out to be far from a "promised land." The influx of thousands of people from the South led to friction over jobs, transport, and housing as the black population tried to spread beyond the confines of the ghettos on the South Side and around the stockyards. An incident on the lakeside in which whites stoned a black youth, who then drowned, exploded into a riot in which white mobs hunted down African Americans, pulled them from streetcars, and pursued them through the streets, often while white policemen looked on. As a result twenty-three black and fifteen white Americans were killed. Almost as shocking, though smaller in scale, was the riot that broke out in Washington, D.C., a week before the explosion in Chicago. Particularly noticeable about the violence in the nation's capital, which lasted three days and resulted in the deaths of four African Americans and three whites, was the involvement of white servicemen, soldiers, sailors, and marines clearly intent on putting African Americans firmly in "their place."

In total at least sixty-two people died in the "Red Summer" of 1919, but although the racial violence abated, it did not end. Although diminishing, lynching continued with fifty-nine in 1920 and fifty-one in 1922. The first antilynching bill was introduced in Congress in 1921 but failed. In 1921 a

three-day riot in Tulsa, Oklahoma, resulted in the deaths of at least fifty white and two hundred black people and the almost complete destruction of the black community of Greenwood. In 1923, 8 African Americans were murdered in the town of Rosewood, Florida, and the 120 surviving black inhabitants fled the town never to return. That no one was ever indicted for these murders hardly comes as a surprise given the fact that the Ku Klux Klan (KKK) was at its height not just in Oklahoma but in many other parts of the country during the 1920s. In 1924 the KKK had an estimated membership of 4 million and could stage parades down Pennsylvania Avenue in Washington, D.C.

The experiences of thousands of black Mississippians in the wake of the floods of 1927 indicated the ingrained racism not just in the South but within government itself. More than 50 percent of those affected by the floods—over three hundred thousand people—were African Americans. The fortunate were located in segregated Red Cross camps and provided with inferior provisions, but while whites were evacuated some thirteen thousand African Americans were held at gunpoint in Greenville, and many were forced to work on the levee—until it broke, sweeping an unknown number away. Planters who feared the loss of their workforce often resorted to violence to prevent them leaving.

Black Americans did not suffer the racist violence passively. Many of those affected by the floods in Mississippi armed themselves during the emergency, and many more left the region afterward to head north. As the numbers of whites who died in the riots suggests, African Americans did as the poet Claude McKay urged in his famous 1919 poem "If We Must Die" and fought back. A "New Negro" emerged in the 1920s, increasingly self-conscious and aware, articulating a sense of identity and race pride that found expression in different organizations and a variety of cultural forms, including music, literature, and art. Among the most striking features of the "New Negro" movement was the emergence of the first black nationalist movement, the Universal Negro Improvement Association (UNIA) led by Marcus Garvey. Garvey arrived in the United States in 1916 from the West Indies and established his base in Harlem, where he called for black pride, economic self-determination, and unity among all people of African origin under the slogan "One Aim, One God, One Destiny." Garvey established various business enterprises, chief among them being the Black Star Shipping Line to trade with Africa and facilitate the return of those African Americans who wished to go back. Nothing came of these grandiose plans, and Garvey was convicted of fraud and jailed before being deported in 1927. Although ultimately a failure, the UNIA appealed to thousands of black Americans,

chiefly from the working classes, and various nationalist offshoots persisted, some appearing significantly later on.

While Garvey preached black pride and racial separatism, other African Americans turned to socialism and class organization as means of overcoming race prejudice. Chief among these were A. Philip Randolph and Chandler Owen, whose newspaper, *The Messenger*, the attorney general branded in 1920 "the most able and most dangerous" of all black publications.[2] Randolph increasingly looked to trade unionism as a means to unite black and white workers. His initial step in 1925 was to unionize the Pullman car porters by establishing the Brotherhood of Sleeping Car Porters (BSCP), with *The Messenger* as its official publication. The American Federation of Labor (AFL) finally granted the BSCP a charter in 1935, and the Pullman Company recognized the brotherhood in 1937. Randolph used his position to work within the AFL to try to open the doors of unions to black workers, but the affiliated unions remained steadfastly segregated or excluded African Americans until well into the 1940s.

Randolph's strategy in many ways reflected the changing economic and demographic patterns in African American life. The migration that had begun in 1915 continued in the 1920s as the economy expanded. Immigration controls introduced in 1921 and 1924 meant that the prewar supply of European workers did not resume. As a consequence, between 800,000 and 1 million blacks left the South in the 1920s, and by 1930 the percentage of African Americans living there had fallen to about 75 percent. Equally important, by 1930 the black urban population nationwide numbered more than 5 million, and the proportion of the black population classed as urban had risen from 27 percent in 1910 to 34 percent in 1920 to 43 percent in 1930. These black city dwellers had an increasingly significant impact on politics, particularly in northern cities. In 1920 approximately 40 percent of the black northern population was concentrated in three cities, New York, Chicago, and Philadelphia, and this proportion grew during the decade. In Chicago the black population doubled, rising from 109,000 in 1920 to 234,000 ten years later; in New York the figures were 152,450 and 327,700, respectively, with most of these people concentrated in Harlem, where the black population reached about 200,000 as 118,792 white people left the neighborhood and 87,417 black people arrived between 1920 and 1930. Detroit, too, saw a rapid increase in its black population as the number of African Americans there rose from under 40,800 to 120,000 during the 1920s. The migration out of the South was halved in the 1930s, but by then the new black city populations already held some political significance as evidenced by the 1928 election of the first black congressman in twenty-eight years, Chicago's Oscar De Priest.

The northern cities also provided a growing middle-class base for black organizations, and probably the most important development in black organization in the 1920s was the growth of the National Association for the Advancement of Colored People (NAACP). Increasingly led by African Americans but committed to integration, the NAACP led protests against the violence of the "Red Summer," and W. E. B. Du Bois expressed the new mood of African Americans through his editorials in *The Crisis*. Abandoning his earlier call to "close ranks," Du Bois now warned that black Americans had returned from fighting and were prepared to fight at home. *The Crisis* had a circulation of over half a million by 1920 and the membership of the NAACP rose from ten thousand in 1918 to ninety thousand in 1919. During the 1920s the NAACP led the campaign against lynching, beginning with the 1919 publication of *Thirty Years of Lynching in the United States: 1889–1918*. In 1920 it held its annual conference in Atlanta, Georgia, to show it would not be intimidated by the Ku Klux Klan or race violence. The following year the association successfully persuaded Congressman L. C. Dyer to introduce an antilynching bill in the House of Representatives, but it failed to pass in the Senate. The field secretary and later executive secretary, Walter White, personally investigated many lynchings and published reports of them in his book *Rope and Faggott* (1929).

In 1925 the NAACP was involved in a case that encapsulated the changing social and economic position of some African Americans in the 1920s and the willingness of black individuals and organizations to fight back against the persistence of white racism. In 1921 a black physician, Dr. Ossian Sweet, moved to Detroit. As the black community grew in numbers, the pressure on housing in the area known as Black Bottom grew. In 1925, Sweet bought a house in a white middle-class area and moved in with his family. However, aware that other African American families who moved there had been met with violence, Sweet was prepared to defend his family and property. When a white mob attacked the house, shots were fired, killing one of the attackers and wounding another. Sweet and his friends were tried for murder, but the NAACP came to his aid and hired famous civil rights lawyer Clarence Darrow for the defense. In 1926 Sweet and his codefendants were acquitted on grounds of self-defense.

The NAACP also supported and encouraged the growth in black artistic expression during the 1920s. Both Du Bois and White penned literary works as well as polemical writings, and *The Crisis* became one of several vehicles for black literature and poetry. A great surge in black writing took place in the 1920s, often celebrating Africa and blackness ("negritude"). Much of this new artistic movement centered on the growing northern urban population,

particularly in New York, where Harlem became the "Negro Mecca" and focus of the "Harlem Renaissance." Here writers like McKay, Countee Cullen, Jessie Fausett, Langston Hughes, Wallace Thurman, Jean Toomer, and Zora Neale Hurston produced a stream of literature reflecting the black experience, while musical performers like Louis Armstrong, Cab Calloway, Duke Ellington, and Ella Fitzgerald provided the sounds that gave the 1920s its title, the "Jazz Age." The vibrant lifestyle and culture of the black ghetto often appealed to white Americans disillusioned with postwar materialism, and aspects of black music influenced white composers like the Gershwin brothers. But the contradiction of the age was well captured in one of the age's most symbolic new cultural forms: the first sound movie in 1927, titled *The Jazz Singer*, starred a white performer, Al Jolson, performing in blackface. The few African Americans who appeared in movies tended to portray servants.

The Wall Street crash of 1929 and the ensuing Great Depression brought the Jazz Age and Harlem Renaissance to a halt and had a significant effect on African Americans. Writing in *I Know Why the Caged Bird Sings* of her childhood in Stamps, Arkansas, during the 1930s, writer Maya Angelou recalls that while the Depression hit whites with "cyclonic impact," it "seeped slowly" into the black community and took two years to have an effect.[3] For most of the African American population (11.8 million in 1930), however, the Depression had an immediate impact as race prejudice and discrimination magnified the economic consequences of industrial and agricultural collapse. As the Depression took hold and unemployment mounted, black Americans were "last hired, first fired" and experienced unemployment at more than twice the rate of white workers. In some places, 50 percent of black workers were unemployed; in others the rate was as high as 65 percent. Overall, in 1935, 30 percent of African Americans, approximately 4 million people, were on relief, but even then they received average weekly relief payments of $9 compared to $15 for whites.

While some northern white workers uttered the slogans "No Jobs for Niggers until Every White Man Has a Job" and "Niggers Back to the Cotton Fields," for the over 75 percent of African Americans still located in the South, falling prices for agricultural products meant that black sharecroppers were further impoverished. As cotton prices dropped from 18 to 6 cents per pound, landlords or banks often evicted black sharecroppers from the land and their homes, and as a result their number fell by almost one hundred thousand during the 1930s. To compound the economic plight of southern black families, throughout the decade increased race hatred brought with it violence and intimidation as the number of lynchings, declining in the

late 1920s, now rose to twenty in 1930 and twenty-four in 1933. Although these numbers dropped back into single digits after 1935, the total for the decade was over 120. The NAACP introduced a new federal antilynching bill in 1933; reintroduced in 1935, it passed in the House of Representatives in 1937, but a filibuster in the Senate finally killed it off in 1938. A further attempt in 1940 met the same fate. Nevertheless, lynching was now clearly a national issue.

Franklin Roosevelt, the successful Democratic Party presidential candidate in 1932, steadfastly refused to back the antilynching measures or any others dealing specifically with the civil rights of African Americans. To do so would have jeopardized his New Deal program of reform aimed at restoring the economy as a whole. However, African Americans benefited from the New Deal to some extent, if only because they were among the neediest. They were also helped by the presence of white progressives such as Harold Ickes, the secretary of interior and a member of the Chicago NAACP, in the Roosevelt administration. First Lady Eleanor Roosevelt, a constant advocate on behalf of African Americans who was obviously able—and willing—to say things that the president was not, provided great support as well. Mrs. Roosevelt became friendly with Walter White of the NAACP and arranged meetings between him and the president, beginning with a fruitless discussion in 1935 of the antilynching bill. Significantly—and symbolically—Eleanor Roosevelt played a leading part in arranging for internationally renowned concert and opera singer Marian Anderson to perform on the steps of the Lincoln Memorial in Washington, D.C., in 1939 after the Daughters of the American Revolution (DAR) had denied her the use of Constitution Hall. Mrs. Roosevelt also withdrew her membership from the DAR.

While the first lady's actions were undoubtedly important—and earned her the affection of black Americans and a considerable amount of hatred from white southerners—more important in many ways were the benefits that came to African Americans from some of the many New Deal agencies. Because all the new federal agencies operated at a local level, those in the South particularly tended to discriminate against African Americans; even national legislation could have a negative or limited impact on blacks. The National Recovery Administration, for example, was known in the black community as "Negroes Ruined Again" or "Negro Run Around" due to the agency's discriminatory practices and because the increases it mandated in wage levels meant that mechanizing industries like tobacco production was often cheaper than employing African American workers. Similarly, the Agricultural Adjustment Administration's policies aimed at reducing farm production to raise prices often encouraged southern landlords simply to

evict their black tenants. In the Tennessee Valley Authority, the great hydroelectric development set to revitalize large parts of the southern economy, African Americans constituted 11 percent of the workforce but received only 9 percent of the wages and worked primarily in janitorial positions. Only 10 percent of African Americans were covered by another major New Deal reform, the Social Security legislation providing old-age and unemployment insurance, because of their concentration in agricultural work or domestic service as self-employed laborers.

On a more positive note, the 1 million black Americans employed by the Works Progress Administration did make up a considerable proportion (26 percent) of the total number of people put to work. Despite early discrimination and the continuation of segregation, the percentage of black Americans among the workforce of the Civilian Conservation Corps rose from 3 to 8 percent, representing a total of 250,000 individuals. Despite discrimination in payments, African Americans constituted something like 30 percent of those on federal relief and a similar proportion of those in the housing provided by the Federal Housing Administration (FHA). For these reasons many African Americans believed that Franklin Roosevelt had done more for them than any president since Lincoln.

Among the most important features of the New Deal was the sense of inclusion that African Americans felt with their increased employment in the federal government itself. The overall number of black federal workers rose from 50,000 to 150,000 between 1933 and 1941, but especially striking was the appointment of African Americans to relatively high positions. The presence of more than forty leading African Americans in cabinet departments or federal agencies—including Mary McLeod Bethune in the National Youth Administration, William Hastie in the Department of Interior, Robert C. Weaver in the FHA, and Robert Vann, editor of the influential black newspaper the *Pittsburgh Courier*, in the Attorney General's Office—led to talk of a "Black Cabinet." The dramatic swing in black voting evidenced the impact of all of this. In 1932, 70 percent of black votes were cast for the Republican Party, but by the end of the decade, this proportion had been reversed, and 70 percent voted for the Democrats. Until well into the late twentieth century, it was the party of Roosevelt (and later John F. Kennedy), rather than the party of Lincoln, that appealed to the black electorate, despite the Democratic Party's continuing, albeit problematic, ties with the white South. The black Democratic vote was particularly significant in the North, and the first black Democratic congressman, Arthur Mitchell from Chicago, was elected to the House of Representatives in 1934. He was suc-

ceeded by William Dawson in 1942, when another Democrat, Adam Clayton Powell of New York, was also elected to the House.

Significant as the political changes of the 1930s were, a growing sense of group consciousness and a resurgent spirit reflective of the earlier "new Negro" also characterized the decade. In the South black sharecroppers formed the Communist-inspired Croppers and Farm Workers' Union in Alabama in 1931 and took part in several violent protests before the group collapsed in 1936. More significant was the Southern Tenant Farmers' Union (STFU) formed in 1934 by an alliance of black and white tenant farmers to resist evictions, foreclosures, and wage cuts. The vice president of the STFU, O. H. Whitfield, was an African American, and its approximately twenty-five thousand black members constituted about one-third of the union's total by 1936. As with the sharecroppers' union, Communist organizers strongly influenced the STFU, and the Communist Party of the USA (CPUSA) did win some support among African Americans for its work both in the South and in the case of Angelo Herndon, a nineteen-year-old African American found guilty in 1933 of fomenting insurrection in Atlanta, Georgia, where he had organized a demonstration of unemployed black and white workers. After five years and considerable publicity, the Supreme Court overthrew his eighteen-to-twenty-year sentence.

The CPUSA also attracted support from the black population for its initial role in a case that became as big a cause célèbre as the Sacco and Vanzetti case had been in the 1920s, the case of the Scottsboro boys. In 1931 nine African American youths between the ages of twelve and twenty-one were convicted of raping two young white women while riding a freight train in Alabama. Eight of the boys were sentenced to death. Whereas previously such a case would probably have passed unnoticed, by the 1930s violence and discrimination against African Americans had become a subject of protest. The NAACP and the International Labor Defense Department of the CPUSA fought the case of the Scottsboro boys throughout the 1930s. Eventually, after an international campaign and three Supreme Court appeals, the death penalties were overturned.

The CPUSA found some support in the black ghettos of the North and among black intellectuals, most notably writers Richard Wright and Ralph Ellison. The party participated in some of the "Don't Buy Where You Can't Work" boycotts and protests in New York, Chicago, and Washington, D.C., and an African American, James W. Ford, ran as the vice presidential candidate for the CPUSA in 1932, 1936, and 1940. Although it failed to attract many votes, black or white, the CPUSA worked with the National Negro

Congress (NNC) and the Southern Negro Youth Congress formed in 1937. However, the party lost what little support it had among African Americans following the Nazi-Soviet Pact in 1939 and even more so after 1941 when it opposed civil rights protests that might threaten the war effort.

The NNC was one of the new organizations to appear as a direct consequence of the Depression. Following a conference on the economic status of African Americans at Howard University in 1935, almost eight hundred delegates met in Chicago the following year and formed the NNC to campaign for the right to jobs, fair wages, trade union membership, and relief without discrimination for African Americans. They chose as their president A. Philip Randolph, leader of the Brotherhood of Sleeping Car Porters. However, political infighting between different groups, particularly those with Communist affiliations, led Randolph to leave the NNC in 1940. While he did not stop fighting to improve the economic position of black Americans, the memory of the political conflicts influenced his strategy in forming the next organization he put together to fight for the inclusion of African Americans in the defense industries of the "arsenal of democracy," the March on Washington Movement.

Behind many of the movements and major campaigns for civil rights of the 1930s, the NAACP remained the most influential and significant group. In 1930 Walter White, one of the key leaders of the antilynching campaign, succeeded James Weldon Johnson as executive secretary and established a significant relationship with the White House. Under White's leadership the NAACP rejected the economic focus advocated by W. E. B. Du Bois (who left his position as editor of *The Crisis* in 1934) and developed a gradualist strategy that combined political lobbying and propaganda with litigation to bring a legal challenge to the doctrine of "separate but equal" that underpinned segregation. Under the direction of the NAACP's chief counsel, Charles H. Houston, a new generation of black lawyers began to mount a series of challenges to segregation in education. Their first victory came in 1938 with *Missouri ex rel. Gaines v. Canada*, requiring that the state provide Lloyd Gaines with equal in-state education at a law school. Subsequent cases in the postwar years dealing with provision of university education paved the way for the landmark *Brown v. Topeka Board of Education* decision in 1954. Other important legal battles centered on the white primary and restrictive housing covenants. In addition the NAACP took part in important cases such as that involving the Scottsboro boys, and in 1930 it also played a role in successfully blocking the appointment of Judge John T. Parker to the Supreme Court because of his previously stated opposition to African American suffrage.

Membership of the NAACP dropped markedly in the late 1920s, rose from twenty-one to fifty-four thousand during the 1930s, but much of its work often seemed slow and behind the scenes and rarely did much to ameliorate the immediate hardships facing the majority of African Americans. Increasingly, frustration and anger grew within the black community, which demonstrated a willingness to take matters into its own hands—as evidenced by the local "Don't Buy Where You Can't Work" boycotts of stores in Chicago, Washington, D.C., and New York City to protest employment discrimination. The northern ghettos also proved a fertile breeding ground for black nationalist and separatist groups and sects, some of them offshoots of Garvey's UNIA. The most significant of these was the Nation of Islam founded in Detroit in 1930 by Wallace Fard Muhammad. He was succeeded in 1934 by Elijah Muhammad, formerly Elijah Poole, who had migrated to Detroit from Georgia in 1923. Muhammad built up a following in Detroit and established another mosque in Washington, D.C.

While the nationalist groups with their apparent rejection of both white society and the desire for integration undoubtedly appealed only to a small following, disillusionment with the experience in northern ghettos could breed violence. In March 1935, the growing sense of bitterness within Harlem's black community exploded in a two-day riot largely directed at white-owned stores and buildings. By 1930 the area a few blocks north of 125th Street, bounded by Seventh and Lenox avenues, had a black population of about two hundred thousand. Many of these families were crammed into tenement buildings, sharing toilet facilities or in some cases lacking such amenities all together. Thousands lived in cellars and basements. Work opportunities were few and poorly paid, and many of these jobs were lost in the Depression. By 1933 more than half of all black families in Harlem, some twenty-five thousand in total, were receiving unemployment relief. Finally an incident involving a black youth in a white-owned store and a confrontation with a white police officer triggered an outbreak of rioting that caused over $2 million in damage to property and left three African Americans dead and over thirty injured. In many ways the first "modern" race conflict in that it was African Americans rather than whites who rioted, the 1935 Harlem riot was a taste of things to come.

While the Harlem unrest perhaps indicated a mood of despair, African Americans in the 1930s also derived some satisfaction from the achievements of their community, and even though not black nationalists, they could still feel a sense of race pride and identity in their people's successes. Writers and artists of the Harlem Renaissance such as Hughes, Hurston, Archibald Motley, and Jacob Lawrence continued to celebrate black culture

in its various forms. New authors like Richard Wright, Ralph Ellison, and Margaret Walker were also emerging and producing the more socially aware literature that culminated in the publication of Wright's "protest" novel and international best seller, *Native Son*, in 1940. At the same time African Americans took pride in the sporting successes of track-and-field athlete Jesse Owens and boxer Joe Louis. The triumphs of both took on a wider, international significance beyond simple sporting prowess. In 1936, Owens, already a three-time record holder, competed in the Berlin Olympics. There, in front of the German Nazi leader, Adolf Hitler, he overturned the myth of Aryan supremacy when he won four gold medals, breaking Olympic records in the 100 meters, 200 meters, long jump, and the 400 meter relay. African Americans also won gold medals in the 800 meters (John Woodruff), 400 meters (Archie Williams), and high jump (Cornelius Johnson). In 1937 Joe Louis defeated James Braddock to become heavyweight champion of the world, and in 1938 he knocked out Max Schmeling in a fight widely represented as pitting opposing ideologies, democracy and Nazism, against each other. However, while Louis became an immediate folk hero for the African American population, the "Brown Bomber" still had to win universal white recognition and follow certain rules of behavior to avoid offending the white sporting fraternity. Only after 1941 was Louis accepted as an all-American hero.

Even before the United States entered World War II in 1941, race was clearly an international issue—and not just in sport. African Americans were keenly aware of developing events overseas and their racial significance. The black press reported widely on developments in Africa and India where Mahatma Gandhi was leading a series of nonviolent protests against British colonial rule. Even the rise and early military triumphs of the Japanese were celebrated in some quarters as victories for nonwhite groups. Black news media and spokesmen also recognized the deeper political significance of the Spanish Civil War, which began in 1936 when the right-wing military nationalist General Franco led the forces that rose against the legitimate Republican government. Some eighty African Americans were among the almost three thousand Americans who went to Spain to fight in the Abraham Lincoln and International brigades against the forces of fascism. Several black Americans died in this lost cause.

The international event that perhaps most moved the black American community was the invasion of Ethiopia by Italian forces under the direction of dictator Benito Mussolini in 1935. Ethiopia had a special significance for African Americans as the one remaining independent African nation. Much of the black press and leading African American spokesmen, includ-

ing Du Bois, Randolph, and singer Paul Robeson, spoke against the Italian aggression, and the New York–based International Council of Friends of Ethiopia made representations to the League of Nations on behalf of the invaded country and its emperor, Haile Selassie. In his "Ballad of Ethiopia," poet Langston Hughes called upon all colored peoples to say to Mussolini, "No! You shall not pass." Sadly, such appeals met with little success, and the annexation of Ethiopia was completed in 1936—although the Ethiopian government never officially surrendered.

As the storm clouds of war gathered over Europe and Asia, African Americans were clearly well aware of the wider issues. Nonetheless, for many the conflict in Europe was not their affair—it was a "white man's war," and as some pointed out, the American and European governments had not rushed to defend Ethiopia. More than this, many African Americans questioned what another war would bring for them, and remembering the events of 1917 to 1919, they answered, "Nothing!"

Unbeknownst to the black population, the War Department had no plans to use African Americans, even if they wanted to serve. In the interwar period the army produced reports supposedly based on the experiences of World War I that confirmed the worst racial stereotypes: black officers were failures; black men lacked the intelligence and courage to make good combat soldiers. By the 1930s planners had determined that segregation was fundamental to efficient military organization and that African Americans should be confined largely to noncombat roles.

If the military was a measure of racial progress, then it accurately reflected the situation in 1939. Such matters as the military plans for their use—or rather nonuse—were hardly uppermost in the minds of most African Americans. Their most pressing concern was generally the lack of freedom and democracy at home and presence of the American equivalents of Hitler in Alabama, Georgia, and Mississippi. The fact that unemployment rates for blacks were twice those for whites, that 87 percent of all African Americans in 1939 lived below the poverty line, that the average life expectancy for black males was fifty-two years compared to sixty-two for white males, that the average amount spent on education per year per white pupil was $38 but only $13 for blacks, that African Americans could still be lynched with impunity, and that large numbers of African Americans were denied the right to vote—these were the issues that most concerned the black population at the end of the 1930s and produced a growing demand for change. African American citizens' limited and segregated role in the U.S. armed forces formed a relatively minor concern in comparison. However, as the United States began to prepare for the possibility that it might be dragged into war,

African Americans now had organizational experience, group consciousness, and a growing political base that they could mobilize behind campaigns to link the world crisis with their own situation in order to demand change. While the war years built on the developments and advances of the previous decades, they also brought enormous new challenges and opportunities for the black population.

~

Mobilizing for War

The Arsenal of Democracy
and the Struggle for Inclusion

Went to the defense factory,
Trying to find some work to do.
Had the nerve to tell me,
'Black boy, nothing here for you.'
My father died, died fightin' 'cross the sea.
Mama said his dying never helped her or me.
I will tell you, brother, well it sho' don' make no sense
When a Negro can't work in the National Defense.

—Josh White, "Defense Factory Blues," 1944.[1]

The invasion of Poland by Hitler's army in September 1939 marked the outbreak of World War II in Europe. Initially determined to remain strictly neutral, many Americans began to express growing concern as the German forces swept first across Poland and then through western Europe. Increasingly Congress relaxed the restrictions of the Neutrality Acts, and President Franklin Roosevelt began to commit American aid to Britain and France through programs like the "destroyers for bases" deal in September 1940. In a radio "fireside chat" on December 29, 1940, President Roosevelt said that the United States should become "the great arsenal of democracy," and in March 1941 the Lend-Lease Act enabled the government to supply Britain and France openly. At the same time steps were taken to prepare American industry for national-defense production, and the first measures were implemented to mobilize the military with the introduction of the Selective

Service in September 1940. These developments posed major questions for the African American population, and black organizations increasingly demanded that they be allowed to participate fully as equals in both the military and industrial mobilization. However, faced with continued discrimination and segregation, black protesters grew more insistent and achieved some significant shifts in policy even before the United States entered the war fully in 1941.

At the time of the outbreak of war in Europe, the situation of African Americans in the military reflected their status in society as a whole. In 1939 the army was segregated, and African Americans could serve only in the four regular army units established after the Civil War. The total number of black soldiers was 3,640, and there were only five black officers, three of them chaplains. Almost four thousand African Americans served in the navy, all as mess men, the only category open to them; they were excluded entirely from the Marine Corps and the Army Air Corps. However, well before 1941 black organizations and leaders began to challenge the military's racial practices, demanding greater inclusion for Africans Americans. The thrust of the campaign was twofold: to increase black participation across all the services and to challenge the policy of segregation.

As early as October 1937, Charles Houston, a veteran of World War I and special counsel for the National Association for the Advancement of Colored People (NAACP), had written to President Roosevelt to ask that an executive order be issued to end discrimination in the armed forces. This campaign was taken up by a new organization, the Committee for the Participation of Negroes in National Defense (CPNND) established in February 1938 by Robert Vann, publisher of the *Pittsburgh Courier*, one of the country's largest black newspapers with a circulation of more than two hundred thousand. Chaired by Dr. Rayford W. Logan, a historian from Howard University and a World War I veteran, the CPNND had branches in twenty-five states and was supported by several leading black organizations, such as the Brotherhood of Sleeping Car Porters (BSCP). However, although Charles Houston was involved, the CPNND lacked the NAACP's official support because of differences on the issue of segregation. While the CPNND was prepared to compromise and accept an expansion of the black military role within a segregated system with a quota of African Americans in all branches of the military, the NAACP insisted on full integration. Nonetheless, the CPNND denounced the military plans to exclude African Americans as degrading and warned the black population that the military "would challenge your right to citizenship."[2] The committee provided a focus for a widespread campaign, holding national meetings that included a

three-day gathering of two thousand delegates at Hampton Institute in late November 1940, speaking before congressional committees, lobbying both parties during the political conventions of that year, and meeting with President Roosevelt. Much of their attention centered on the Selective Training and Service Act (Burke-Wadsworth Act) of 1940, the first peacetime draft introduced in American history.

Prior to the passage of the act, some thirty thousand African Americans had tried to enlist but were turned away. The introduction of the draft on September 16, 1940, was preceded by a concerted effort by black newspapers and organizations like the CPNND and NAACP to capitalize on the forthcoming presidential and congressional elections to challenge the discrimination African Americans had experienced in the military ever since World War I. The black spokesmen hoped to achieve their aims by securing the inclusion of clauses prohibiting racial bias in the legislation. Sympathetic politicians, such as Senator Robert Wagner of New York, introduced a number of antidiscrimination clauses, but these were initially rejected. However, proposals made by Rayford Logan and presented by Republican congressman Hamilton Fish were finally included in the bill when it passed on September 14, 1940. While Section 3(a) said that any male person between the ages of eighteen and thirty-six would have the opportunity to volunteer for service, Section 4(a) stated simply that "in the selection and training of men under this act, there shall be no discrimination against any person on account of race or color."[3] Neither clause made any specific reference to segregation.

On September 27, 1940, Walter White of the NAACP, A. Philip Randolph of the BSCP, and Arnold Hill, an advisor to the National Youth Administration and acting secretary of the National Urban League, had a meeting with President Roosevelt at the White House to press for the complete integration of the military and an end to discrimination in the defense industries. They presented the president with a seven-point program calling for the training of black officers, the assignment of black officers according to ability rather than race, the opening of all branches of the Army Air Corps to black Americans, the inclusion of black administrators in the Selective Service system, the admission of black women as nurses in the army, navy, and Red Cross, and finally a mandate that all army units be required to accept and select officers and enlisted personnel without regard to race. Apparently sympathetic, the president promised to respond after conferring with military and government officials. In an official announcement given to the press on October 9, the War Department announced that African Americans would be admitted to the army in the same proportion as that in the population as a whole; that service would be open in all branches of

the army, combatant as well as noncombatant; that officer training would be expanded, though black officers could only serve in black regiments; and that African American pilots would be trained and formed into a black branch of the Air Corps. However, the announcement stated clearly that it was "not the policy to intermingle colored and white enlisted personnel in the same regimental organizations." In other words, segregation would continue; any changes were thought likely to "produce situations destructive to morale and detrimental to the preparation for national defense."[4] Worse, the implica-

Walter White. LOC 96509827.

tion was that the three black leaders who met with President Roosevelt had endorsed this policy.

The black press reacted angrily to this development, as did White, Randolph, and Hill, who responded to charges of having sold out with a vigorous denial, stating that "such discrimination and segregation is a stab in the back for democracy."[5] The Republican Party seized upon the issue to embarrass their political opponents in the run-up to the election, and the presidential aide who released the statement was forced to retract the claim that the black leaders had approved the continuation of segregation. In order to regain the loss of black political support, the White House quickly acted to confirm the establishment of a black aviation program at Tuskegee, the promotion of Col. Benjamin O. Davis as the first black general, and the appointments of Judge William H. Hastie, dean of Howard Law School, as civilian aide to the secretary of war and of Col. Campbell Johnson, executive secretary of the YMCA in Washington, D.C., as assistant to the director of Selective Service. These actions did enough to ensure the majority of black voters' support for President Roosevelt in 1940, but the issue of segregation in the armed forces and the treatment of black military personnel remained an issue throughout the war.

Some African Americans also made an individual stand against the operation of the draft and segregation in the forces: in January 1941, Ernest Calloway, the educational director of the Chicago local of the Transport Employees of America and a member of a group called Conscientious Objectors against Jim Crow, refused to accept induction under what he called the antidemocratic structure of the army and claimed exemption from service. His request was denied, and he was jailed. The *Chicago Defender* suggested that Calloway spoke for a substantial number of African Americans. The press also supported the case of Lewis Jones of New York. On October 10, 1942, the *Baltimore Afro-American* reported Jones's statement to the draft board that he was "simply a colored American who insists on his constitutional rights to serve his country as a citizen unsegregated and unhumiliated in a Jim Crow Army."[6] A sympathetic court reluctantly found him guilty and sentenced him to serve three years in jail. A handful of other individuals who refused to serve in the segregated forces received similar sentences.

At least three African Americans were reported to have committed suicide rather than serve in the segregated forces. Less dramatic was the position taken by future leading black historian John Hope Franklin. Having just received his PhD from Harvard but determined to do his bit in the war, Franklin was turned away from the navy recruiting office in 1941 because he lacked the qualification of the right color. His subsequent application for a

position in the War Department was ignored. At that point he determined if his country did not want him, he did not want it either and managed to secure a draft deferment.

The most significant legal challenge to segregation in the forces came from Winfred W. Lynn, a thirty-six-year-old gardener from Long Island, New York. In June 1942, Lynn refused to report for induction on the grounds that the army's black quota system violated the nondiscrimination clause in the Selective Service Act, but he declared his willingness to serve in any unit that was not segregated by race. Lynn was represented by his brother Conrad, a lawyer and a legal counsel for the NAACP, although the national NAACP, having agreed not to test the draft, was not involved (in fact the Lynns were expelled from the NAACP for being unpatriotic). The federal district court judge refused to hear the case until Lynn reported for induction, which he duly did, entering the army in December. His brother, supported by the Lynn Committee against Racial Segregation in the Army, which included A. Philip Randolph, applied for a writ of habeas corpus, but the U.S. Circuit Court of Appeals for New York denied their motion in February 1944. In a 2–1 decision the court ruled that Section 4(a) of the Selective Service Act prohibited discrimination but not specifically segregation. A National Committee for Winfred Lynn, which included Randolph, writer Carey McWilliams, sociologist Horace Cayton, scholar Alain Locke, and Oswald Garrison Villard, then mobilized support behind what they called "the Twentieth Century Dredd Scott Case" to take the case before the Supreme Court in May 1944.[7] The court ruled the case moot on the grounds that as Lynn was now a soldier in the South Pacific, he could not appear in court. A request to rehear the case in 1945 was denied. Some officials in the Selective Service and Judge Advocate's offices felt that if the court had ruled, it probably would have supported Lynn.

One African American who objected to service on both racial and religious grounds was Randolph's assistant, thirty-one-year-old Quaker activist Bayard Rustin. In 1942, Rustin, a member of the pacifist Fellowship of Reconciliation and its newly formed civil rights offshoot, the Congress of Racial Equality (CORE), refused to submit to armed service or to do any work that would contribute to the war effort and was jailed for three years. While in jail he organized protests against segregated dining provision for prisoners and, after his release, soon became involved in a number of civil rights activities that would pave the way for some of the campaigns of the 1960s.

While the black press generally supported these individuals, it was less inclined to view some others sympathetically, dismissing them as fanatics or crackpots. Among the most important groups opposing military service

to fight what they saw as a white man's war was the precursor of the Nation of Islam or Black Muslims, then known as the Temple of Islam. In 1942 the group's leader, Elijah Muhammad, and more than sixty of his followers were sentenced to three to five years in jail for draft evasion in Chicago. Members of related black nationalist groups in Detroit, Newark, and New York were convicted of similar offences. Overall fewer than 200 people evaded the draft on racial or religious grounds. The total number of black violators of the Selective Service Act between 1941 and 1946 was 2,208—quite a high percentage (18.1) of the total number of violations recorded (12,183), perhaps reflecting some African Americans' feeling that they had little to fight for.

The implementation of the draft and military policies were not the only subjects that concerned African Americans before the attack on Pearl Harbor plunged the nation into war in December 1941. Groups like the CPNND and NAACP also campaigned for greater opportunities for African Americans in the defense industries as well as their full inclusion in the military. Black labor organizations, particularly Randolph's BSCP, joined them in this struggle. Randolph had been instrumental in securing the meeting at the White House with President Roosevelt in September 1940 through the good offices of Eleanor Roosevelt. In September 1940 the president's wife had attended the BSCP annual meeting, which called upon President Roosevelt to end discrimination in the military. Now the union leader turned his focus on the racism in employment, particularly in the defense industries.

Despite all the efforts of the New Deal, at the beginning of 1940 8 million people remained unemployed, 7 million of them white and 1 million black. As defense plants opened, white workers were given priority over African Americans, and "first fired" became "last hired." While unemployment among whites began to fall, it remained stationary for blacks, and the proportion of African Americans unemployed (22 percent) was almost twice that of whites in 1940. In 1941 the number of African Americans on relief was twice that of whites nationally, and in cities like New York and Detroit, it was four times as many. Despite instructions from the U.S. Office of Education to the contrary, discrimination also ensured that little of the federal money allocated for defense training went to schools for African Americans; they could only find jobs largely in unskilled, hot, and heavy industries or in service work. Lester B. Granger of the National Urban League estimated that 75 percent of the defense industry was closed to African Americans, and of the 150,000 men placed in the defense industries between October 1940 and March 1941, only 4 percent were black. In correspondence with Harry S. Truman, then the chair of the Senate Committee to Investigate the Defense Program, Robert C. Weaver, a leading figure in Roosevelt's "Black

Cabinet," argued in May 1941 that the existence of restrictive practices in practically all defense industries created economic waste and threatened national unity.

The economic discrimination existed in all parts of the country. In New York ten factories with a combined workforce of 30,000 workers only employed 142 African Americans. In Los Angeles there were only about one hundred African Americans among the eighty-five hundred shipyard workers. In the shipyards in the South, black Americans were employed in small numbers and generally as laborers; few, if any, worked as welders. One shipyard in Mobile with ten thousand workers only employed twenty-two African Americans. As late as January 1942, over half of the hundreds of industries with large war contracts stated in response to a U.S. Employment Service questionnaire that they did not and would not employ African Americans. In Cleveland, Ohio, two-thirds of the city's defense contractors employed not one African American in a skilled or semiskilled capacity. The case of the aircraft industry was indicative: the Douglass Aircraft Company, with a workforce of 33,000, employed only 10 African Americans; Boeing Aircraft had not one black worker among the 41,000 in its Seattle plant; nationally, only 240 black laborers worked in the entire aircraft industry. Not surprisingly, the NAACP singled out airplane manufacturing when it called upon President Roosevelt to issue an executive order prohibiting employment discrimination in the defense industries in May 1940. The NAACP's request for presidential action received no immediate response.

Incensed by this situation and encouraged by the *Pittsburgh Courier* and the CPNND, African Americans held mass meetings in a number of different towns and cities, and further demonstrations were planned for National Negro Defense Sunday on February 9, 1941. The NAACP independently also held its own National Defense Day with meetings in twenty-four locations across the United States taking place on January 26, 1941. However, when on January 15, 1941, Randolph issued a call for ten thousand African Americans to march on Washington to demand the right to fight and work in defense of their country, the reaction of the black press and leadership was lukewarm. Walter White and the NAACP did not immediately support Randolph's initiative, and an editorial in the *Chicago Defender* on February 8, 1941, suggested that to get ten thousand "Negroes assembled in one spot, under one banner with justice, democracy and work as their slogan would be the miracle of the century." Even the *Pittsburgh Courier*, as late as June 14, 1941, suggested the idea of a march was a "crackpot proposal," but by then events had moved on.

At the beginning of March 1941, Randolph reissued his call for a demonstration in the BSCP journal, *Black Worker*. Walter White, who had hoped for another meeting with President Roosevelt to secure some executive action to deal with job discrimination but was told that the president was

A. Phillip Randolph, labor leader. LOC 97519529.

too busy, now began to support Randolph's campaign. Together with Ray-ford Logan, Lester B. Granger, and others, he joined Randolph to establish the March on Washington Committee, and on May 1 the group called on African Americans to march on the capital on July 1. The organization was deliberately kept all black, largely to limit the influence of Communist Party members whom Randolph regarded as a potential threat to unity. He also argued that African Americans had to fight and win their own battles and began to suggest that the number of marchers could be as many as one hundred thousand.

The Roosevelt administration grew increasingly alarmed by the threat of a large demonstration in the nation's capital, fearing that it not only would be politically embarrassing but could result in racial violence. Black New Deal administrator, housing expert, and economist Robert C. Weaver was placed in charge of Negro employment and training in the Office of Pro-duction Management (OPM), and on June 12 the president made public a memorandum sent by William Knudsen and Sidney Hillman, the heads of the OPM, to defense contractors requiring them to use black workers fully. The next day Eleanor Roosevelt and Mayor Fiorello La Guardia of New York met with Randolph and White to try to halt the protest, but the black leaders would not be persuaded. Finally, on June 18, 1941, Randolph and White had another meeting with the president in the White House. Among the offi-cials present were Secretary of the Navy Frank Knox, William Knudsen, and Sidney Hillman. They first discussed the continued segregation of the armed forces and the contradiction inherent in fighting what White called "Hitler's theories of race" while practicing a similar philosophy. When the subject of segregation in the navy came up, the president allegedly suggested, in a rather revealing comment, one way to expand the role of African Americans above the rank of mess man and to get black and white seamen to "know and respect each other": "We've got some good Negro bands in the navy. Why don't we make a beginning by putting some of the bands aboard battle-ships?"[8] However, the main subject of discussion was Randolph's threat to lead a march on Washington. When asked how many people might march, Randolph replied, "One hundred thousand." Assuming Randolph might be bluffing, Roosevelt asked White how many people would really march, and he too replied, "One hundred thousand." Neither White nor Randolph would agree to call the march off, and facing a demonstration that would be both deeply embarrassing to his administration and potentially dangerous in terms of public order, Roosevelt asked them to draft an outline of an execu-tive order. After further discussion and some redrafting, the president issued

Executive Order 8802 on June 25, 1941, and the march on Washington was called off just five days before it was due to take place.[9]

The executive order declared that U.S. government policy mandated full participation in the defense industries without discrimination on grounds of "race, creed, color, or national origin." It also prohibited discrimination in employment in the federal government and defense industries and established a Fair Employment Practices Committee (FEPC) to receive and investigate complaints and redress grievances. The black press widely greeted the order as a major breakthrough. According to the *Pittsburgh Courier*, a new day had dawned, while the *Chicago Defender* described the order as one of the most significant pronouncements in the interest of African Americans in over a century. Some considered it a second Emancipation Proclamation; others did note the order's shortcomings, particularly the absence of any reference to the armed forces. Some African Americans, including members of the March on Washington Movement (MOWM)—one, Bayard Rustin, was very close to Randolph himself—argued that the march should not have been canceled. Randolph, however, believed that significant gains had been made and more could be made in the future. Some historians have argued that in reality a shrewd president had granted limited concessions and averted a major confrontation.

The debate has persisted over the years. Most of the argument focuses on the role and achievements of the FEPC. However, there is fairly general agreement about the significance of Randolph and the MOWM. At the time, the black union leader was awarded the NAACP's Spingarn Medal and an honorary doctorate from Howard University. He was also recognized by the Schomburg Collection in New York and placed on the *Chicago Defender*'s honor roll; New York's *Amsterdam News* simply called him "the nation's No. 1 Negro leader," and elsewhere he was described as a "saint."[10] Of undoubted significance was the fact that the threat of large-scale, nonviolent, mass protest had produced results, and not surprisingly some people compared Randolph to the Indian leader Mahatma Gandhi. But this mass movement never actually massed, and, of course, we will never know whether the march would have taken place on the scale Randolph forecasted. The numbers of those who gathered at subsequent rallies suggest that it would have achieved the target he claimed. Even if it had taken place, the march would not have been the first: the Bonus Army of World War I veterans *had* marched, bringing between fifteen and twenty thousand to the capital in 1932, and during World War I, between ten and fifteen thousand black and white civil rights campaigners in New York City had famously staged a silent march to

protest lynching. Unlike those earlier demonstrations, the MOWM had achieved a tangible victory of some significance in the form of the executive order and FEPC. This precedent had considerable importance for civil rights campaigns in the years ahead, something Randolph recognized at the time when he said that "the future strategy and technique of the Negro must be in the field of demonstration, both non-violent mass activity and disciplined non-violent demonstrations."[11]

The MOWM's success resulted no doubt from A. Philip Randolph's commitment and determination, the momentary unity and common focus among civil rights organizations, and the evident growing support for a march among African Americans. It was also due to the unique world-affairs context in which the United States, led by Franklin Roosevelt, was taking on the role of defender of democracy against the threat of a racist ideology. The president best expressed this on January 6, 1941, in his State of the Union address outlining the "four freedoms": freedom of speech, freedom of worship, freedom from want, and freedom from fear. It remained to be seen whether the FEPC would live up to those high ideals or even deliver what the executive order had laid out.

The FEPC had some built-in weaknesses, most obviously the fact that it was a temporary wartime body with jurisdiction only over the defense industries and federal government. In addition, the committee's size was limited and its budget relatively low. Originally consisting of 5 members, then 6, then 7, at its height the total staff, including field staff, numbered fewer than 130. The committee also underwent several changes of membership: the first chairman, Mark Ethridge (owner of Louisville's *Courier-Journal*), was succeeded by Malcolm MacLean (president of Hampton Institute) in February 1942; he was replaced by Monsignor Francis J. Haas (May 1943), and in this second FEPC, Sarah Southall (International Harvester Co.), P. B. Young (editor of Norfolk's *Journal and Guide*), and Samuel Zemurray (head of United Fruit Company) replaced Earl Dickerson (a black Chicago alderman) and David Sarnoff (president of RCA). Hass was succeeded by Malcolm Ross in October 1943. Philip Murray of the Congress of Industrial Organizations (CIO), William Green of the American Federation of Labor (AFL), and Milton Webster of the BSCP were the only constant members.

Ethridge, although regarded as a "liberal" southerner, was fairly conservative, once remarking publicly that no power on earth could force southerners to give up segregation. The committee itself was sometimes divided on how best to operate and also fell victim to political infighting and administrative struggles. In 1942 the FEPC was transferred without warning to operate under the War Manpower Commission (WMC) headed by Paul V. McNutt.

Many black observers saw this as an attempt to muzzle the committee, something Roosevelt denied. In reality the charges were correct: McNutt was not sympathetic, and the committee did very little under his control. The committee's apparent demise prompted Randolph to organize mass rallies in New York and Chicago to "Save FEPC" on June 12, 1942. Smaller gatherings met later in other cities, including St. Louis and Washington, D.C., and in May 1943 President Roosevelt issued Executive Order 9346 reaffirming the principles of the original order and establishing a new committee under the Office of Emergency Management, an executive agency. The new FEPC was given a budget of almost half a million dollars and granted the power to hold hearings, make findings, and recommend measures to the WMC.

To some extent these political machinations reflected how important both its defenders and its critics considered the FEPC. Historian Merl E. Reed suggested that the FEPC was not only the most controversial wartime federal agency but perhaps also the most contentious in modern history. Certainly, it provoked a great deal of opposition throughout its existence, particularly from southerners both inside and outside of Congress—a foretaste of the later reaction to the Supreme Court's 1954 *Brown v. Topeka Board of Education* decision. Gov. Frank Dixon of Alabama called the FEPC crackpot and accused the government of meddling in the South's racial policies; other southern politicians described the FEPC as communistic or suggested it could lead to racial bloodshed; some suggested that blacks and whites working together would lead to racial intermarriage. Members of the FEPC even received death threats from white supremacists. Opposition to hearings into discrimination in the southern railroad industry led to their postponement in January 1943. When they were finally held in Washington in September, twenty companies and seven unions received cease-and-desist orders; sixteen companies and three unions refused. The companies maintained that the promotion of black workers was not just impracticable but impossible: the appointment of black locomotive engineers or train conductors would disrupt relations with employees and antagonize rail customers. The matter was referred to President Roosevelt, but nothing came of it.

Even more revealing of the opposition the FEPC faced in the South was the dispute at the Alabama Drydock & Shipping Company in Mobile in 1943. In response to the committee's urging, the company reluctantly promoted twelve black workers to the position of welder and put them to work on the night shift with white workers. The result was an outbreak of rioting quelled only when federal troops moved in after two days. The dispute was settled when, with FEPC agreement, segregated work crews were created. The FEPC also met resistance outside of the South. In Cincinnati, Ohio, for

example, when challenged by the committee about their hiring practices, several employers failed to respond as requested or did so half-heartedly. Some employers cited workers' or union opposition for their failure to comply with FEPC directives, and indeed much evidence supported these claims. In a number of cases in Cincinnati, as in Mobile, the employment or upgrading of black workers resulted in strike action, at times necessitating the involvement of the National War Labor Board to bring about a settlement.

Labor unions as well as employers were often the focus of FEPC hearings and investigations, even though two senior union representatives, Murray and Green, were committee members. Unions affiliated with the AFL either excluded black workers all together or admitted them only in segregated branches. The newer, more radical CIO had adopted a nondiscriminatory policy, which it reaffirmed during the war. However, imposing such policies on its membership was not always easy. In one case, for example, members of the CIO-affiliated Industrial Union of Marine and Shipbuilding Workers in Baltimore downed tools when two African Americans were simply admitted to the welding school. When the union expelled some of the strikers, further demonstrations ensued. The most serious case involving the CIO occurred in Philadelphia in 1944 when its members struck after the hiring of eight black streetcar workers, paralyzing the city and requiring troops to prevent violence and get the transport system running again. In such cases the FEPC often seemed powerless, reflecting the fact that it could only threaten to cancel or withhold defense contracts for noncompliance, something it never did.

Despite all this, it would be wrong to judge the FEPC a complete failure. First, the executive order and FEPC had huge symbolic importance and, if nothing else, provided a statement of intent. There was to be no single federal body with similar power and responsibility until the establishment of the Equal Employment Opportunity Commission in 1964. Second, although the committee's essentially reactive rather than proactive methods—it responded to complaints brought to it—were a weakness, it nonetheless focused national attention on the issue of discrimination in employment by holding public hearings across the country. These were not simply meaningless gestures. The inquiries in Los Angeles in October 1941 and in Chicago, New York, and Birmingham in 1942 all served to publicize the extent of discrimination and brought a great deal of moral pressure to bear by naming and shaming companies with racially discriminatory employment practices. Equally, the work of regional offices had some impact on local industries and unions. Even where success was limited, such as with the opening of defense training programs through the U.S. Office of Education, it highlighted the issue within government circles, even though the president prevented these

regional offices from making their findings public. Although unsuccessful in a number of conspicuous cases, the FEPC succeeded in others, both directly and indirectly. At least one major employer, International Harvester, reexamined its hiring policies because of the FEPC's influence. The committee also examined more than six thousand cases of discrimination and brought a satisfactory settlement to almost two thousand of them. Almost as important in some ways, a number of states such as New York introduced their own fair-employment-practices legislation and committees during or soon after the war.

It is impossible to demonstrate what impact the FEPC had in terms of actual job numbers. Most gains in employment for African Americans came only after 1942 as labor shortages began to have a serious effect—more than half of black workers' gains were in areas of acute shortage. Nonetheless, both qualitative and quantitative advances were made in the employment of African Americans during the war, probably due to the combination of declared government policy, the actions of the FEPC, pressure from black organizations, and the demands of war itself. Certainly African Americans recognized how important the agency was and campaigned to maintain it during the war and to establish a permanent body afterward. However, despite the enormous significance of Executive Order 8802, the FEPC, and the relaxation of some of the military's racial policies prior to 1941, white prejudice often seemed as firmly entrenched in many areas of American life as ever. Even after the United States had entered the war, it seemed that African Americans would be denied an equal role in the fight and that any changes in racial patterns would be met with resistance.

The Japanese attack on Pearl Harbor on December 7, 1941, changed the entire context of black protest. U.S. entry into the conflict met with general declarations of 100 percent loyalty and recognition of the importance of the issues at risk. Although some African Americans believed it was a white man's war, the majority believed otherwise. A. Philip Randolph wrote an article in the *Pittsburgh Courier* on December 20, 1941, titled "The Negro Has a Great Stake in This War," and pointed out that although American democracy might be limited, it did allow the right to campaign for civil rights. As if to emphasize that fact, the outbreak of open hostilities with Germany and Japan did not bring a cessation of the demands for racial change. Rather, the struggle against the Axis powers became increasingly linked to the struggle for equality at home. While the New York *Amsterdam News* said on December 13 simply that the United States was "one nation indivisible," the front page editorial of the *Pittsburgh Courier* the same day summed up the mood with the headline "We Are Americans, Too!" followed by a pledge to

continue "unrelenting warfare against the enemies within our gates." The newspaper also carried a statement by Walter White of the NAACP that while African Americans would give unqualified support to the war effort, they should at the same time continue the struggle for full citizenship rights. He said African Americans would fight for their country but at the same time demand the right to fight as equals in all branches of the military. In an editorial in *The Crisis* in January 1942, Roy Wilkins reaffirmed the NAACP position and specifically rejected the line adopted by W. E. B. Du Bois in his World War I "Close Ranks" editorial. Wilkins stated clearly that now was not the time to be silent about the breaches in democracy in the United States; instead, it was the time to speak out—"the fight against Hitlerism begins in Washington, D.C." Other papers—like the *Chicago Defender* in its December 13, 1941, editorial "For Democracy and Unity"—linked expressions of loyalty and promises not to impede the war effort with insistence that African Americans be allowed to serve their country fully, at the same time referring to "the broken promises of the past."

Tying the war to the continued struggle for civil rights became the predominant theme of the black press. A letter from a James G. Thompson of Wichita, Kansas, published by the *Pittsburgh Courier* on January 31, 1942, posed the dilemma for many African Americans when he asked, "Should I sacrifice to live 'half American'?" Referring to the "V for victory" sign displayed prominently in countries fighting "for victory over aggression, slavery and tyranny," the writer urged "colored Americans [to] adopt the double VV for a double victory. The first V for victory over our enemies from without, the second V for victory over our enemies from within." The *Courier* seized upon this symbolism and on February 14, 1942, launched the "Double V" campaign for "victory at home and abroad." In its statement the newspaper affirmed its determination "to protect our country, our form of government and the freedoms which we cherish for ourselves and the rest of the world" and called for a "two-pronged attack against our enslavers at home and those abroad who would enslave us." The statement ended, "WE HAVE A STAKE IN THIS FIGHT. . . . WE ARE AMERICANS TOO!" The newspaper claimed that public response to the campaign was overwhelming; its office had been inundated with hundreds of letters and telegrams expressing support, and over 88 percent of people polled were against any soft-pedaling on their demands. The "Double V" symbol, widely displayed in the newspaper, was taken up elsewhere in Double V clubs and by several more black newspapers in a campaign that ran until 1943.

The *Chicago Defender* also published a letter from a reader on March 7, 1942, in which the writer asked, "With America trying to spread the gospel

of the Four Freedoms world-wide, why should we cease our fight for them right here at home? While we 'Remember Pearl Harbor' let's 'Remember Jim Crow' too." Events gave this suggestion particular meaning and pointed up the struggle that African Americans faced. At the end of January 1942, the *Defender* had reported the lynching of a twenty-six-year-old mill worker, Cleo Wright, in Sikeston, Missouri, for allegedly sexually assaulting a white woman. Already wounded following a struggle with the police, Wright was seized from jail, dragged behind a vehicle, and burned to death. At an NAACP meeting in St. Louis in February, a new national slogan of "Remember Pearl Harbor but don't forget Sikeston, Mo." was proposed, and on March 14 the *Defender* published this as "Remember Pearl Harbor and Sikeston, too."

The black press and civil rights organizations continued to call for an end to segregation throughout the war. However, after the widespread outbreak of racial violence in 1943 and as the military campaigns abroad began to take their toll, the tone of protest moderated. To some extent this reflected pressure exerted by the Roosevelt administration and government agencies and even threats of possible legal action. Demands for change did not, however, stop altogether. In 1944, for example, the NAACP was still calling for the end of segregation in the army and navy, as well as challenging Secretary of War Henry Stimson on his slurs against black combat troops, including the suggestion that they were incapable of mastering modern weapons. After a series of critical articles, on March 18, 1944, the *Pittsburgh Courier* called for Stimson's resignation, but the *Courier's* "Double V" campaign, which had inspired many Americans, effectively disappeared after 1943, as the emphasis fell more on fighting the war abroad than fighting at home. The black press did, however, report events and leave their readers to make up their own minds. In addition to covering racially motivated strikes at home, papers like the *Chicago Defender* and *Pittsburgh Courier* detailed the discrimination and racially motivated incidents African American troops faced in Britain, Australia, and elsewhere. The press also continued to emphasize the view that African Americans had a stake in the war and could come out of it with expectations of change.

While many African Americans hoped the war would enable them to demonstrate their patriotism and strengthen claims for equal citizenship, some white Americans resisted any changes to the racial status quo sufficiently to force African Americans to question their support for the conflict. Even as the United States entered the war, Col. E. R. Householder of the Adjutant General's Office, speaking before a meeting with twenty black newspaper editors and publishers in Washington, D.C., on December

13, 1941, could reaffirm the continued policy of segregation and remind his listeners that "the Army is not a sociological laboratory."[12] The fear of jeopardizing white morale and provoking violence appeared a greater force against change than the fear of black protest was for it. Violence occurred anyway. Cleo Wright's murder was one of six lynchings in 1942, and the year had begun with a riot in Alexandria, Louisiana, in which hundreds of whites, aided by police, had attacked black soldiers. Twelve African Americans were reportedly killed, although there seems to be no official record of this. Perhaps the truth did not matter; there were enough similar incidents for the black writer C. L. R. James to sum up a widespread feeling among African Americans when he asked,

> Why should I shed my blood for Roosevelt's America, for Cotton Ed Smith and Senator Bilbo, for the whole Jim Crow, Negro-hating South, for the low-paid, dirty jobs for which Negroes have to fight, for the few dollars of relief and insults, discrimination, police brutality, and perpetual poverty to which Negroes are condemned even in the more liberal North?[13]

As the war progressed in tandem with continued organized black pressure for change, a growing voice of militancy could be heard as some African Americans became increasingly angry, bitter, and disillusioned. Equally, many whites seemed determined to resist change at all costs. The additional stresses and strains of wartime coupled with the tension between these two opposing forces created an explosive situation that culminated in widespread violence in 1943 and seriously undermined wartime national unity.

CHAPTER THREE

∽

Fighting for Freedom
Changing Military Policy
and the Black Experience, 1941–1945

If you ask me, I think Democracy is fine,
I mean Democracy without the Color Line.
Uncle Sam says "We'll live the American way—
Let's get together and kill Jim Crow today."

—Josh White, "Uncle Sam Says," 1944.[1]

Josh White's song, in an outline of the situation in the armed forces at the start of World War II, neatly captures how the war highlighted the gap between American war aims and practices. In White's song, as far as the Army Air Corps (Army Air Force after June 1941) was concerned, African Americans' place was "on the ground"; in the navy, "all they got is a mess-boy's job for me"; and in the army it was "two camps for Black and White." The fact that in fighting Nazism the Allies opposed an openly racist enemy—a point emphasized in the often reiterated declarations in defense of democracy and the "four freedoms"—only served to highlight contradictions between the United States' policies and practices and strengthened African Americans' demands for change. As a black soldier serving at Fort Still, Oklahoma, would write to the *Pittsburgh Courier* in a letter published on August 30, 1941, many black soldiers would just as soon fight and die for their rights in the United States as on some foreign battlefield. The determination to bring about change during the war years brought unprecedented challenges to the status quo in the military. At the same time, the experience of service in the armed forces at home and abroad had an enormous impact on

African Americans. Although the War Department repeatedly insisted that the services would not be "a laboratory for reform," in practice the demands of war brought about changes in policy that made the military just that, and by the end of the war, the armed forces often led the way in racial reform. But the black military experience was to be bittersweet, a mixture of progress and resistance that did much to strengthen African Americans' demands for equality and bred a growing determination to effect change in the postwar years.

Among the immediate issues facing African Americans was the implementation of the draft. The appointment of Campbell C. Johnson, executive secretary of the YMCA in Washington, D.C., to the Selective Service Office to oversee the interests of black draftees was largely window dressing as he could do little to address some of the fundamental issues. African Americans sat on only 250 of the 6,442 draft boards and on only three in southern states. The discriminatory patterns in the draft were fairly clear. For example, in 1940, 51.6 percent of African American draftees were designated Class I, available for immediate service, whereas the proportion for whites was 32.5 percent. As a consequence of draft boards' attitudes, as well as of the wider effects of discrimination, the number of black draftee deferrals was relatively low. In January 1943, only 4.7 percent of the men deferred on occupational grounds were black; in January 1944 the proportion was still only 7.3 percent. At the same time, draft boards rejected a larger proportion of African Americans (18.2 percent) than whites (8.5 percent), reflecting the educational and health deficiencies of men drawn from the poorest sections of American society. Almost one-third of the African Americans rejected for service were turned away for lack of education. By 1943 manpower shortages were such that the army introduced a special training program to ensure inductees had basic reading and writing skills. Almost 136,000 African Americans took part in this program with a success rate of 85.1 percent compared to 81.7 percent for whites. Nonetheless, segregation meant that instead of being dispersed across all branches and regiments in the army, poorly educated black soldiers were concentrated in the all-black units, a fact that on occasion impacted performance and thus reinforced existing racist stereotypes in the military.

By the time the United States actually entered the war, a number of concessions had been made to African Americans' demand that they be allowed to participate in the military effort equally. In March 1941 the then Army Air Corps began to recruit African Americans for aviation training in a segregated program at the Tuskegee College Army Air Field in Alabama, and the following year African Americans were accepted for general service

in the navy and Marine Corps. With the exception of those in the Army Air Corps, black army officers received training in integrated camps, although on-base facilities often remained segregated. However, progress in most areas remained slow. The number of black officers soon exceeded the number of possible assignments open to them in black regiments, and many were passed over for promotions that would rank them above white officers. Racial policy also limited the full utilization of the ordinary soldier as the number of black soldiers in the army had risen from 97,725 in November 1941 to 467,883 a year later. However, at 6 percent of total army personnel, this proportion lagged far behind that of African Americans in the population. Moreover, the proportion of black soldiers in service as opposed to combat units actually increased, rising from 48 percent in 1942 to 75 percent in 1945. By 1945 there were 650,000 African Americans in the army, but only 50,000 played some sort of combat role. The number of black officers had risen from five men to seven thousand.

Even had it in fact been practiced, the War Department's avowed policy of segregation without discrimination was not acceptable to the majority of African Americans. Some black spokesmen did accept segregation, if only as a first step toward full acceptance, but others believed this was simply defeatism. The black media widely expressed the view that segregation always entailed discrimination, and although the creation of the black aviation units was welcomed as a move in the right direction and a widening of opportunities for African Americans, it was still seen as a limited concession and an opportunity missed. This was the view of the black civilian aide to the secretary of war, William H. Hastie, who increasingly chafed against the military restrictions on black service.

From the start of his appointment in 1940, Hastie had called for the integration of the army, but his proposals were rejected. Hastie also fought to train more black officers and was critical of the policy that prevented black officers from being placed in command of whites. Constantly made aware of the discrimination experienced by soldiers, Hastie grew more and more frustrated; he was also increasingly seen as an agent of the National Association for the Advancement of Colored People (NAACP) and kept uninformed of developments affecting black service personnel. In August 1942, the Advisory Committee on Negro Troops was set up under Assistant Secretary of War John J. McCloy as a way of bypassing Hastie. Only after he had protested was Hastie permitted to attend the committee meetings, but he was not officially a member. Although increasingly aware of the inefficiency resulting from segregation, the committee refused to question the policy. When the Army Air Corps indicated that it would establish a segregated officer-training

Standing on the steps of the Capitol, lobbying for antilynching legislation, are left to right: William Hastie, Walter White, Raymond McKeough, and Joseph Gavagan.

school, whereas the other branches of the army had integrated training, Hastie submitted his resignation on January 5, 1943, to take effect from the end of the month, an event that received a great deal of coverage in the black press. He was awarded the Spingarn Medal for his refusal to accept racial bigotry in the War Department. Hastie was succeeded by his assistant, Truman K. Gibson, who proved to be a less critical voice, and the plan for the segregated training school was dropped.

Hastie and other black leaders were well aware of the reality of the black military experience. Black soldiers experienced discrimination and prejudice not only within the army itself but also when they encountered white civilians, particularly in the South, where many of the military camps were located and more than 80 percent of black trainees were sent. With generally white and often southern officers, African Americans were constantly addressed as "boy" or "nigger," given menial jobs, passed over for promotion, and frequently humiliated. They were expected to follow the Jim Crow laws and accept the racial mores of the South without question, no matter where they came from. In town, the African American soldiers were generally lim-

ited to the black quarters and subject to local law enforcement, which could be brutal in the extreme. In just one of several similar incidents, on July 3, 1943, in Summit, Georgia, the police chief shot and killed a black soldier, Willie L. Davis, after he became involved in a dispute. No action was taken against the policeman.

Travel from army bases into nearby towns and back was always fraught with risk as southern segregation often led to conflict about access to buses and seating. Such problems occurred regardless of rank: one black soldier training as an officer at Fort Benning, Georgia, recalled that the only way back to base from Columbus was by taxi, and taxi drivers refused to take black and white soldiers together. Bus transport was equally problematic. African American soldiers who protested against or ignored segregated seating could be arrested, beaten, or worse. An example of the worst sort of treatment a black soldier might expect occurred on July 8, 1944, when a white bus driver shot and killed Pvt. Booker T. Spicely in Durham, North Carolina, for failing to move to the back of the bus quickly enough. The driver claimed he shot in self-defense and was acquitted. This was not a lone incident. Beginning in April 1941 with the lynching of Pvt. Felix Hall near Fort Benning, black soldiers fell victim to violence at the hands of white civilians, bus drivers, military police, or civilian police. William Hastie listed several cases of brutality, including the murder of black soldiers in Georgia and North Carolina, and Walter White described the killing of a black soldier, Charles Reco, by a police officer in Texas following an argument with a bus driver, the shooting death of Pvt. Raymond Carr in Louisiana, and the beating of a nurse, Lt. Nora Green, in Montgomery, Alabama. White police beat three black members of the Women's Army Corps (WAC) in one southern town for not moving quickly enough from the white waiting room to the "colored" room.

An often repeated story tells of African Americans in the South who witnessed German prisoners of war receiving better treatment than they themselves did, something even some white Americans found contradictory. The poet Witter Bynner in "Defeat" could ask, "Whom are we fighting this time, for God's sake?" and warned against "the token of the separate seat."[2] Such slights could provoke stronger action from black servicemen, and in August 1944 thirty Italian prisoners of war at Fort Lawson in Washington were injured following an attack by black troops who resented the better treatment given their supposed enemies. Of forty-three soldiers tried, twenty-three were convicted for the attack, although their sentences were subsequently reduced.

Obviously not always prepared to suffer passively, African American servicemen often fought back in confrontations and committed acts of disobe-

dience in response to real or perceived acts of discrimination. In November 1942, after a number of incidents involving African Americans and white civilians and police in Phoenix, Arizona, men of the 364th Infantry seized their weapons and shot and wounded fourteen people. Two soldiers and a civilian were killed. Fifteen of the black soldiers were tried, fourteen were sentenced to jail terms, and one received the death penalty. President Franklin Roosevelt commuted the death sentence. The 364th was then posted to Camp Van Dorn in Mississippi. Many of the black soldiers came from the North, and already demoralized and suffering from poor leadership, they were prepared for trouble. In a dispute between one of them and a local sheriff, the soldier, Pvt. William Walker, was shot dead. Other members of the regiment then armed themselves and were only restrained by armed riot military police and the intervention of their black chaplain. The regiment was quickly shipped to the Aleutian Islands shortly afterward. Rumors that many men of the 364th had been massacred at Camp Van Dorn surfaced in the 1990s, but an official investigation found no evidence to support such claims.

Clearly the level of violence in and around the camps where African American troops were based was considerable. One historian suggested that 209 racial military confrontations occurred between 1942 and 1945, and in 1943 alone several individuals, black and white, were killed in over 68 different clashes and riots in or around different camps, leading "official" military historian Ulysses Lee to write of a "harvest of disorder."[3] In one case in June 1943, disaffected black soldiers at Camp Stewart, Georgia, called the "Georgia Hell-Hole" by the troops, responded to constant discrimination by ambushing military policemen (MPs) sent in to discipline them. One MP was killed and several were wounded. Such incidents were not limited to the South: three soldiers died in a gun battle at Fort Dix in New Jersey after racial tension escalated into open violence. So great was the scale of conflict that an official War Department memorandum reported that most black troops had hidden ammunition and weapons to prepare for race conflict.

Violence, or the threat of it, was not the only response to the racial discrimination experienced by African Americans in the military. Black soldiers, mostly from Michigan, serving in the 94th Engineer Battalion near Gurdon and Prescott, Arkansas, participated in a number of clashes with local people and police in August 1941. Finally, feeling threatened by the harassment of state police, more than forty black soldiers simply went absent without leave and traveled back to their original base in Michigan.

Individual servicemen also refused to accept racist treatment passively. In July 1944 future baseball star 2nd Lt. Jackie Robinson had an altercation with a bus driver near Camp Hood, Texas, after refusing to move to the back

of the bus. Robinson insisted on his rights as an officer when white enlisted military policemen subsequently tried to arrest him, and he protested further when the soldiers abused him racially. As a result Robinson was court-martialed for refusing to obey orders and showing contempt to a white officer. He was found not guilty, but rather than being returned to his unit, the 761st Tank Battalion, he was posted to another base as a sports instructor, then honorably discharged in November 1944.

Others besides soldiers protested against their treatment in the service. In July 1944 two ships being loaded with ammunition by black seamen working as stevedores in Port Chicago, California, blew up. The enormous blast damaged over three hundred buildings and resulted in the deaths of 320 people, including 202 ammunition loaders and their 9 white officers. When the remaining men were ordered to resume loading ships the following month, 258 of them refused on the grounds that they were improperly trained and inadequately protected for such work. In September fifty were charged with mutiny, and after a six-week trial they were convicted and sentenced to between five and fifteen years in prison with dishonorable discharges. An appeal by the NAACP led to a reduction in the sentences, and the men were released under a general amnesty in 1946. President Bill Clinton granted the last surviving "mutineer" a full pardon in 1999.

In many ways these wartime protests by African Americans indicated a growing determination to be treated as equals, and in some respects they were forerunners of the massive protests launched in the 1960s. For example, in March 1945 black officers of the 477th Bomb Group repeatedly entered a "whites only" officers' club at Freeman Field, Indiana, and requested service. Despite their being refused and arrested, more black officers entered the facility and were also arrested. Over 160 men were placed under arrest, but when the action spread to the 619th Bombardment Squadron, the War Department ordered the charges dropped. The one conviction was set aside. This nonviolent protest took the form later repeated in the sit-ins that began with such momentous impact in Greensboro, North Carolina, in 1960.

Sgt. Henry Jones summed up the experience of many black service personnel when he wrote to Eleanor Roosevelt on March 8, 1943, detailing the experiences of men of the 349th Aviation Squadron at Carlsbad Army Airfield, New Mexico. Their commanding officer had established a Jim Crow camp in which the black servicemen were constantly abused and denied equal access to recreational facilities; for example, of the one thousand seats in the camp theater, African Americans could sit in only twenty at the rear. The black troops were denied access to the Post Exchange and suffered all the indignities of segregated southern transport, often having to walk back to

base. As Jones said, the black troops were not asking for any special privilege but merely to enjoy the rights of any American soldier. Mrs. Roosevelt raised the issue with George C. Marshall on several occasions but did not get a response.

Military officials were not, however, oblivious to the feelings of black service personnel. Throughout the war, surveys taken to determine the attitudes of black soldiers found that 20 percent thought the army unfair, while 60 percent had mixed feelings. Less than 70 percent felt the war was as much their affair as anyone else's. In his famous 1944 study of race in the United States entitled *An American Dilemma*, Swedish sociologist Gunnar Myrdal quoted the epitaph coined by African Americans during the war: "Here lies a black man killed fighting a yellow man for the protection of a white man."[4] Aware of the low morale and possible growing disaffection of black servicemen and women, the War Department began to introduce measures to lessen tensions and addressed issues raised by Sergeant Jones and others. Following recommendations of the McCloy Committee, in 1944 the army began to introduce bus services between military camps and neighboring towns on a first-come, first-served basis for service personnel only, and in July of that year the committee ordered an end to any designation of facilities by race. They could, however, be assigned by unit, and such issues were left to local commanding officers to decide.

Other morale-boosting measures included the production of a film, *The Negro Soldier*, in 1944. Written by and featuring the black screenwriter Carlton Moss and produced under the aegis of famous white director Frank Capra, the film presented a historical overview of black participation in the United States' wars before focusing on their contribution to World War II. Entirely positive in tone, it contrasted U.S. liberty and democracy with Hitler's Nazi ideology, glossed over negative aspects of the past such as slavery, and made no mention of the contemporary discrimination or segregation in the armed forces. However, while today the film may seem little more than simplistic propaganda, it was not viewed that way at the time. The sensitivity of the subject delayed its making and release, but when it was shown, first to service personnel and then to the wider public, the response was generally favorable. Black commentators compared it particularly with the poor record of Hollywood movies in depicting African Americans. The film became mandatory viewing in the army and was then released for public showing. Although it did not get the circulation that other wartime documentaries did, reportedly millions eventually saw the film. It was successful or effective enough to be followed by *The Negro Sailor* (1945) and the even more emotive *Teamwork* (1946).

Among those appearing in *The Negro Soldier* was world heavyweight boxing champion Joe Louis. In 1942 Louis donated the winnings of his successful bout with Buddy Baer to the Navy Relief Fund. In a much-used after-fight quote, Louis stated that the United States would win the war, saying, "We all got to do our part, and then we'll win. 'Cause we're on God's side."[5] The next day he enlisted in the U.S. Army. Overnight Louis was transformed from an African American hero into a national one, but the army used him in public relations and morale-boosting activities aimed especially at black troops. He also appeared on war posters and in the film *This Is the Army* alongside future president Ronald Reagan. In recognition of his patriotic work, the army awarded Louis the Legion of Merit in 1945.

Although never an outspoken critic of the army's racial policies, Louis did insist on boxing before integrated audiences, and he also supported Jackie Robinson during his court-martial. As part of his duties, Louis toured U.S. bases in Britain and experienced firsthand what many Africans Americans found when they went abroad wearing the uniform of their country: he was barred from a segregated movie theater until he protested. Initially the War Department was reluctant to send black troops overseas and particularly to commit them to combat roles. Foreign governments and officials, including those in Australia, Britain, China, Liberia, and the West Indies (Antigua, Jamaica, Trinidad), had also on occasion expressed the wish that no black troops be sent to their countries for fear of the impact on local populations. However, the demands of the war eventually outweighed the reservations of both American and foreign officials. Approximately five hundred thousand African American service personnel saw service overseas during the war. Their experience had an enormous effect not only on the service men and women themselves but also on race relations and the nation's racial policies.

From 1942, during the buildup to the invasion of Europe and after, almost 3 million Americans passed through the British Isles, among them several thousand African Americans—the number peaked in 1945 at around 132,000. As the British black population at the time was estimated to be only about seven to ten thousand mainly concentrated in a few port cities and London, the presence of the American troops was a novelty. Although often treated as curiosities, African American troops generally received a very warm welcome from the British people—they were, after all, there to help win the war. They were also better clothed, better fed, and better paid than most British people. For many war-weary Britons, the African Americans, like their white counterparts, had everything: money, cigarettes, candy, gum, razor blades, nylons, ice cream; they also brought with them music and

the "jitterbug" dance craze. Both their novelty and their generosity often made the black soldiers very popular, and they were often preferred to white GIs because they were polite and courteous while white Americans were often seen as loud and brash. When Walter White toured Britain in 1944 he concluded that for many African Americans, their time in England provided a first experience of being treated like normal human beings and friends by white people. Thus, American forces' attempts to introduce Jim Crow–style segregation into British life created resentment among the black soldiers and their British hosts, who objected to what they called a "color bar."

The issue of American race practices was discussed even within the British cabinet, and questions about segregation were also raised in parliamentary debates in the House of Commons and in the British press. While some government ministers favored acceptance of the American system, others objected. Ultimately the U.S. military authorities were left to control their own forces, while British police were instructed not to impose segregation in nonmilitary facilities. A program of education was undertaken on both sides through leaflets, and a film shown to all visiting American service personnel entitled *Welcome to Britain* included the race issue and suggested that wartime was the moment to forget race differences. Despite this, many facilities in Britain became segregated, with some pubs designated for black troops, others for whites, and even fish-and-chips shops operating "black only" and "white only" days in some places. Separate day clubs and Red Cross centers were also established in a number of towns, and some towns were declared "off-limits" for blacks and others for whites. Even so, on numerous occasions African Americans suffered verbal or physical abuse by white Americans who took offence at their presence in a pub or restaurant or on a train, especially if accompanied by white women. These confrontations led at least twice to major outbreaks of violence resulting in the deaths of two black soldiers, both of which were reported in the black press back home. In conversation with Walter White, Gen. John Lee, commander of the Service of Supply troops, described the situation between black and white troops in England as dangerous, adding that it was slowing up preparations for the invasion of Normandy and making the United States unpopular with the British people.

One aspect of the American presence that caused the British particular concern was the application of American law to black troops in certain situations. The Visiting Forces Act gave the U.S. military authorities complete legal jurisdiction over their forces, even in cases involving assault on British citizens. A number of incidents involved rape, which in Britain was not a capital offence. In May 1944 Leroy Henry, a black soldier, was convicted of raping a woman near Bath and sentenced to death. However, strong evi-

dence suggested that the attack had not been a rape; locals petitioned on the soldier's behalf, and the matter was raised in the British press. Doubts about the safety of the conviction were so strong that Gen. Dwight Eisenhower himself intervened, the sentence was overturned, and Henry was returned to the ranks. When two other black GIs were found guilty of raping a sixteen-year-old girl in Cheltenham, Gloucestershire, in April 1944 and sentenced to death, several groups of local people wrote to the press to protest on the grounds that the punishment was based on the men's color. The American authorities denied any suggestion of race bias, and the two men were executed.

Whatever the claim of the U.S. Army, the statistics suggest bias indeed existed. While black troops constituted only 8 percent of all the American forces in the European Theater of Operations (ETO), they accounted for 21 percent of all those convicted of crimes and 42 percent of those convicted of sex crimes. Of the eighteen men executed in Britain, eleven were African American, and three were Hispanic. Seven of the African Americans were executed for rape. The pattern of discrimination was evident in the disproportionate number of African Americans executed in total during the war: out of the ninety-one military executions, seventy-three, or 80 percent, were of African Americans. Even less serious cases showed evidence of bias, and Walter White reported innumerable instances in which African American troops received harsh punishments for minor offenses while whites got off or in which black soldiers were court-martialed for protesting against discrimination. Despite the experiences of racism largely at the hands of their white countrymen in Britain and subsequently in Italy and Germany, many black soldiers commented on the feelings of freedom they experienced in Europe, which often significantly affected their attitudes upon their return home.

Because the majority of African Americans worked in the Service of Supply regiments, comparatively few of the troops who took part in the D-day landings were black—approximately five hundred of the almost thirty thousand who landed on Omaha beach and about twelve hundred of the thirty-two thousand on Utah beach. However, among those who landed was one all-black unit, the 320th Barrage Balloon Battalion, which helped provide cover from air attack for the invading forces; they were followed quickly by the many men who helped unload ships and get supplies to the front line. The Allies' rapid push west meant that it was difficult to maintain supplies, and in August 1944 the "Red Ball" plan was devised to ensure supplies reached the front from the beaches of Normandy. For over eighty days nearly nine hundred trucks a day drove virtually nonstop in the "Red Ball Express" convoys from the coast to Paris and beyond to keep the front line

U.S. General Dwight Eisenhower visits the supply port of Cherbourg. LOC 2002706912.

supplied. More than 75 percent of the drivers were African Americans in the Army Transportation Corps.

By August 1944 more than two hundred thousand African Americans had arrived in the ETO, and twenty-two black combat units took part in fighting the German forces. Among them was the first black unit to go into combat, the all-black 761st Tank Battalion, attached to Gen. George Patton's Third Army and nicknamed "Patton's Panthers." They landed in Normandy in October 1944, fought in a number of major engagements through France, Belgium, Holland, and into Germany, and were among the first American troops to reach the concentration camps in April 1945. By the time war in Europe had ended, three officers and thirty-one enlisted men from the 761st had been killed in action, and over two hundred men had been wounded. In 1997 Sgt. Ruben Rivers was posthumously awarded the Medal of Honor, and the following year the 761st received a presidential citation.

In December 1944 Hitler launched a last desperate offensive against the Allied forces in the Ardennes, pushing them back into Belgium. During the Battle of the Bulge, as it became known, many U.S. Army soldiers suffered casualties or were taken prisoner. As a result urgent manpower replacements were needed, and the army called for volunteers from among the African Americans filling noncombat roles to serve in platoons alongside white soldiers at the front. Almost five thousand African Americans volunteered, and even though for some the transfer meant loss of rank, twenty-five hundred men served in thirty-seven platoons beside larger white units. This experiment in integration proved a success, and a survey of the men concerned found that racial prejudices actually diminished the more blacks and whites were together. Despite this, the platoons were demobilized or returned to their former units at the end of the war in Europe.

In the Mediterranean African Americans in the Ninety-second Division landed in Italy in July 1944 and took part in the major Allied offensive in September. After some initial successes, German forces pushed the division back in February 1945, and the white press reported these setbacks widely in critical terms. William Hastie's successor as civilian aide to the secretary of war, Truman Gibson, went to Italy and, after some investigation, gave a press conference in March 1945 in which he seemed to accept that the Ninety-second had failed. He repeated the remarks of an earlier report stating that many of the soldiers had shown a tendency to "melt away" under fire. When criticized in the black press for these remarks, Gibson clarified that he thought any failures were the inevitable consequences of segregation, the lack of combat training, and the poor educational qualifications of many of the black soldiers.

African American soldiers on patrol near bombed buildings, somewhere in Europe. U.S. Army Signal Corps. LOC 2003689099.

Most historians have subsequently agreed with this assessment, pointing to the low morale of the black soldiers and the particularly poor leadership of the regiment by white officers who expressed little faith in the troops under their command. The Ninety-second's treatment while at Fort Huachuca, Arizona, contributed to the low morale subsequently reflected in its members' military performance in Italy. Many of the men in the division scored well below average on the standard IQ tests, but even able soldiers grew disenchanted due to their poor treatment by officers and the local population. One soldier recalled, regarding a particularly difficult element within the division known as the "Casuals," "If they had been treated as human beings, as soldiers in the United States Army, they would not have become a problem."[6] In Italy, as elsewhere, the introduction of segregation and racial prejudice also inflamed black soldiers' bitter feelings. Other writers have also emphasized that any failures could be attributed to the harsh terrain, poor tactics, and fierce German defense. Moreover, they record many instances in which the black soldiers repeatedly went forward in the face of enemy fire.

Whatever their reported failings, the men of the Ninety-second Infantry Division won a total of 12,096 military decorations and citations, including three Distinguished Service Crosses (the second-highest award for gallantry), sixteen Legion of Merit medals, and 145 Silver Stars. The king of Italy awarded the entire regiment a Cross of Merit in War, and several soldiers remarked on the empathy they shared with the local population, who viewed them as liberators. Among the men of the Ninety-second to be honored was Lt. Vernon Baker, who won a Purple Heart, Bronze Star, and Distinguished Service Cross. In 1997 Baker became the first living African American to be awarded the Medal of Honor for his extraordinary heroism and outstanding courage and leadership at Viareggio during the Italian campaign. Another

Tuskegee Airmen, 1945. Toni Frissell. Reproduction Number: LC-F9-02-4503-330-5 (8-6).

seven Medals of Honor were awarded posthumously at the same time to African Americans for their service during World War II.

Also among the African Americans who served in Europe were those in the newly formed black Army Air Force unit. The first squadron to see combat was the 99th Fighter Squadron led by Gen. Benjamin Davis's son, Benjamin O. Davis Jr., who flew over sixty missions and rose to the rank of colonel. The 99th was joined by three additional black squadrons, the 100th, 301st, and 302nd, which together became the 332nd Fighter Group under Davis's command. Altogether the 332nd flew over fifteen thousand sorties in North Africa, Italy, and Germany, shot down 111 enemy planes, and inflicted considerable damage to installations and weapons on the ground. The unit received a presidential citation and among the various awards to its pilots were 95 Distinguished Flying Crosses and 865 Legion of Merit awards.

Although the greatest number of African Americans served in the ETO, many also contributed to the war in the Pacific. As in Europe, the majority served in noncombat roles but still made a vital contribution to eventual victory. Between 1942 and early 1944, for example, more than ten thousand black engineers took part in building the 270-mile-long Ledo Road from Assam into China. Other African American units served in quartermaster units and port companies and participated in vital amphibian landings on Japanese-held islands. But black soldiers also saw combat in the Pacific. After two years of training and constant harassment in the United States, the Ninety-third Infantry Division was finally committed to action in the Pacific campaign, and after landing at Guadalcanal, where they performed stevedoring duties unloading ships, the men took part in the island-hopping campaign through the Solomon Islands toward the Philippines. Although Walter White recalled that some attempted to malign its achievements, the division performed very creditably and did not attract the adverse attention that the Ninety-second had. Nor did it attract much positive comment despite the fact that several men were awarded military honors for their service.

Even during the bitter Pacific campaigns, racism among the American forces flared up, leading to open conflict. White recorded details of the discrimination experienced by black base companies in Guam in 1944. Not only were the black soldiers abused, but white marines actually threw hand grenades and smoke bombs into their camps. On Christmas Eve a black camp was invaded, and the next day shots were fired from a passing jeep with a mounted machine gun. When African Americans set out for the nearby town to exact revenge, they were halted at a roadblock, and forty-four of them were arrested and faced a court-martial. Despite all the evidence and

having White as defense counsel, the men were convicted and sentenced to prison, an outcome later overturned on appeal brought by the NAACP.

Black women also experienced discrimination when finally allowed to enter the armed forces. When in May 1942 Congress established the Women's Army Auxiliary Corps, which became the Women's Army Corps a year later, 40 black women were among the first 440 enrolled for officer training. Over 150,000 black women served in the WAC as enlisted personnel. Among the officers was Charity Adams Earley, who rose to lieutenant colonel, the highest rank possible in the WAC, in December 1945. As a black woman and an officer, Earley experienced negative reactions from white Americans on a number of occasions in the United States, particularly when traveling by rail. Fortunately for her, the abuse she experienced was purely verbal, but she recalled that one black WAC officer had been beaten while waiting in a segregated waiting room in a small southern town because white people were angry that, as a captain, she would expect white people to salute her. Earley also wrote that while she was in charge of the 6888th Central Postal Directory Battalion, which served in Birmingham, England, local people asked that visitors from the unit be allowed to stay out until 12:30 a.m. because they wanted to see whether what they had been told was true, namely "that Negroes had tails that came out at midnight."[7] (Black soldiers also reported hearing such stories, even in the battle zone in Italy.) When, over her protests, the Red Cross provided a separate all-black hotel to accommodate members of the WAC visiting London, Earley persuaded troops under her command not to use it. The 6888th was responsible for redirecting mail to all U.S. personnel in the ETO, a number estimated at about 7 million. According to the official WAC record, "The unit broke all records for redirecting mail"[8] before moving on to serve in France, where it continued to work to get mail to men at the front. After the war Earley was awarded a scroll of honor by the National Council of Negro Women in 1946 for her distinguished military service.

Due to the restrictions imposed by the army until 1944, only a small number of African American women were allowed to serve in the Army Nurse Corps, and they were restricted to hospitals or wards devoted exclusively to the treatment of black soldiers. Some black nurses served in Liberia, and in June 1944 a unit was sent to England to look after wounded German prisoners of war. Eventually black nurses were sent to Australia, Burma, and New Guinea, but at the end of the war, only about five hundred of the fifty thousand army nurses were African American. Even African Americans working in hospitals could experience discrimination, and when sixty black WACs,

European Theater of Operations, nurses in England, 1944. NAACP Collection, Prints and Photographs Division. Reproduction Number: LC-USC4-6175/LC-USZ62-119985 (8-5).

trained as medical technicians, were ordered to take on menial cleaning tasks in Fort Devens, Massachusetts, they staged a sit-down strike. Six of the women were eventually court-martialed and sentenced to one year hard labor until protests from black organizations led to the reversal of the convictions and dropping of all charges.

Resistance to including black women in the Women's Reserve of the U.S. Navy also persisted almost until the end of the war. Women Accepted for Volunteer Emergency Service (WAVES) was established in July 1942. However, Secretary of the Navy Frank Knox steadfastly blocked the inclusion of African American women until his death, and replacement by the more liberal James Forrestal in April 1944 made progress in this area possible. When President Roosevelt continued to delay, his Republican opponent in the 1944 presidential election, Gov. Thomas E. Dewey, took up the issue,

and shortly after the election, black women were allowed into the WAVES on an integrated basis. In December 1944 the first two black officers, Harriet Pikens and Frances Wills, were sworn in and joined by seventy-two enlisted women—in a total force of ninety thousand.

If the navy was slow to admit black women, it did show some progress regarding black men. In 1940 four thousand African Americans served in the navy, almost all as mess men or in the engine rooms. Another 12,500 African Americans served in the naval construction units, the Seabees, and almost one thousand in the Coast Guard. On April 7, 1942, the navy announced that African Americans would be admitted to all branches of the reserve sections of the naval, marine, and coast guard services, and starting in 1943 African Americans were admitted on a proportional basis with the first black naval officers appointed in February 1944. Initially the only way to fully deploy African Americans while maintaining segregation was to crew ships entirely with black seamen, and in 1944 the destroyer escort USS *Mason* and submarine chaser *PC 1264* were manned with black crews. In August of that year, however, black and white sailors were formed into integrated crews on twenty-five auxiliary vessels. By the end of the war, there were 165,000 African Americans in the navy and 5,000 in the Coast Guard, but 95 percent of these were still mess men, and only 5 percent were in general service. There were only fifty-four black naval officers and seven hundred in the Coast Guard in 1945.

Under the combined pressures of black protest, political influence, and the real necessities of the war itself, the racial policies of the U.S. armed forces had been questioned and in some cases forced to change. It was increasingly apparent that it was not possible to maintain segregation and achieve the full use of all available resources. Attempts to do so threatened the morale of the black population and also undermined the United States' democratic principles. By the end of the war, all branches of the forces were reviewing their policies and at least considering the possibility of integration. Equally significant was the profound effect the war had on the 1 million African Americans who served in the military. Some found the experience totally disillusioning; for others it was more positive. Despite everything, many gained an education, a skill, an experience of life beyond the United States, and often, quite simply, a degree of self-respect. In letters to the black newspapers, some servicemen wondered what benefits their service would bring; others declared their refusal to return to the status quo, claiming they would have what was rightfully theirs. As one soldier said, "I went into the Army a nigger; I'm coming out a *man*."[9]

CHAPTER FOUR

~

Conflict on the Home Front
Resistance, Riot, and Social Change

For me the war period was a very compelling, very exhilarating era. There was a feeling that you had hold of something that was big and urgent and was not going to last forever. There were opportunities for change which could not exist after the war was over.

—Alexander Allen, in *The Home Front: America during World War II*, 1984.[1]

World War II brought enormous opportunities for all Americans. In addition to throwing the military's racial policies and practices into sharp relief, it also focused attention on discrimination on the home front in employment and housing. While the issue of armed service highlighted fundamental questions about citizenship rights, the growing labor shortages in the defense industries, combined with black protests and the federal government's positive action to enforce equal employment, led to an opening of economic opportunities that in turn encouraged a massive movement of population, both black and white, out of the South and into northern and western towns and cities. Thrown together in strange living and working conditions, the new arrivals were forced to make readjustments as their changing circumstances amid the ever-present stresses of wartime challenged old values and expectations. Although the nation's fight for democracy and freedom encouraged some positive change in racial attitudes and values that found expression in public actions, statements, and publications, resistance and conflict also persisted on the shop floor, on public transport, over housing, and in the streets. A

negative reaction seemed to accompany every step forward, and just as wartime gains encouraged a sense of hope, setbacks created anger, bitterness, and despondency among the black population.

On occasion the despair led to violence on an individual and group level as racial antagonism on both sides exploded into open confrontation that both challenged the United States' standing as the defender of democracy and directly threatened to hinder the war effort itself. The widespread and continuous violence and confrontation on the home front and in the armed services supports the argument that the more accurate description of World War II as a "race war" should replace the widely held perception of it as a "good war." At the same time, this conflict forced an often reluctant government to take measures to reduce tensions, and many white Americans began to question whether the old racial patterns could survive. As Swedish sociologist Gunnar Myrdal suggested in his famous study, *An American Dilemma*, commissioned by the Carnegie Endowment in 1938 but published in 1944, there was bound to be "a redefinition of the status of African Americans as a result of the war."[2]

Increasingly after 1941, job opportunities in the defense industries began to open up for African Americans. Some of these gains were certainly due to government policy and the establishment of the Fair Employment Practices Committee (FEPC) after President Franklin Roosevelt issued Executive Order 8802; increasingly, however, they stemmed from the growing war emergency and developing labor shortages as war mobilization reached its height. The biggest advances came after 1942, particularly in areas of acute labor shortage. Between 1940 and 1945 the proportion of all African Americans employed in manufacturing increased by 135 percent, and the black press reported that black employment was at an all-time high as the number of unemployed fell from almost 1 million to 151,000. The actual number of African Americans employed rose from 4.4 million in 1942 to 5.9 million in 1945, and they accounted for over 8 percent of all defense workers.

The gains in employment were uneven and varied from industry to industry and area to area. Most occurred in the heavy industries, such as shipbuilding, where the number of black workers rose from six to fourteen thousand between 1942 and 1943. Eventually African Americans constituted almost 12 percent of shipyard workers. Much smaller, but still significant, advances occurred in the aircraft industry as leading aircraft manufacturers reversed their earlier discriminatory policies. The number of black aircraft workers rose from virtually zero to five thousand by 1943, and by 1945 it had reached one hundred thousand, just under 6 percent of the total. However, some aircraft manufacturers maintained segregated patterns of employment

and excluded African Americans from supervisory roles, while others, some even in the South, integrated their workers and allowed black supervisors. In Chicago, where labor leaders, local politicians, and the FEPC played an active role, black employment rose from over 80,000 to 222,600, or from 8.6 percent of the labor force in 1943 to 13.1 percent in 1944; in Baltimore the numbers rose from 9,000 to 36,000, and from 6 percent of the labor force

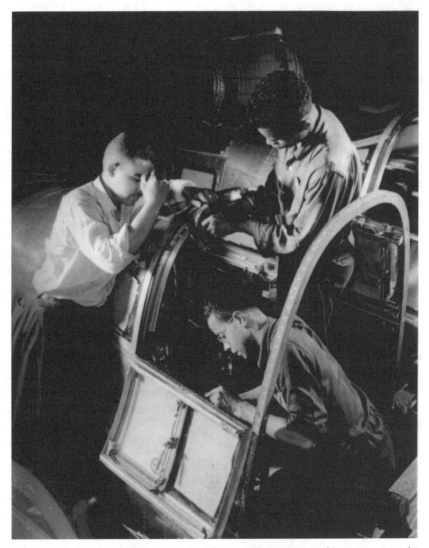

African Americans working on an aircraft, May 1942. www.archives.gov/research/ african-americans/ww2-pictures/images/african-americans-wwii-248.jpg.

to 15 percent. In Cincinnati, Ohio, on the other hand, FEPC representatives could still find employers refusing to hire African Americans in March 1944.

The pressure of wartime demand alone did not break down racial barriers—effecting change still required protest. In a number of places the intervention of the FEPC was necessary, but elsewhere African American groups took the initiative. In Portland, Oregon, the National Shipyard Organization for Victory worked to open up the Kaiser shipyards; in San Francisco the Committee against Segregation and Discrimination led by the local president of the National Association for the Advancement of Colored People (NAACP), Joseph James, succeeded in forcing the previously all-white shipyard unions to open their doors to African Americans; in Oakland, the Shipyard Workers Committee against Discrimination led by a Communist and head of the local National Negro Congress, Ray Thompson, achieved a similar outcome. All three groups shared clear links with the "Double V for Victory" campaigns, as did the Los Angeles Negro Victory Committee formed in 1941 to challenge racial discrimination in industry. Led by Rev. Clayton Russell, a minister in central Los Angeles, and Charlotta Bass, publisher of the *California Eagle*, the largest African American newspaper in the state, the committee coordinated protest meetings in support of demands for defense-industry job-training centers in Watts and the hiring of black conductors and locomotive drivers on the Los Angeles Railway. It also campaigned against segregated housing and racial quotas in city employment and forced the U.S. Employment Service to stop placing black women exclusively in janitorial and service positions in defense plants.

Often, as was the case in West Coast shipyards, black organizations had to struggle to break down the discriminatory policies of trade unions as much as those of employers. Although the number of African Americans in unions rose during the war from 500,000 to 1.25 million and both the American Federation of Labor (AFL) and Congress of Industrial Organizations (CIO) had agreed to work to remove barriers against their employment in defense industries, the pattern of racial discrimination among union members remained a depressing feature of the war years. At the three annual AFL conventions from 1941 to 1943, A. Philip Randolph repeatedly listed various instances in which AFL unions excluded African Americans or discriminated against them in some way, but to no avail. He was told no action was necessary. The CIO was more positive, frequently passing resolutions at its annual convention condemning discrimination and establishing a committee to eliminate it from within the organization itself. CIO-led union drives helped to ensure the employment of African Americans in a number of areas,

and when members of the CIO Industrial Union of Maritime and Shipbuilding Workers at the Bethlehem shipyards in Baltimore struck because black workers had been admitted to the welding school, the union expelled the strikers. The threat of similar action prevented a strike at the Chrysler plant in Detroit in 1942. However, the union proved powerless when in May 1943 twenty-five thousand white workers at the Packard Motor Company in Detroit struck to protest the hiring of four black women and the upgrading of three black men; ending the strike required the combined efforts of the FEPC, local politicians, and management.

"Hate strikes" against the employment or promotion of black workers occurred in a number of industries across the country, regardless of union or government policies. The most serious occurred at the Alabama Drydock & Shipping Company in Mobile in 1943 and the Philadelphia Transportation Company in 1944. When twelve black workers were promoted to the position of welder in the Mobile shipyards in response to FEPC instructions, white workers struck—despite CIO union directives—and some began to riot. Federal troops moved in after a second day of violence, and eventually the black workers were reassigned. In August 1944 white transport workers in Philadelphia went on strike in defiance of their union and employers, the FEPC, and the War Manpower Commission after the promotion of eight African Americans to trolley drivers; in doing so they paralyzed one of the nation's biggest centers of war production. President Roosevelt sent in eight thousand troops and threatened to revoke strikers' draft deferments before the dispute ended. On this occasion, the outcome was a victory against racism, and within a year the company employed almost one thousand black workers. Nonetheless, too often it seemed that some white workers, as the saying went, would rather see Hitler and Hirohito victorious than work beside African Americans.

Despite these conflicts, after decades of exclusion, the war years marked the beginning of a significant period of economic advance for African Americans. The gains made were in both quantity and quality. During the war the number of African Americans working in domestic service declined, while the number in skilled and semiskilled occupations doubled; as black economist and government official Robert C. Weaver noted, more occupational diversification of black labor occurred during the war than in the preceding seventy-five years.[3] Among the biggest growth areas for black employment was federal government itself: the number of African Americans it employed rose 400 percent from sixty to three hundred thousand, and one survey in 1944 found that almost 20 percent of federal employees were black. More importantly, many worked in positions other than the traditional janitorial

and custodial jobs, the vast majority in war agencies: in the Office of Price Administration, for example, 70 percent of the 1,250 black workers had clerical and administrative roles. With more work in better jobs went better wages, and the average earnings of black workers doubled during the war. As one African American woman, Sybil Lewis, recalled, "The war and defense work gave black people opportunities to work on jobs they never had before. It gave them opportunity to do things they had never experienced before . . . [and] their expectations changed."[4]

Clearly, the wartime economic changes did not exclude black women. The number of black women employed rose from 1.5 to 2.1 million during the war. Often increased opportunities for employment only came for black women after black men and white women had found work, so they only accounted for about 4 percent of the 7 million women in war production in 1944. Many of these jobs entailed work that white women refused to do and thus often resembled the hot, heavy, dirty labor undertaken by black men. For instance, there were substantial increases in the number of black female workers in the car industry and in the foundries and shipyards as the percentage of African American women in industrial occupations rose during the war from 6.6 to 18 percent. Although barriers to black female employment remained, such opportunities did mean that many African American women could leave domestic service or waitressing and earn more, sometimes nine or ten times more, in industrial occupations. Sybil Lewis, for example, moved from Oklahoma, where she earned $3.50 a week as a maid, to Los Angeles, where she earned $48 as a riveter with Lockheed Aircraft before becoming a welder in the shipyards. Videll Drake moved from Dallas and her $7.75 per week job as a maid and waitress to Los Angeles, where she started at sixty cents an hour working as a riveter for North American Aviation—suggesting, as one black worker remarked, that "Hitler was the one that got us out of white folks' kitchens."[5] At Lockheed the number of black female workers had risen from fifty-four in 1941 to seventeen hundred in 1943; at North American the number had risen from eight women to twenty-five hundred.

Work shifted to the factory not just from the kitchen but also from the farm, and as Sybil Lewis recalled, black women discovered another way of life. In 1940 43.3 percent of black men and 21 percent of black women were employed in agriculture, but four years later the figures had fallen to 31.3 and 10.9 percent, respectively. These statistics reflect only part of a much larger and significant development, namely, the massive movement of the black population from the country to the town and from the South to the North and now, substantially for the first time, to the West. Of course, to some extent this movement continued that which had begun during World War I,

Women welders at the Landers, Frary, and Clark plant, New Britain, Connecticut. LOC owi2001033044/PP.

but the increase in scale was remarkable and included new directions, leading some writers to describe it as the second "Great Migration" lasting from 1940 until 1970. Between 1940 and 1945, approximately 1.5 million African Americans moved out of state, and half a million of these (17 percent of black southerners compared with only 3 percent of whites) left the South; between

1940 and 1950, 1.5 million African Americans, the same number as in the previous three decades, left the South. This movement gravitated toward the centers of war production, so California, with half the nation's shipbuilding and aircraft manufacturing, attracted 338,000 African Americans. Los Angeles saw its black population increase by over 133,000 to 196,856; the number in San Francisco grew from just under 5,000 to just over 32,000 in the same period. In percentage terms this far exceeded the movement of whites into these cities, and the same held true for the states of Oregon and Washington, both of which experienced a large influx of black migrants. Even in other areas of population growth, such as Detroit and Washington, D.C., the scale of increase in black population exceeded that of whites quite considerably, and the increases in major northern centers were also much greater than they had been during World War I. In both Detroit and Chicago the number of African Americans who arrived during the war years alone numbered more than sixty thousand; by 1950 Chicago's black population had increased by well over two hundred thousand. Smaller towns and cities in the North, such as Buffalo, New York, and Milwaukee, Wisconsin, also experienced wartime increases in black population that, although relatively small numerically (8,000 and 4,000, respectively), represented a large proportional increase over their prewar black populations (17,694 and 9,000). Even in the South, where overall the black population declined, urban centers such as Birmingham, Mobile, and New Orleans experienced a rise in numbers. Be they northern, western, or southern, large or small, these sudden surges in black population often had the same wider social consequences.

While some strides toward economic equality between the races were made during the war, at least narrowing, if not closing completely, the gap between the two, social equality was rarely on the agenda in the workplace anymore than it was in the military. Many whites clearly were not prepared to work with blacks, and when they were, it was rarely, if ever, as equals. Sybil Lewis, like many others, found that California did not quite match expectations—everywhere there was prejudice and discrimination. Although there was no consistent pattern in Los Angeles, African Americans (and Mexican Americans) were often barred from restaurants, bars, and movie theaters, and it was not unusual to see signs announcing Wednesday as "Mexican night" and Thursday as "colored night." One black woman remembered being refused admission to a theater in Sacramento because of her color; she was later dismissed from her job in Los Angeles for interracial socializing. Alexander Allen of the National Urban League found that the racism of peacetime had carried over into the defense industries in Baltimore: even if you had a degree in electronics, if you were black, you were sent to join the common laborers

and unskilled workers. William Barber, a prewar migrant to Philadelphia and one of the African Americans employed as a trolley driver, recalled white passengers getting off rather than ride with a "nigger"; others spat at him. He continued working because he felt he was a pioneer paving the way for others to follow. He stayed on the job for forty years.[6]

African Americans experienced white resentment not just on the shop floor or in the workplace. The rapid population increases in war centers exacerbated problematic social conditions that had developed during the Depression. Among the most serious issues was housing, an area particularly hard hit during the economic collapse of the thirties. While the housing crisis affected all Americans, for African Americans poor housing indicated their place at the bottom of the economic and social pile. In the South many lived in wooden shacks, often without toilets or running water; northern black urban populations had crammed into poorer, more and more overcrowded ghettos, their movement limited by poverty, social conventions, and restrictive housing covenants that prevented the sale of properties to nonwhites. When African Americans fortunate enough to have the means of moving did so, they often met with white resistance and violence, as did Dr. Ossian Sweet in Detroit in 1925. African Americans had benefited from the New Deal public housing programs, but these barely scratched the surface of an endemic problem. These issues intensified during the war.

Housing was a major national concern during the war. Insufficient or inadequate housing magnified labor shortages as war workers moved to areas where they could find decent homes. In major centers of war production, the lack of housing often reached crisis proportions. Press reports described families living in single rooms, sometimes without proper facilities; the hotbed system of several people sharing a single bed was widely reported. In 1942 a National Housing Agency was established to coordinate a federal war housing program, and during the war more than 1.3 million publicly and privately financed war homes were built. Because of patterns of discrimination and their late entry into the labor market, African Americans did not fully benefit from these developments—by the end of 1944 only 8.6 percent (115,389) of the war homes went to blacks, the majority of these being publicly rather than privately financed. As a result, housing conditions for African Americans often deteriorated. One survey found that for African Americans in a number of cities, including Chicago, Cleveland, Detroit, and St. Louis, they had gone from bad to worse.

Despite increased earnings, African Americans often had limited choice of accommodation. In California, for instance, black newcomers found themselves forced into areas formerly inhabited by Japanese Americans (who

had been relocated to internment camps). In San Francisco ten thousand African Americans moved into a district previously inhabited by five thousand people and in which more than half the homes were rated as substandard. Blacks in the city occupied just under five thousand defense homes, and they were segregated. In Los Angeles, which had far more black migrants, only 3,825 war homes were provided for African Americans. So Katie Mac Miles, a new arrival from Houston in 1942, found public housing in Los Angeles, but it was segregated. She remained there until 1956. On the other hand, Christina Hill, who came from Texas to Los Angeles at the same time, earned enough at North American Aviation to buy a house in an integrated neighborhood in South Central Los Angeles.

One journalist reported some of the worst wartime housing could be found in Washington, D.C., where he discovered five or six people in a room sharing one bed. Attempts to build homes for African Americans outside the capital were abandoned due to white opposition, and of the almost sixty thousand war homes built in Washington, only four thousand, half of them temporary buildings, were for blacks. A similar story was told in Buffalo, New York, where local opposition to National Housing Agency plans to build segregated homes for black workers delayed construction for two years while accommodation stood empty in white projects. In Chicago, too, whites resisted African Americans' attempts to move into white areas. Between May 1944 and July 1946, forty-six black homes in white neighborhoods were fire-bombed. Public housing remained limited despite the huge number of black migrants to the city. When one project of 1,658 units opened in January 1941, there were nineteen thousand applicants.

Some of the worst housing conditions were found in Michigan's Detroit–Willow Run area, which attracted over half a million migrants, more than fifty thousand of them black. The huge Ford aircraft manufacturing plant at Willow Run outside of Detroit had an enormous workforce, employing forty-two thousand people at its peak. Initially, thousands of these were housed in a government-built dormitory while others slept in tents, trailers, and garages. Eventually, more war housing was provided, but white opposition ensured that none went to black workers. In Detroit itself, 44,607 war homes were built, but African Americans occupied only just over three thousand. The majority of the city's two hundred thousand African Americans squeezed into an area on the east side ironically named Paradise Valley; as a result housing issues became a major source of friction in the city. In January 1942, when the Sojourner Truth Housing Project, named for the famous black abolitionist, was opened for African Americans in a white neighborhood, the resulting protests led to its being reassigned to whites. Pressure from African

Americans forced a reversal of the order, but when the black tenants tried to move in at the end of February, a hostile crowd of whites prevented them from taking occupancy. Eventually, in April, 6 black families took possession of their properties under the protection of more than two thousand police and national guardsmen, and another 160 families followed shortly.

Although it perhaps epitomized the "arsenal of democracy" in production terms, Detroit already had a history of racial conflict, particularly over employment. White migrants from the South brought their prejudices with them, and were further encouraged by the presence of the Ku Klux Klan and home-grown demagogues like Catholic priest Father Charles Coughlin. Strikes over the hiring or upgrading of African Americans had halted production at the U.S. Rubber Company, the Vickers Company, Hudson Motors, and others, and white street gangs had attacked blacks on several occasions. Some African Americans responded by "bumping" whites on sidewalks. Finally, on Sunday, June 20, 1943, the simmering tensions in the city exploded following a clash between blacks and whites in Belle Isle amusement park. As rumors spread through both communities, thousands of whites took to the streets, pulling black workers from street cars and attacking African Americans in automobiles. African Americans responded by looting or burning white-owned stores. By Tuesday three-quarters of the city had been affected, and the riot did not come to an end until six thousand federal troops were brought in. By then thirty-four people were dead, twenty-five of them black (seventeen killed by police) and nine white. Hundreds were injured, almost two thousand people were arrested, $2 million worth of property had been damaged, and the war effort had been dealt a serious blow.

Detroit, although possibly the worst case, did not provide the only example of the heightened race conflict during the war. In 1943 more than 240 racial incidents—ranging from "hate strikes" and industrial conflicts to full-scale riots—occurred in forty-seven towns and cities. The *Pittsburgh Courier*'s headline on June 26, 1943, read simply, "Race Riots Sweep Nation"; on the same day, New York's *Amsterdam News* wrote of a "national race war." Just the week before the riot in Detroit, Los Angeles witnessed an outbreak of violence in which white sailors and soldiers attacked mainly Mexican American, but also some African American, youths dressed in "zoot suits," flamboyant suits with long jackets, wide trousers, and tight cuffs, often topped with a wide-brimmed hat. The attacks began on June 3 after weeks of negative news coverage of the activities of zoot suit gangs, or pachucos, and although no deaths were reported, several hundred people were injured and about 150 were arrested, all Mexican American. Just a few days later in Beaumont, Texas, where tensions ran high due to increased population, greater

employment of African Americans, and conflict on city transport, all exacerbated by food shortages and the strains of war, several thousand workers from the local shipyard gathered downtown on June 15, 1943, after a white woman claimed she had been raped by a black man. Over two days the mob attacked the black section of town, destroying property and beating African Americans unfortunate enough to be caught. Two people were killed, one black and one white, before the violence finally came to an end.

Chester Himes captured a sense of the workplace tensions and the wartime mood of African Americans in his novel *If He Hollers Let Him Go*, published in 1945. In this story Robert Jones, a black shipyard worker who had migrated to Los Angeles from Cleveland, Ohio, seethes with anger over the constant discrimination and exercise of power by whites, who can make him stand and wait for change on the streetcar, or force him to step off the sidewalk to let them pass, or ignore him, or, worse, insult him at work. Every time he steps outside, Jones sees a challenge he must accept or ignore, and everyday he must decide "Is it now? Is now the time?"[7] Even driving to the shipyard involves conflict with white drivers. For Jones, it is a white man's world, and they resent him just for standing in it. The shipyard is a scene of constant racial and sexual tension, and eventually a white woman worker falsely accuses Jones of rape. Given the choice, he opts for the army rather than a prison sentence.

African Americans' anger became all too evident in New York City in August 1943. Although New York had experienced many problems similar to those of other towns and cities, the pattern of violence was rather different. In 1940 the black population of 450,000 was crowded into the poorer city neighborhoods, with more than 60 percent living in Harlem. Although New York City did not see a huge influx of population during the war, many of the prewar conditions still applied, and wartime inflation increased the cost of living for a population that reaped little benefit from the war boom. In the summer of 1942, the NAACP found that only 142 out of almost 30,000 war workers in the New York area were African American. As one black inhabitant of the city wrote, although an American, if he lived in New York, he had to pay higher rent, yet live in squalid accommodation, and could find employment only in menial roles. Among the greatest causes of black resentment in Harlem was the brutality of the police force. Local black newspapers regularly reported cases of police violence against African Americans in 1943, and on August 1, 1943, simmering black resentment came to a head when word of an incident involving a white police officer shooting a uniformed black soldier spread like wildfire through the black community. Un-

like the riots in Detroit and elsewhere in which whites played a major role, the Harlem riot represented an implosion of black anger directed mainly at white-owned property within the black ghetto. Over several hours shops were looted and vandalized, and more than $5 million worth of damage was done. Five people, all black, were killed, more than five hundred were injured, and five hundred were arrested. Ending the riot did not require the use of troops, but black leaders Walter White and Roy Wilkins actively assisted the police and Mayor Fiorello La Guardia in bringing peace to the streets.

It is tempting to see each of these riots as different; indeed, in some ways they were—one was a commodity or property riot, another a labor or military riot; one was white on black, another black on white. In reality, however, they all had much in common. First, the race riots should be viewed alongside the widespread and increased outbreak of labor disputes in 1943, reflecting in many ways the general anxieties and tensions of the war: concerns for absent family members in the armed forces, the disruptions of wartime migration, the pressure of long hours of work, shortages of material goods, rationing, and wartime price inflation. The duration and outcome of the war itself also remained far from clear. Population movement and pressure on housing and public transport aggravated all of these anxieties. The violence of war may even have encouraged rioting: surveys revealed that the majority of those who rioted were young males, and Walter White and Thurgood Marshall of the NAACP suggested that the rioters were young men facing the prospect of going into service or expressing their resentment of others who had seemingly avoided it. For those too young to serve or whom the draft had rejected, perhaps rioting was an expression of masculinity. Whatever their precise and often unique causes, race and ethnic conflict lay behind all of the riots and reflected the inflamed racial climate of the war years.

The riots in 1943 were really just the most conspicuous manifestation of the mounting racial conflict throughout the war. On the one hand, African Americans found wartime expressions of democracy and changes in patterns of employment encouraging and anticipated further change. On the other hand, they were frustrated and embittered by white resistance, by the persistence of Jim Crow and the constant reports of discrimination against black civilian workers and military service personnel, and by the many cases of white violence during the war. In addition to the incidents involving black soldiers and southern police officers or bus drivers, there were a number of wartime lynchings: five in 1942, three in 1943, two in 1944. The black press regularly reported occurrences like the treatment of famous black tenor Roland Hayes, who was thrown out of a shoe shop in Rome, Georgia, in July 1942 for sitting in the whites-only area, then arrested and beaten by police.

Institutional racial violence also continued through the war. In 1940 Odell Waller, a twenty-five-year-old sharecropper in Virginia, shot and killed his landlord, Oscar Davis. Davis had refused Waller the fifty-two sacks of wheat that were his share of the crop, then apparently reached into his pocket for what Waller believed was a gun. Davis had also evicted the Waller family from their home. Convicted of first-degree murder, Waller was sentenced to death. Despite a campaign on his behalf and the intercession of Eleanor Roosevelt who persuaded President Roosevelt to appeal directly to the governor of Virginia for clemency, Waller was executed on July 2, 1942.

Not surprisingly, African Americans responded to events like these with anger and bitterness, but they also grew more determined to fight back. The FBI reported a widespread mood of rebelliousness among the black population, which it and other commentators tended to attribute to foreign-inspired agitators. The reaction of the press, including some black newspapers, to the riots was generally critical of both white participants, dismissed as extremists, and black participants, described as looters and vandals, criminals bent on wanton violence and destruction without reason or defense. Many respondents to a survey in Detroit after the riot put the conflict down to black belligerence. While one or two observers did point to the underlying social and economic causes, others blamed the influence of radical agitators who exploited these conditions for their own ends. Some writers, however, noted a new mood among the black population: as George Schuyler had written in the *Pittsburgh Courier* on May 27, 1942, the old days of "scared, timid, ignorant Negroes are gone forever." Commenting on the Hayes incident, poet Langston Hughes wrote,

> Negroes
> Sweet and docile,
> Meek, humble, and kind.
> Beware the day
> They change their minds![8]

A poll reported in the *Courier* on October 24, 1942, found that almost 90 percent of African Americans surveyed felt that they should not soft-pedal on demands for complete freedom and citizenship, and a government survey of black New Yorkers found that over 40 percent thought it more important to make democracy work at home than to defeat Germany and Japan. Throughout the war years there was widespread evidence of mounting day-to-day resistance by African Americans as those on military bases and in civilian centers responded to racial insults, attacks, and discrimination by protesting

and fighting back. Often this conflict erupted in public spaces such as buses and trolley cars or parks. These became contested places, called "theaters of resistance" by historian Robin Kelley, who noted in Birmingham, Alabama, that these conflicts increased throughout the war and involved not just black servicemen but also a considerable number of black women.[9] Young people, too, seemed radicalized by the war: the zoot suiters' extravagant style, for example, demonstrated an oppositional culture that flaunted their freedom and rejected the austerity of rationing as well as the discipline and conformity of military life. This phenomenon was not limited to Mexican American youth in California: in June, the Baltimore police took action against African American zoot suit gangs, and in Detroit and Philadelphia clashes erupted between black teenagers in zoot suits and white gangs.

The young Malcolm X, then Malcolm Little, was a zoot suit–wearing hipster in New York, drinking liquor, smoking marijuana, and dressed in extravagant outfits with long jackets, pants thirty inches wide at the knee and twelve at the ankle, colored knob-toed shoes, all topped off with a wide-brimmed hat. Like many young African Americans, he also enjoyed the jazz bands of the day and later recalled the abandon with which black crowds danced to Count Basie, Lionel Hampton, and Duke Ellington at the Roseland State Ballroom in Boston or the New York Savoy. Some jazz musicians, notably Charlie Parker, Thelonious Monk, and Dizzy Gillespie, expressed their blackness while rejecting the conformity and structured musical form of the swing bands for an exclusive, more improvised and discordant form of jazz or bop that white musicians had not adopted. But the youthful rebellion was not just one of style: Malcolm X recounted what his friend and he thought about the war: "Whitey owns everything. He wants us to go and bleed for him? Let *him* fight." When Malcolm received his draft papers, he reported to the draft board in his zoot suit, behaved outrageously to feign insanity, and told the psychiatrist he wanted to be sent down south "to organize them nigger soldiers, you dig? Steal us some guns, and kill up crackers!"[10] Malcolm was classed 4-F and never heard from the army again. As an eighteen-year-old participant in the Harlem riot said in a subsequent interview on his pending induction into the army, "I do not like it worth a dam [sic]. I'm not a spy or a saboteur, but I don't like goin' over there fightin' for the white man—so be it."[11]

Of course, such behavior could be dismissed as belonging simply to a criminal minority, but there was sufficient concern in government about the unrest among the African American population and its attitude to the war for some to suggest that the black press should be muzzled. As early as May 1942, Roosevelt and his cabinet had expressed alarm about what they

deemed the "subversive language" of the black newspapers, and there were some calls to suspend mailing rights for black publications and to indict their publishers for sedition. Although such demands were rejected, at a meeting with black editors in January 1943, Walter White did urge the newspapermen to tone down their rhetoric. Certainly after the violence of 1943, the black press did appear less radical in its demands, but that might also have stemmed from the growing employment opportunities, the widening of black military service, and the war situation itself. The influence of the press was still sufficient for President Roosevelt to meet with members of the Negro Newspaper Publishers Association himself in 1944. While the African American representatives were critical of any form of disunity that threatened victory, they insisted it was still their duty to fight for equal rights and that anything else would undermine the very democratic principles at stake in the war.

The federal government's response to black demands for further civil rights action was limited after 1941. Even in the aftermath of the riots, Roosevelt refused to speak out, although black leaders repeatedly asked that he address the subject of race violence in a radio broadcast or speech to the nation. Proposals for a federal investigation of race conflict or a committee on race relations were ignored. Instead a presidential aide, Jonathan Daniels, was given a watching brief on race matters. For Roosevelt, the priority was winning the war, and he did not want to jeopardize southern congressional support for necessary war measures or to divert attention from the military effort by tackling the issue of race. States and cities were largely left to respond to the conflicts at home, and by the summer of 1944, over two hundred local organizations or agencies had been established to deal with race. Although the formation of such bodies clearly acknowledged that there was an issue to address, they did little to tackle the root causes of the problem. They functioned mainly to inform, educate, and exhort. The federal government also concentrated its efforts on similar activities. The Office of War Information produced a major publication entitled *Negroes and the War* in the form of a large-size, seventy-page, illustrated pamphlet. Written by A. Philip Randolph's former colleague Chandler Owen, *Negroes and the War* stressed the progress made rather than all that remained unachieved. Like the film *The Negro Soldier*, the pamphlet contrasted Nazi ideology with American ideals and compared Hitler's statements with Roosevelt's to illustrate that defeat in the war would lead to a worsening of the African Americans' situation. *Negroes and the War* also stressed black participation in the war effort, as did the films *Henry Browne, Farmer* (1942), *Negro Colleges in Wartime* (1943), *The Negro Soldier* (1944), *The Negro Sailor* (1945), and *Teamwork* (1946).

A number of white voices were raised in favor of doing more to improve race relations during the war. The most significant belonged to Wendell Willkie, the 1940 Republican presidential candidate and a major figure during the war before his death in 1944. In speeches, articles, and a book entitled *One World*, Willkie argued that the pressures of war could and should bring about the end of discrimination in industry and the armed services. Others agreed with him: as early as November 15, 1941, the famous author Pearl S. Buck wrote a letter in the *New York Times* calling on the government to guarantee equal economic opportunities and ensure that African Americans would not suffer insults just because of their color. An April 3, 1942, *New York Times* editorial argued that the United States' racial problem had to be solved if the country was to avoid "the sinister hypocrisy of fighting abroad for what it is not willing to accept at home." The June 1942 issue of *Fortune* was simply entitled "The Negro's War," and another journal, *Survey Graphic*, devoted its November 1942 issue to addressing "Color: Unfinished Business of Democracy." Swedish sociologist Gunnar Myrdal picked up this theme in his detailed, two-volume study of race in the United States, *An American Dilemma* (1944), subtitled *The Negro Problem and Modern Democracy*. Commissioned by the Carnegie Foundation in 1938, Myrdal's work provided a detailed study of the economic, social, and political obstacles that prevented the realization of the American creed as espoused in the Declaration of Independence—equality, life, liberty, and the pursuit of happiness. In arguing that racism impoverished the United States as a whole, he suggested the "Negro problem" was in fact a white problem. His book was cited extensively in the Supreme Court's *Brown v. Topeka Board of Education* 1954 ruling that separate-but-equal education was unconstitutional. The Supreme Court was already beginning to topple some of the bars to racial equality during the war and in *Smith v. Allwright* in 1944 ruled that the all-white Democratic Party primary in Texas effectively denied African Americans the vote.

Already during the war it was clear that some young African Americans would not wait for Supreme Court decisions and wanted to see Americans practice what they preached immediately. In addition to individual acts of resistance, more organized, direct forms of action emerged, hinting at what would come twenty years later. In Washington, D.C., Howard University students led by a law student, writer, and civil rights activist, Pauli Murray, who had previously been arrested for failing to go to the back of a bus in Virginia in 1940 and was later involved in the Freedom Rides of the 1960s, staged a sit-in in a restaurant in 1943 and another in 1944. The war clearly influenced the protestors in their actions. Urging "We Die Together, Let's Eat Together," they asked whether returning soldiers would be able to walk

as free men in their native streets, and their flyers read, "Our boys, our bonds. Our brothers are fighting for you. Why can't we eat here?" Another asked, "Are you fo' 'Hitler's way' or the 'American way'?" Some whites reportedly joined the demonstration.[12]

In 1942 an interracial group of students met in Chicago to establish the Congress of Racial Equality (CORE). Among them were James Farmer and Bayard Rustin, members of a Quaker pacifist group, the Fellowship of Reconciliation, which adopted the nonviolent approaches of Mahatma Gandhi. Like their counterparts in Washington, D.C., when negotiation failed, they staged a number of sit-ins to challenge segregation at Jack Sprat's Café and other Chicago restaurants. Rustin and Farmer had already started to articulate the philosophy and method of nonviolent mass action and the need for struggle to achieve change, some of which was evident in the proposals of the March on Washington Movement and the CORE statement of purpose of 1942. These different groups pioneered the nonviolent direct-action methods that resurfaced twenty years later.

However, if the early signs of a new civil rights movement could be seen during the war years, so too could the indicators of white resistance. While strikes and riots reflected general white responses, southern politicians and editors were also making clear their determination to resist changes to the racial status quo. Although some southerners, such as the members of the Southern Regional Council formed in 1944, supported the end of the poll tax and white primary as well as moves toward integration in public transport, others did not—and the Regional Council was not prepared to criticize segregation until 1949. In 1944 the South Carolina House of Representatives issued a statement reaffirming the state's commitment to maintaining white supremacy, and other southern politicians like James Eastland and Theodore Bilbo, the senators from Mississippi, or Eugene Talmadge, governor of Georgia, echoed these sentiments. They supported Gov. Frank Dixon of Alabama, who spoke out against the activities of the FEPC and threatened to lead a breakaway Democratic Party in the South in opposition. Thus, rather than uniting the nation, clearly the war often heightened racial divisions at home. While the social and economic changes often brought benefits to the black population, the battle lines were being drawn between those demanding further progress and those determined to resist. It remained to be seen how these differences would be resolved in the postwar period and beyond.

CHAPTER FIVE

~

The Postwar Years
and Changing Civil Rights
"An American Dilemma"

> A change will come out of this war. If it doesn't, if the politicians and
> the people who run this country are not forced to make good the shib-
> boleth they glibly talk about freedom, liberty, human rights, then you
> young men who live through it will have wasted your precious time, and
> those who don't live through it will have died in vain.

> —William Faulkner, letter to Malcolm Franklin, July 4, 1943.[1]

The end of the World War II with Victory over Japan Day on August 15,
1945, brought a combination of relief and uncertainty for all Americans.
Many Americans, like the most famous southern author, William Faulkner,
looked to a new and better future—in his case, in race relations as well as
other areas of American life. Other people were not so positive in outlook.
Although the United States had emerged from the war as the most powerful
economic and military power and one relatively unscathed in comparison
to the other nations involved, the future was unclear. While the end of the
conflict meant the return home of husbands, fathers, and brothers, it also
raised questions about what would follow. Many people suffered from a "depression psychosis" and believed that with the end of the war and the closure
of war industries, the United States might return to the mass unemployment
of the 1930s. Some commentators anticipated unemployment reaching 10
million. Those groups that had made employment gains during the war,
such as women, some labor groups, and racial minorities, were particularly
anxious that they would once again be last hired and first fired in postwar

layoffs. Even the future of the surviving New Deal programs seemed unclear at the war's end.

In addition to having concerns about the domestic situation after 1945, many people were unclear about the United States' postwar position in international affairs and its likely consequences. While most wanted to demobilize the armed forces quickly and return to a national policy of limited foreign involvement and a focus on domestic concerns, clearly the global situation in 1945 had changed and would not allow this. Among the most significant consequences of the world war was the effective end of American isolationism. The power vacuums created by the defeat of Germany in Europe and Japan in Asia, as well as the military, economic, and political weakness of former great nations such as Britain and France, altered the balance of power and cast the United States in a totally different role. It would indeed be what Henry Luce, publisher of *Time* magazine, had called the "American Century." But American dominance was not guaranteed: the defeat of Hitler had brought the armies of the Communist Soviet Union into eastern and central Europe, and relations between the two new superpowers declined rapidly after 1945.

Adding to the domestic and international problems facing the United States, Franklin D. Roosevelt, the man who had led the country through depression and war to become the greatest president of the twentieth century and the longest serving president of all time, died on April 12, 1945. The responsibility of leadership in the transition from war to peace fell to Roosevelt's relatively unknown and untried vice president, Harry S. Truman. African Americans felt Roosevelt's loss particularly keenly and were concerned about his successor's credentials in race relations. Although Roosevelt had done little specifically for them, black Americans had benefited from several New Deal policies along with the concern for people at the bottom of the economic pile evident in Roosevelt's programs. Moreover, Executive Order 8802, the Fair Employment Practices Committee (FEPC), and the few changes in military racial policies made during the war had been the most significant measures to affect African Americans since the period of Reconstruction. For many African Americans as well as whites, Roosevelt had been a source of hope.

Political commentators in 1945 and since have not characterized Harry S. Truman as an inspirational figure. Often dismissed as a haberdasher from the border state of Missouri, Truman was a little-known senator when he became Roosevelt's running mate in 1944. He had been selected in preference to the incumbent vice president, Henry Wallace, as a more conservative choice, who would appeal to southerners. He had risen to some prominence early

in the war as chair of the Senate Committee to Investigate the National Defense Program, where he had made something of a reputation defending smaller businesses. Truman's record on civil rights did not stand out one way or the other. There was some suggestion that he had paid the membership fees of the Ku Klux Klan while a county judge in Kansas City in the 1920s, but that might merely have been a necessary part of the machine politics of the day. Though he did not speak out on race issues, he appeared to be a defender of equality of opportunity but also of segregation. As president, however, he soon had to confront the issue, and in doing so he gave the black population considerable reason to hope.

In addition to their general anxieties at the end of the war, African Americans had particular cause for concern. Many feared that wartime jobs would be lost, or that there would be little work for returning black servicemen, or, even worse, that World War II might be followed by racial violence like that of the Red Summer of 1919 after World War I. These were not irrational fears. A study of seven war centers during reconversion found that in all but one, African Americans suffered greater job losses than whites, and in a number of places the seniority of black workers was ignored in postwar layoffs. The movement of black former servicemen into peacetime employment lagged far behind that of white veterans, and most of the job placements available to them were for unskilled or service work.

Perhaps not surprisingly, African Americans made up 25 percent of reenlistments in the first year after the war, despite the discrimination that still existed in the military. However, many of the African Americans who had served with the expectation that they would be better off after the war realized their ambitions by virtue of the Selective Serviceman's Readjustment Act, better known as the GI Bill of Rights. The GI Bill provided a readjustment allowance of $20 per week, loans for home purchases, and grants to cover school, college, or university tuition. Many black veterans availed themselves of these opportunities. Surveys indicated that over 40 percent of black enlisted men hoped to return to school, and by 1947 twenty thousand had entered college. Only 20 percent of black soldiers planned to return to their previous jobs, and many indicated that they intended to move. In 1947 an estimated seventy-five thousand black veterans had reportedly left the South. African Americans who had served in the forces were not prepared to accept prewar patterns of race relations. As one soldier remarked, "I figure that if I can go int' Uncle Sam's army to try an' fight for America, I can come back and be treated as an American. Not as somebody that's throwed aside."[2]

Another factor that undoubtedly encouraged African Americans to leave the South was a rising tide of racial violence in the immediate postwar years

as some of the African Americans' worst fears seemed about to materialize. Between 1945 and 1947 at least twenty-five racial killings took place, the majority of them in the South. Many of the victims were black veterans, suggesting that some whites feared the effect that military service might have had on African Americans. A historian recently recorded the memories of black men who had returned home in uniform after the war and the resentment and fear they faced from whites—one was stopped in the street by a white man who admired his medals and then reminded him, "You're still a nigger."[3] On a number of occasions, black servicemen suffered at the hands of police officers—the National Association for the Advancement of Colored People (NAACP) recorded countless incidents of random racist violence, often involving police or state troopers. In one case an African American visiting Louisiana from San Francisco was arrested and held for three days simply for driving a fairly new car. Even worse, five black veterans died in separate incidents at the hands of the police in Birmingham, Alabama, in January and February 1946 alone. On February 24, 1946, in Columbia, Tennessee, an argument between a black navy veteran and a white former soldier led to an armed confrontation between police and the black community as a whole. The police were joined by the state's national guard, which over a two-day period arrested a hundred African Americans, two of whom were shot dead in jail. Twenty-seven African Americans were charged with attempting to murder police officers, and Thurgood Marshall and Walter White of the NAACP went to Tennessee to organize their defense. Eventually all but one were acquitted.

Worse atrocities followed. Maceo Snipes, a thirty-seven-year-old African American who served in the army in the Pacific during World War II, returned home to Taylor County, Georgia, in 1946 and became the first black person to vote in the county. However, on July 18, a day after casting his ballot, he was shot and died two days later. No one was arrested or charged for his murder. A week later, on July 25, 1946, twenty-eight-year-old army veteran George Dorsey, his wife Mae Murray Dorsey, and twenty-four-year-old Roger Malcolm and his twenty-year-old wife, Dorothy, were murdered in Monroe, Georgia, because they had behaved in an "uppity" manner. But whereas such events might have been ignored in the years after World War I, the climate of opinion had now changed. Appalled by reports of these events, President Truman sent FBI investigators to Georgia, but no convictions were secured. (The case was reopened in the 1990s and again in 2001, but no one has been convicted.) On August 8, 1946, in Louisiana, a mob attacked a black army veteran, John C. Jones, and his cousin, Albert Harris, after they were accused of rape. Jones died of his injuries, but Harris survived.

The Return of the Soldier, *1946. Charles White. LC-USZC4-4886 (8-19).*

The NAACP initiated an investigation and persuaded Harris to act as a witness. A federal grand jury indicted Deputy Sheriff Oscar Henry Haynes Jr., Minden chief of police Benjamin Geary Gantt, and several others for the murder, but they were acquitted.

Another case of race violence against a black veteran in the South attracted considerable national attention in 1946. Isaac Woodward (sometimes written "Woodard"), a twenty-seven-year-old black soldier who had served

fifteen months in the South Pacific, was honorably discharged from the army with the rank of sergeant in February. Travelling by bus from Georgia, still in uniform, he became involved in an altercation with the bus driver, who then called the police at a stop in Batesburg, South Carolina. The police beat Woodward with their clubs, damaging his eyes and leaving him permanently blind. Again the NAACP took up Woodward's case, and in July 1946 a national campaign involving actor and radio broadcaster Orson Welles and many others was launched to get justice for the army veteran. In August more than twenty-five thousand people heard Billie Holiday, Cab Calloway, Count Basie, and white folk singer Woody Guthrie, among others, appeal on Woodward's behalf at a benefit concert at the Lewisohn Stadium in New York City. Guthrie wrote a song, "The Blinding of Isaac Woodward," and recalled he received the loudest applause of his career when he performed it at the concert. In September Walter White met President Truman and brought the case to his attention. Independently of the NAACP, W. E. B. Du Bois and Paul Robeson launched the American Crusade to End Lynching and gathered three thousand delegates, including Albert Einstein, in Washington, D.C., on September 23. Shortly afterward, in another meeting with Truman, Robeson warned that the temper of black Americans had changed, and if the government did not act, they would. The president angrily ended the meeting. Despite this disagreement, the Woodward case shocked the president, who instructed the attorney general to launch an investigation. Eventually the sheriff was brought to trial, but as in previous instances, he was acquitted.

Several common points stand out in these different events. The mood of the majority of white southerners was clear—historian John Egerton has written of an "epidemic of random murder and mayhem" sweeping the region in an attempt to keep African Americans in their place and quell any demand for change from black veterans.[4] The violence clearly appalled many white Americans, including the president. Also striking, however, is the NAACP's role in trying to bring culprits to justice, which reflected a new mood among African Americans. After the war the NAACP adopted the slogan "Victory begins with you. Help win the peace . . . and full equality for minorities."[5] NAACP membership rose from fifty thousand in 1940 to four hundred thousand in 1946, across eleven hundred branches. The Detroit branch alone had twenty thousand members, but even in the South the organization grew in strength. In Louisiana, for example, thirty-three branches had a membership of 10,000 in 1946; by 1954 this had risen to 12,500 members in fifty branches.

African American veteran Isaac Woodard, who was beaten and blinded by police, applying for maximum disability benefits, seated with David Edwards; standing (l to r) Oliver W. Harrington, Edward Nottage, and Woodard's mother, Mrs. Isaac Woodard. LOC 2001695131.

Behind the increase in NAACP membership was a new sense of determination among African Americans after the war. "Our people are not coming back with the idea of just taking up where they left off. We are going to have the things that are rightfully due to us or else, which is a very large order, but we have proven beyond all things that we are people and not just the servants of the white man" wrote a soldier "somewhere on Okinawa" in a letter published by the *Pittsburgh Courier* on May 19, 1945. Black veterans in the South often demonstrated that they expected to be treated as equals and many, like Maceo Snipes, encouraged by the Supreme Court's decision in *Smith v. Allwright* outlawing the all-white Texas primary, took part in voter-registration drives in the immediate aftermath of the war. In February 1946 one hundred black veterans marched on the county courthouse in Birmingham, Alabama, to register to vote, but most were rejected on questions related to the Constitution and its interpretation. Several hundred veterans

also mobilized to vote in Atlanta, Georgia, and the number of black registered voters in Georgia increased from 20,000 in 1945 to 135,000 in 1946; in Texas the number rose from 30,000 to 100,000. Similar drives across the South raised the percentage of black registered voters from 3 to 12 percent by 1946 and to 25 percent (1.2 million) by 1952. Although this was a beginning, progress remained limited as evidenced in Louisiana, where the black vote increased by 6,532 to 7,561 in 1945—a mere 0.9 percent of the electorate; by 1948, despite continued intimidation and violence, this number had risen to 22,000, or 2.4 percent of the electorate.

Among the many veterans determined to effect change after the war was Medgar Evers, who had enlisted with his brother, Charlie, in 1943 and saw service in Europe. Discharged in 1946, Evers returned to Decatur, Mississippi, determined to exercise his rights as an American. He and Charlie managed to register but were barred from voting by a mob of two hundred whites. "All we wanted to be was ordinary citizens," he reportedly said. "We fought during the war for America and Mississippi was included. Now after the Germans and the Japanese hadn't killed us, it looked as though the white Mississippians would."[6] Denied the right to vote, the brothers joined the NAACP, and Medgar Evers became a prominent civil rights activist. In 1963 he was assassinated by Byron de la Beckwith, a white racist—and ironically, also a World War II veteran. Other black veterans who became prominent in the later civil rights campaigns in Mississippi were Amzie Moore and Aaron Henry.

Many white Americans also came back from the war with a different racial outlook or recognized that the Jim Crow system of race relations in the United States was no longer acceptable. A white lieutenant and war hero pointedly told Mississippi senators Theodore Bilbo and James Eastland at a 1945 reception in his honor that he and other white soldiers had changed their ideas about black people a lot during the war, and he recalled that "the colored boys fight just as good as the white boys."[7] The South's leading white author, William Faulkner, together with friends in Oxford, Mississippi, insisted in 1947 that the names of black soldiers be included on a new war memorial with those of local whites who died. They were, but separately, at the bottom of the list. Even former governor of Alabama Frank Dixon acknowledged that the Nazis had undermined the theory of a master race, and Texan politician and future president Lyndon Baines Johnson also recognized the significance of African Americans' military service. He told an aide in his inimitable fashion, "The Negro fought in the war, and now that he's back here with his family he's not gonna keep taking the shit we're dishing out. We're in a race against time. If we don't act, we're gonna have blood

in the streets."[8] In 1957 as Senate leader, Johnson helped to push through the first civil rights act, and as president he signed even more significant legislation into law.

While President Johnson is remembered for the 1964 Civil Rights Act and 1965 Voting Rights Act, which in many ways marked the culmination of the struggle that emerged after 1945, President Truman's contribution to improving race relations is often forgotten. In 1945 he confirmed that the FEPC would continue through the period of reconversion and called for a permanent committee—but a southern filibuster in Congress in 1946 quashed attempts to establish such a body. Truman also appointed William Hastie to the governorship of the Virgin Islands. More significantly, genuinely shocked by reports of race violence in the South, on December 5, 1946, the president established a committee to study, report, and recommend measures for protecting civil rights. Before the committee reported, Truman became the first president ever to address the NAACP when he spoke to a crowd of ten thousand from the steps of the Lincoln Memorial in Washington on June 29, 1947. In a speech broadcast on national radio, Truman called

President Harry S. Truman addresses the closing session of the thirty-eighth annual conference of the NAACP. Missouri Digital Heritage Collection. MDIHTZ73-2563.

for the removal of the last barriers standing between millions of Americans and their birthright, and insisting the country could not wait for the slowest states to act, he said the federal government must show the way. This was a clear break with the past and a challenge to the defenders of states' rights.

In October 1947 the President's Committee on Civil Rights delivered its report, *To Secure These Rights*, a comprehensive document that, like Gunnar Myrdal's *An American Dilemma*, examined all aspects of life and listed four essential rights due to every American: the right to safety and security of person; the right to citizenship, its responsibilities, and its privileges, including military service and the franchise; the right to freedom of conscience and expression; and the right to equality of opportunity. The report condemned segregation and discrimination in all aspects of American life and recommended measures to ensure fair employment and education, guarantee voting rights, end restrictive housing covenants, and take action against lynching. The committee particularly singled out military service for comment and called for an end to segregation and discrimination in the armed forces. President Truman took immediate action and had the Justice Department support the successful challenge to restrictive housing covenants in the Supreme Court's decision in *Shelley v. Kraemer*. On February 2, 1948, the president included many of the committee's recommendations in a special civil rights message to Congress. Calling discrimination "utterly contrary to our ideals," President Truman linked the need for civil rights reform with his foreign policy and the United States' position in the world when he said, "If we wish to inspire the peoples of the world whose freedom is in jeopardy, if we wish to restore hope to those who have already lost their civil liberties, if we wish to fulfill the promise that is ours, we must correct the remaining imperfections in our practice of democracy."[9]

The international situation was clearly a factor in encouraging action on American race relations. By 1948 the Cold War between the United States and the Soviet Union was already under way, and the president had announced the Truman Doctrine committing the United States to resisting and containing communism on a global front in 1947. The African American leadership, keenly aware of the United States' new world role after the war, was already working to place U.S. race relations on the international agenda. The creation of the United Nations in 1945 and the Universal Declaration of Human Rights in 1948 seemed to a number of black leaders and organizations to offer an opportunity to challenge the United States' segregationist policies on the international stage, and many hoped that the United Nations would act to protect minority rights. Walter White and other members of the NAACP recognized this possibility and appointed W. E. B.

Du Bois as director of special research to coordinate activities. However, the Communist-led National Negro Congress (NNC) had already decided to present a petition to the UN Commission on Human Rights protesting the oppression of African Americans and did so in 1946. The United Nations responded by requesting proof of human rights abuses in the United States and pointed out that such appeals could only come from governmental organizations. When the NNC collapsed shortly afterward, the NAACP took up the challenge, and Du Bois prepared *An Appeal to the World* in 1947, outlining the situation of African Americans and calling upon the United Nations for redress of grievances. It was hoped that the U.S. delegation would be able to present this petition, but the appeal was also supported by Belgium, China (Formosa), Egypt, Ethiopia, Haiti, India, Norway, Pakistan, and the Soviet Union, which introduced the document in October 1947. American officials blocked the Soviet representatives' request that the appeal be placed on the UN agenda, and opposition from the State Department and from Eleanor Roosevelt (who threatened to resign from the NAACP's board if the organization persisted in the appeal) meant that this action came to nothing. Furthermore, the linking of such a protest with communism indicated the growing restraint being placed on civil rights protest in the postwar years.

The NAACP's failure to persist in the appeal to the United Nations or to be too critical of the Truman administration caused a rift between White and Du Bois, who increasingly supported Truman's Progressive Party opponent in the 1948 election, Henry Wallace. However, the international arena remained important for African Americans' campaign for civil rights. In 1949, for example, Du Bois, now no longer with the NAACP, filed a petition with the United Nations on behalf of Rosa Lee Ingrams, a black woman who had killed her white attacker, and she and her two teenage sons had been charged with murder. Despite the clear case of self-defense, the Ingramses had received the death penalty, which was reduced to life imprisonment. Although the United Nations could not take any action, Du Bois's actions won publicity, and the family was eventually released from prison in the 1950s.

In 1951, a delegation headed by the singer Paul Robeson and the black Communist leader William L. Patterson presented a second petition, *We Charge Genocide: The Crime of Government against the Negro People*, to the United Nations on behalf of the Civil Rights Congress (CRC). The CRC was a largely Communist-based group formed in Detroit in 1946 as an amalgamation of the International Labor Defense, the National Federation for Constitutional Liberties, and the National Negro Congress, mainly to provide legal defense for African Americans charged with capital crimes. The petition outlined the history of lynching in the United States, but little came

of it. The NAACP and other groups denied that racial violence was deliberate American policy, and the inclusion of a domestic jurisdiction clause in the UN charter ensured that the organization could not investigate human rights abuses in the United States.

There is considerable debate among historians about the impact of the Cold War on the campaign for civil rights, particularly its effect on the NAACP. Some writers have suggested that, fearful of criticism from McCarthyite and conservative groups, the organization abandoned any association with left-wing groups and individuals but in doing so missed an opportunity for reform. On the other hand, recent studies of the NAACP question this view and suggest that the organization struggled to keep civil rights on the political agenda through a difficult time. It is also worth bearing in mind that people like A. Philip Randolph and others had tried to disassociate themselves and the groups they represented from Communist elements well before 1945. The NAACP leadership, for example, pointed to the conflicts that had arisen between left-wing groups and themselves during the Scottsboro trials in the 1930s, and many African Americans could recall the way the Communist Party of America had followed the Moscow line and chopped and changed its positions on civil rights in the lead-up to war. The NAACP, like many other organizations, such as the Congress of Industrial Organizations and indeed the Democratic Party itself, increasingly associated itself with the political center in support of President Truman's Cold War policies. Besides, black organizations had every reason to support a president who, against all odds, had taken a remarkable stand on civil rights.

In the run-up to the 1948 presidential election, Harry Truman took a decision that seemed at the time the equivalent of political suicide. Apparently taking the advice of his special counsel, Clark Clifford, Truman deliberately set out to win the black vote by further supporting civil rights measures. Following up his civil rights message, the president supported the inclusion of a mild civil rights plank at the Democratic Party convention in June. When that was replaced by an even stronger measure, several southern delegates stormed out of the proceedings and established the States Rights Party, or Dixiecrats, with Strom Thurmond of South Carolina as their candidate. The liberal wing of the party having already bolted in favor of Wallace's Progressives, it appeared that Truman could not win. However, in July 1948 the president issued two executive orders on civil rights, 9980 ordering an end to discrimination in the federal government and establishing the Fair Employment Board within the Civil Service Commission, and 9981 to bring equality of treatment and opportunity into the armed forces.

While the Fair Employment Board fell short of the permanent FEPC that black campaigners had hoped for, it still held some significance. Executive Order 9981, on the other hand, was regarded as a major victory and the culmination of years of effort before, during, and after the war. The issue of segregation had been under review in all branches of the military when the war ended, but the proposal to introduce a peacetime draft with the Universal Military Training Bill in 1948 reopened the issue for African Americans. A. Philip Randolph and a former army captain, Grant Reynolds, had established the Committee against Jim Crow in Military Service and Training, and they spearheaded a nationwide campaign against segregation in the forces by calling for a program of civil disobedience. In an angry meeting with Truman in March 1948, Randolph warned the president that African Americans would refuse to serve unless segregation was ended. He reiterated this statement before the Senate Armed Services Committee later that month and suggested the possibility of a mass civil disobedience campaign like that led by Mahatma Gandhi in India. Randolph indicated that, if necessary, he was personally prepared to go to jail for encouraging resistance to the draft. NAACP surveys indicated that Randolph had a considerable amount of support among the black population.

How much Randolph's campaign influenced President Truman is hard to say, given other factors such as wartime experiences, the problems associated with stationing segregated troops overseas, supposedly as defenders of democracy, and increased political pressures after the Republican Party promised integration of the military as a campaign commitment. Nonetheless, when the executive order was issued, Randolph ended the campaign and disbanded his new organization. He may have acted prematurely as, despite the *Chicago Defender*'s headline announcing that the president had wiped out segregation, the executive order did not actually *end* the policy but only began the process. Rather like Roosevelt's Executive Order 8802 before it, the new order promised rather more than it delivered. While the order declared equality of treatment and opportunity in the armed services regardless of race or color to be federal policy, it was to be implemented as "rapidly as possible, having due regard to the time required to effectuate any necessary changes *without impairing efficiency or morale*" (my italics). Integration was implied rather than explicitly mentioned. A committee was established to see how the new policy might best be introduced. Again, it was the pressure of war with the outbreak of conflict in Korea in 1950 that speeded up the whole process, but integration still was not totally achieved until well into the mid-1950s.

Whatever the limitations of the executive order, Truman confirmed the worst fears of the Dixiecrats and fulfilled the highest expectations of many

African Americans. He was the first president to campaign actively in the black community when he addressed black audiences in Harlem during the 1948 campaign. Together with his public statements and presidential action, he did enough to win the majority of black votes, and that contributed significantly to his upset election victory that year. However, once elected Truman seemed unable or unwilling to deliver on the other elements of his civil rights program. Faced with growing opposition from Republicans and conservative Democrats in Congress, Truman, like Roosevelt before him, refused to jeopardize key elements of his other policies, particularly in foreign affairs, by pushing civil rights issues further. Roy Wilkins and other black leaders tried to organize support for a permanent FEPC and other measures through the National Emergency Civil Rights Committee, and in January 1950 they mobilized more than four thousand representatives in Washington, D.C., but to no avail. The onset of the Korean War and the domination in domestic politics of Senator Joseph McCarthy from 1950 on pushed hopes of reform onto the back burner.

Although Truman's actual achievements in civil rights were perhaps more symbolic than real, they were clearly not insignificant. In addition to the president's own actions, the Supreme Court issued a number of significant decisions in the 1940s and 1950s, undermining the practice of racial segregation and exclusion. As well as deciding against white primaries in *Smith v. Allwright* in 1944, the Court ruled against segregation in interstate transport in *Morgan v. Commonwealth of Virginia* in 1946 and against restrictive housing covenants in *Shelley v. Kraemer* in 1948. In *Sipuel v. Oklahoma Board of Regents* (1948), *McLaurin v. Oklahoma State Regents* (1950), and *Sweatt v. Painter* (1950), it issued a number of rulings challenging segregation in education that paved the way for the landmark decision in 1954's *Brown v. Topeka Board of Education*.

As important as these measures were, other factors encouraged black optimism. While signs indicated that the immediate postwar layoffs affected African Americans disproportionately, employment levels rose again as the United States moved toward its status as the "Affluent Society" in the 1950s, and although still concentrated at the bottom of the economic pile, most African Americans were better off than they had been in the 1930s. Many benefited from increases in minimum wage levels in 1949 and again in 1950, as well as from laws prohibiting discrimination in employment passed in eleven states and twenty-eight cities by 1951. As the economies in northern and western states once again boomed, the flight from the South continued, accelerated no doubt by the mechanization of the cotton industry, which displaced labor. Although this migration added to already swollen urban

ghettos, African American families accounted for more than a quarter of those housed by new federal housing initiatives after 1949.

While legislative reform, presidential action, and Supreme Court decisions all offered encouragement to African Americans, there were wider signs of a changing racial climate in the postwar United States. In 1945, when white high school students boycotted their school in Gary, Indiana, due to the admission of black pupils, famous singer Frank Sinatra gave a concert in the school auditorium that helped to end the protest. He performed "The House I Live In," a song written in 1943 that celebrated the United States as a nation of all races and religions, where one's neighbors are both white and black. A short film in which Sinatra appealed for racial and religious tolerance was also released that year. The event with greatest social impact, however, was the breaking of racial barriers in baseball with Jackie Robinson's carefully managed inclusion in the Brooklyn Dodgers by the club president Branch Rickey in 1947. Army veteran Robinson was chosen because of his undoubted sporting ability, but also because of his temperament and character. He was followed by Leroy "Satchel" Paige and Lary Doby, who joined the Cleveland Indians in 1948, and other players who joined the Dodgers shortly after Robinson. The complete integration of sport still had some way to go, but there is little doubt that, in the *Pittsburgh Courier*'s words celebrating Robinson's appointment on April 19, 1947, "there have been a whole lot of changes in the thinking of Americans on the question of color, creed and national origin in the past decade."

Having said all this, considerable evidence remained that the United States had a very long way to go before black citizens were accepted as equals. The *Chicago Defender*'s triumphant front page celebrating Executive Order 9981 on July 31, 1948, also carried an account of a would-be lynch mob searching woods for their "prey" in a southern town. In Chicago itself, attacks on black homes in the late 1940s revealed a continued and deep-seated resentment among whites, with almost five hundred racial incidents recorded between 1945 and 1950, most involving housing. Race riots also occurred in a number of military bases between 1946 and 1948, both in the United States and overseas.

If evidence was needed of how much was still required in race relations, the story of Harry T. Moore and the Groveland Four provided it. Moore was a long-term civil rights activist and school teacher in Florida, where he had made a name for himself as an NAACP organizer who campaigned for equal salaries for school teachers and against lynching. In 1945 he organized the Progressive Voters League in Florida and led a voter-registration drive that brought about an immediate increase of five thousand black registered

voters. As a result he and his wife were sacked from their teaching jobs. Moore became a full-time NAACP organizer. In 1949 he became involved in the case of four young African Americans accused of raping a seventeen-year-old married white woman in Groveland; two of the men, Walter Irvin and Sam Shepherd, had recently returned from serving in the army. The third accused was a sixteen-year-old visitor to the area, Charles Greenlee. The fourth man, Ernest Thomas, was shot and killed before he could be arrested. Despite strong evidence of their innocence, the three surviving African Americans were quickly found guilty by an all-white jury; Shepherd and Irvin were sentenced to death and Greenlee to life imprisonment. The NAACP took up the case and, with the help of sympathetic newspaper reporting, secured a retrial. The convictions were confirmed but overturned a year later by the Supreme Court, and a new trial was scheduled for 1951. On the way to the court, Sheriff Willis McCall claimed that Shepherd and Irvin attempted to escape. He shot and killed Shepherd and wounded Irvin. In the retrial Irvin was found guilty and again sentenced to death. The NAACP managed to secure a stay of execution from the Supreme Court, and eventually Irvin's sentence was commuted to life. He was released from prison in 1968, Greenlee having been released in 1962. Harry Moore in the meantime launched a campaign to bring Sheriff McCall to trial, but in 1951 he and his wife were both killed when a bomb blew up their home. Members of the Ku Klux Klan were reportedly responsible, but no convictions were secured. Sheriff McCall remained in office until he was dismissed in 1973 after a black prisoner was kicked to death in his custody.

If the events in Florida seem exceptional, they perhaps suggest that little had changed between the case of the Scottsboro Boys in the 1930s and that of the Groveland Four. However, the war years had effected a shift in attitude among many white Americans; brought about decisive change in the role of the president, federal government, and courts in race relations; accomplished an almost complete reversal in military race policies; and resulted in enormous economic and demographic change in the African American population. More than this, the war and Cold War years placed the United States' racial practices firmly in the international spotlight and forced the country to confront the issues posed in Myrdal's *An American Dilemma*. African American leaders and organizations emerged from the war determined to secure rewards for their service and share the fruits of victory. However, sections of the population, particularly in South, clearly did not accept these challenges and remained intransigent in their racial ideology. The 1954 Supreme Court decision that rejected the separate-but-equal doctrine underpinning the entire Jim Crow system revealed the full extent of their opposition—as well

as the determination of African Americans to achieve their postwar dreams. Precedents for future action were there in the March on Washington Movement, the wartime protests, and the early sit-ins. In 1947 the Congress of Racial Equality mounted its first "Freedom Ride" to test Supreme Court decisions on segregation in interstate transport in Virginia, North Carolina, and Kentucky. Although it attracted little attention and had less success, it was a harbinger of things to come. Building on the experience and philosophies of men like A. Philip Randolph, Walter White, Medgar Evers, and Harry T. Moore, and increasingly supported by the federal government and large sections of the white community, a new generation of black (and white) civil rights activists emerged to take up the struggle to ensure the achievement of the hopes William Faulkner had written of.

Conclusion

The African American experience in World War II clearly had enormous significance in shaping developments in the coming decades. However, a considerable amount of debate persists among historians about just how crucial these years were. While some write of turning points and watersheds, others see continuity or even put forward either the 1930s or 1940s as more significant. To some extent, of course, this debate is simply academic. We can say without doubt that the war had an enormous impact on all Americans, black and white, and that race shaped the African American experience. Neither a beginning nor an end in civil rights history, the war took further issues raised in the 1930s and beyond and paved the way for future developments. The war years brought massive economic, demographic, and ideological shifts in the makeup of the American population. The removal of millions of men and women into the armed forces and their service overseas in itself generated considerable upheaval. The war boom accelerated the movement of populations into the defense industries, precipitating huge growth in urban centers, new and old, and intensifying problems in the workplace, housing, and public recreation.

For African Americans all of these things carried an additional dimension: military service raised questions that had been posed throughout American history concerning segregation, limits to service, and their significance in relation to black claims for citizenship and equal rights. The expansion of war industries and the booming economy raised issues of equal economic opportunity and the role and place of minorities in a time of war. The wartime migrations posed again the subject of equal access to housing, transportation, and social facilities. The war itself focused attention on issues of race

prejudice, discrimination, and exclusion. African American leaders, organizations, and institutions, mindful of the disappointments of World War I, seized upon these issues to strengthen their demands for reform. From the March on Washington Movement through the "Double V" campaign and beyond, African Americans linked fighting and winning the war with their call for fair and equal treatment for the black community. New organizations began to develop the techniques and philosophy of nonviolent mass protest that laid the foundations for later protests. Black service personnel returning from Alaska and the Aleutians, from Europe and Asia, arrived back on American soil expectant and determined to see change, as were the men and women who had contributed to the war effort at home. While many whites supported them, others did not. The tensions over these matters often exploded in violence among both the civilian and military populations, forcing the American people to address in one way or another the "American dilemma" of how to reconcile the American creed of democracy and equality with racial intolerance. Though not new to be sure, these questions had never been posed so sharply and intensely over such an extended period or on such a scale. And still unanswered, these questions increasingly dominated the postwar years, as African Americans became more and more determined to see them addressed. If the war did not bring total, overwhelming, and complete change, it brought enough to establish the preconditions for another generation to demand that the United States indeed practice the very principles it espoused at home and continued to defend abroad. The achievement of so much in terms of presidential action and changing federal policy during and immediately after the war seemed to indicate a new commitment to racial equality. The election of an African American as president and commander in chief some sixty years later in 2008 might suggest that this mission has finally been accomplished, but even that apparent watershed event should be seen as part of an ongoing process rather than an end in itself.

~

Documents

W. E. B. Du Bois, "Close Ranks" (May 1918)

Here the African American leader and editor of the NAACP journal, The Crisis, articulates the Wilson administration's view of World War I and seems to suggest that demands for equality should be put on hold in the hope that black service will be recognized. Although some black newspapers, such as the Chicago Defender, *had expressed similar views, a number of black editors openly rejected this position and described Du Bois as a traitor. Their anger was all the greater when it was discovered that Du Bois had been offered (but in the end did not accept) a commission in the Army Military Intelligence Bureau as advisor on racial affairs.*

This is the crisis of the world. For all the long years to come men will point to the year 1918 as the great Day of Decision, the day when the world decided whether it would submit to military despotism and an endless armed peace—if peace it could be called—or whether they would put down the menace of German militarism and inaugurate the United States of the World. We of the colored race have no ordinary interest in the outcome. That which the German power represents today spells death to the aspirations of Negroes and all darker races for equality, freedom and democracy. Let us not hesitate. Let us, while this war lasts, forget our special grievances and close our ranks shoulder to shoulder with our white fellow citizens and the allied nations fighting for democracy. We make no ordinary sacrifice, but we make it gladly and willingly, with our eyes lifted towards the hills.
Source: The Crisis 16 (May 1918): 111.

~

W. E. B. Du Bois, "Returning Soldiers" (May 1919)

Disillusioned by the treatment of African American soldiers while on service in France, and even more so by their treatment at home after the war, Du Bois reveals a complete change of attitude in this editorial and, like many others, expresses the view of an emerging "New Negro."

We are returning from war! *The Crisis* and tens of thousands of black men were drafted into a great struggle. For bleeding France and what she means and has meant and will mean to us and humanity and against the threat of German race arrogance, we fought gladly and to the last drop of blood; for America and her highest ideals, we fought in far-off hope; for the dominant southern oligarchy entrenched in Washington, we fought in bitter resignation. For the America that represents and gloats in lynching, disfranchisement, caste, brutality and devilish insult—for this, in the hateful upturning and mixing of things, we were forced by vindictive fate to fight also.

But today we return! We return from the slavery of uniform which the world's madness demanded us to don to the freedom of civil garb. We stand again to look America squarely in the face and call a spade a spade. We sing: This country of ours, despite all its better souls have done and dreamed, is yet a shameful land.

It *lynches.*

And lynching is barbarism of a degree of contemptible nastiness unparalleled in human history. Yet for fifty years we have lynched two Negroes a week, and we have kept this up right through the war.

It *disfranchises* its own citizens.

Disfranchisement is the deliberate theft and robbery of the only protection of poor against rich and black against white. The land that disfranchises its citizens and calls itself a democracy lies and knows it lies.

It encourages *ignorance.*

It has never really tried to educate the Negro. A dominant minority does not want Negroes educated. It wants servants, dogs, whores and monkeys. And when this land allows a reactionary group by its stolen political power to force as many black folk into these categories as it possibly can, it cries in contemptible hypocrisy: "They threaten us with degeneracy; they cannot be educated."

It *steals* from us.

It organizes industry to cheat us. It cheats us out of our land; it cheats us out of our labour. It confiscates our savings. It reduces our wages. It raises our rent. It steals our profit. It taxes us without representation. It keeps us consistently and universally poor, and then feeds us on charity and derides our poverty.

It *insults* us.

It has organized a nation-wide and latterly a world-wide propaganda of deliberate and continuous insult and defamation of black blood wherever found. It decrees that it shall not be possible in travel nor residence, work nor play, education nor instruction for a black man to exist without tacit or open acknowledgment of his inferiority to the dirtiest white dog. And it looks upon any attempt to question or even discuss this dogma as arrogance, unwarranted assumption and treason.

This is the country to which we Soldiers of Democracy return. This is the fatherland for which we fought! But it is our fatherland. It was right for us to fight. The faults of our country are our faults. Under similar circumstances, we would fight again. But by the God of Heaven, we are cowards and jack-asses if now that that war is over, we do not marshal every ounce of our brain and brawn to fight a sterner, longer, more unbending battle against the forces of hell in our own land.

We *return*.

We *return from fighting*.

We *return fighting*.

Make way for Democracy! We saved it in France, and by the Great Jehovah, we will save it in the United States of America, or know the reason why.

Source: The Crisis 18 (May 1919): 13–14.

~

A Black Woman Writes to Radio Broadcaster Eric Seberite [Sevareid] Concerning "Jobs for Defense" (April 1, 1941)

Even before the United States entered the war, African Americans were asking questions about discrimination in the defense industries. Last hired and first fired, qualified black workers were being passed over in favor of whites. Here a young woman writes to a radio broadcaster outlining her husband's experiences and feelings and offers some acute observations on the significance of this, given the United States' professed beliefs in the lead-up to war. A subsequent radio program, "Here's Your Answer: The Negro in War Production," in August 1942 emphasized the need to utilize all manpower in total war.

I have for the past two Saturdays listened to your interviews on labor problems.

Now I am a young colored woman. My husband is 32 years of age and is a graduate of West Virginia State College (1933) majoring in Mechanical

Arts, but unfortunately never had a chance to execute his ability in his cho-sen field [sic] profession due to the fact that he hasn't found an opening in that field, and never had a chance to earn enough money to buy tools and go in business for himself.

I told my husband about the discussion I heard on the radio and asked him to register, and here was his answer: "What good would it do me to register. They don't hire colored people in factories for National Defense. I know quite a few who has tried but failed because of their color."

Now this doesn't seem to me to be the Democratic way unless you can find a different meaning for the word "Democracy." After all they are human, live and breathe like any body else, and above all this is the only country we know, whereas the Germans, Italians, and Russians in fact any other nationality can come into this country and whether they are citizens or non-citizens get top jobs any place they wish, and do undercover work against the Government, and the negro [sic] never thought of such things, yet they can't get a decent job.

I am wondering if you can possibly get a discussion on this particular prob-lem so the negro will know where he stands in this drive in National Defense for the safety of Democracy.

Source: Letter to Eric Seberite, April 1, 1941, in Papers on Fair Employment Practices Committee, File 1B4i, War Manpower Commission National Ar-chives Record Group 211.

⁓

A. Philip Randolph Calls for a March on Washington (1941)

Concerned about the widespread discrimination in the defense industries and in the armed forces, A. Philip Randolph, the head of the Brotherhood of Sleeping Car Porters and a leading civil rights spokesman, proposed a mass protest march on Washington by African Americans. As the government failed to act, other black organizations took up Randolph's call, and together they formed the March on Washington Movement, scheduling a march for July 1, 1941.

A Call to the March
July 1, 1941

We call upon you to fight for jobs in National Defense.

We call upon you to struggle for the integration of Negroes in the armed forces, such as the Air Corps, Navy, Army and Marine Corps of the Na-tion.

We call upon you to demonstrate for the abolition of JimCrowism in all Government departments and defense employment.

This is an hour of crisis. It is a crisis of democracy. It is a crisis of minority groups. It is a crisis of Negro Americans.

What is this crisis?

To American Negroes, it is the denial of jobs in Government defense projects. It is racial discrimination in Government departments. It is Widespread Jim-Crowism in the armed forces of the Nation.

While billions of the taxpayers' money are being spent for war weapons, Negro workers are being turned away from the gates of factories, mines and mills—being flatly told, "NOTHING DOING." Some employers refuse to give Negroes jobs when they are without "union cards," and some unions refuse Negro workers union cards when they are "without jobs."

What shall we do?

What a dilemma!

What a runaround!

What a disgrace!

What a blow below the belt!

"Though dark, doubtful and discouraging, all is not lost, all is not hopeless." Though battered and bruised, we are not beaten, broken or bewildered.

Verily, the Negroes' deepest disappointments and direst defeats, their tragic trials and outrageous oppressions in these dreadful days of destruction and disaster to democracy and freedom, and the rights of minority peoples, and the dignity and independence of the human spirit, is the Negroes' greatest opportunity to rise to the highest heights of struggle for freedom and justice in Government, in industry, in labor unions, education, social service, religion and culture.

With faith and confidence of the Negro people in their own power for self-liberation, Negroes can break down the barriers of discrimination against employment in National Defense. Negroes can kill the deadly serpent of race hatred in the Army, Navy, Air and Marine Corps, and smash through and blast the Government, business and labor-union red tape to win the right to equal opportunity in vocational training and retraining in defense employment.

Most important and vital to all, Negroes, by the mobilization and coordination of their mass power, can cause PRESIDENT ROOSEVELT TO ISSUE AN EXECUTIVE ORDER ABOLISHING DISCRIMINATIONS IN ALL GOVERNMENT DEPARTMENTS, ARMY, NAVY, AIR CORPS AND NATIONAL DEFENSE JOBS.

Of course, the task is not easy. In very truth, it is big, tremendous and difficult.

It will cost money.

It will require sacrifice.

It will tax the Negroes' courage, determination and will to struggle. But we can, must and will triumph.

The Negroes' stake in national defense is big. It consists of jobs, thousands of jobs. It may represent millions, yes, hundreds of millions of dollars in wages. It consists of new industrial opportunities and hope. This is worth fighting for.

But to win our stakes, it will require an "all-out," bold and total effort and demonstration of colossal proportions.

Negroes can build a mammoth machine of mass action with a terrific and tremendous driving and striking power that can shatter and crush the evil fortress of race prejudice and hate, if they will only resolve to do so and never stop, until victory comes.

Dear fellow Negro Americans, be not dismayed in these terrible times. You possess power, great power. Our problem is to harness and hitch it up for action on the broadest, daring and most gigantic scale.

In this period of power politics, nothing counts but pressure, more pressure, and still more pressure, through the tactic and strategy of broad, organized, aggressive mass action behind the vital and important issues of the Negro. To this end, we propose that ten thousand Negroes MARCH ON WASHINGTON FOR JOBS IN NATIONAL DEFENSE AND EQUAL INTEGRATION IN THE FIGHTING FORCES OF THE UNITED STATES.

An "all-out" thundering march on Washington, ending in a monster and huge demonstration at Lincoln's Monument will shake up white America.

It will shake up official Washington.

It will give encouragement to our white friends to fight all the harder by our side, with us, for our righteous cause.

It will gain respect for the Negro people.

It will create a new sense of self-respect among Negroes. But what of national unity?

We believe in national unity which recognizes equal opportunity of black and white citizens to jobs in national defense and the armed forces, and in all other institutions and endeavors in America. We condemn all dictatorships, Fascist, Nazi and Communist. We are loyal, patriotic Americans, all.

But, if American democracy will not defend its defenders; if American democracy will not protect its protectors; if American democracy will not give jobs to its toilers because of race or color; if American democracy will not insure equality of opportunity, freedom and justice to its citizens, black

and white, it is a hollow mockery and belies the principles for which it is supposed to stand.

To the hard, difficult and trying problem of securing equal participation in national defense, we summon all Negro Americans to march on Washington. We summon Negro Americans to form committees in various cities to recruit and register marchers and raise funds through the sale of buttons and other legitimate means for the expenses of marchers to Washington by buses, train, private automobiles, trucks, and on foot.

We summon Negro Americans to stage marches on their City Halls and Councils in their respective cities and urge them to memorialize the President to issue an executive order to abolish discrimination in the Government and national defense.

However, we sternly counsel against violence and ill-considered and intemperate action and the abuse of power. Mass power, like physical power, when misdirected is more harmful than helpful.

We summon you to mass action that is orderly and lawful, but aggressive and militant, for justice, equality and freedom.

Crispus Attucks marched and died as a martyr for American independence. Nat Turner, Denmark Vesey, Gabriel Prosser, Harriet Tubman and Frederick Douglass fought, bled and died for the emancipation of Negro slaves and the preservation of American democracy.

Abraham Lincoln, in times of the grave emergency of the Civil War, issued the Proclamation of Emancipation for the freedom of Negro slaves and the preservation of American democracy.

Today, we call upon President Roosevelt, a great humanitarian and idealist, to follow in the footsteps of his noble and illustrious predecessor and take the second decisive step in this world and national emergency and free American Negro citizens of the stigma, humiliation and insult of discrimination and JimCrowism in Government departments and national defense.

The Federal Government cannot with clear conscience call upon private industry and labor unions to abolish discrimination based upon race and color as long as it practices discrimination itself against Negro Americans.

Source: Black Worker 14 (May 1941): 4.

⌒

President Franklin Roosevelt Issues Executive Order 8802 Outlawing Discrimination in the Defense Industry (1941)

Following a meeting in the White House with A. Philip Randolph and Walter White on June 19, 1941, at which they made clear their determination to lead a

march on Washington in protest against discrimination in the defense industries,
President Franklin Roosevelt acceded to their demand for an executive order. Using
his power as commander in chief in time of war, the president declared the official
U.S. policy to be against discrimination in defense production and established a
Fair Employment Practices Committee to see the policy implemented. Some black
newspapers greeted the order as a "second emancipation proclamation," and while
that might be an exaggeration, it was indeed significant as the first presidential act
on civil rights since Reconstruction.

Executive Order 8802
Reaffirming Policy of Full Participation in the Defense Program by All Persons, Regardless of Race, Creed, Color, or National Origin, and Directing Certain Action in Furtherance of Said Policy

June 25, 1941

WHEREAS it is the policy of the United States to encourage full participation in the national defense program by all citizens of the United States, regardless of race, creed, color, or national origin, in the firm belief that the democratic way of life within the Nation can be defended successfully only with the help and support of all groups within its borders; and

WHEREAS there is evidence that available and needed workers have been barred from employment in industries engaged in defense production solely because of considerations of race, creed, color, or national origin, to the detriment of workers' morale and of national unity:

NOW, THEREFORE, by virtue of the authority vested in me by the Constitution and the statutes, and as a prerequisite to the successful conduct of our national defense production effort, I do hereby reaffirm the policy of the United States that there shall be no discrimination in the employment of workers in defense industries or government because of race, creed, color, or national origin, and I do hereby declare that it is the duty of employers and of labor organizations, in furtherance of said policy and of this order, to provide for the full and equitable participation of all workers in defense industries, without discrimination because of race, creed, color, or national origin;

And it is hereby ordered as follows:

1. All departments and agencies of the Government of the United States concerned with vocational and training programs for defense production shall take special measures appropriate to assure that such programs are administered without discrimination because of race, creed, color, or national origin;

2. All contracting agencies of the Government of the United States shall include in all defense contracts hereafter negotiated by them a provision obligating the contractor not to discriminate against any worker because of race, creed, color, or national origin;

3. There is established in the Office of Production Management a Committee on Fair Employment Practice, which shall consist of a chairman and four other members to be appointed by the President. The Chairman and members of the Committee shall serve as such without compensation but shall be entitled to actual and necessary transportation, subsistence and other expenses incidental to performance of their duties. The Committee shall receive and investigate complaints of discrimination in violation of the provisions of this order and shall take appropriate steps to redress grievances which it finds to be valid. The Committee shall also recommend to the several departments and agencies of the Government of the United States and to the President all measures which may be deemed by it necessary or proper to effectuate the provisions of this order.

Franklin D. Roosevelt
The White House,
June 25, 1941.
Source: Federal Register 6, no. 125 (June 27, 1941): 4544.

⌒

A. Philip Randolph Asks, "Why Should We March?" (1942)

Although the march on Washington scheduled for July 1, 1941, was called off, the March on Washington Movement (MOWM) continued in being and held a number of rallies through 1941 into 1942. Here A. Philip Randolph lays out the MOWM's aims, and while the movement had a declining significance, Randolph articulates the view of many African Americans in linking the war with the campaign for civil rights.

Though I have found no Negroes who want to see the United Nations lose this war, I have found many who, before the war ends, want to see the stuffing knocked out of white supremacy and of empire over subject peoples. American Negroes, involved as we are in the general issues of the conflict, are confronted not with a choice but with the challenge both to win democracy for ourselves at home and to help win the war for democracy the world over.

There is no escape from the horns of this dilemma. There ought not to be escape. For if the war for democracy is not won abroad, the fight for democracy cannot be won at home. If this war cannot be won for the white peoples, it will not be won for the darker races.

Conversely, if freedom and equality are not vouchsafed the peoples of color, the war for democracy will not be won. Unless this double-barreled thesis is accepted and applied, the darker races will never wholeheartedly fight for the victory of the United Nations. That is why those familiar with the thinking of the American Negro have sensed his lack of enthusiasm, whether among the educated or uneducated, rich or poor, professional or nonprofessional, religious or secular, rural or urban, north, south, east or west.

That is why questions are being raised by Negroes in church, labor union and fraternal society; in poolroom, barbershop, schoolroom, hospital, hairdressing parlor; on college campus, railroad, and bus. One can hear such questions asked as these: What have Negroes to fight for? What's the difference between Hitler and that "cracker" Talmadge of Georgia? Why has a man got to be Jim Crowed to die for democracy? If you haven't got democracy yourself, how can you carry it to somebody else?

What are the reasons for this state of mind? The answer is: discrimination, segregation, Jim Crow. Witness the navy, the army, the air corps; and also government services at Washington. In many parts of the South, Negroes in Uncle Sam's uniform are being put upon, mobbed, sometimes even shot down by civilian and military police, and on occasion lynched. Vested political interests in race prejudice are so deeply entrenched that to them winning the war against Hitler is secondary to preventing Negroes from winning democracy for themselves. This is worth many divisions to Hitler and Hirohito. While labor, business, and farm are subjected to ceilings and doors and not allowed to carry on as usual, these interests trade in the dangerous business of race hate as usual.

When the defense program began and billions of the taxpayers' money were appropriated for guns, ships, tanks and bombs, Negroes presented themselves for work only to be given the cold shoulder. North as well as South, and despite their qualifications, Negroes were denied skilled employment. Not until their wrath and indignation took the form of a proposed protest march on Washington, scheduled for July 1, 1941, did things begin to move in the form of defense jobs for Negroes. The march was postponed by the timely issuance (June 25, 1941) of the famous Executive Order No. 8802 by President Roosevelt. But this order and the President's Committee on Fair Employment Practice, established thereunder, have as yet only scratched the surface by way of eliminating discriminations on account of race or color in

war industry. Both management and labor unions in too many places and in too many ways are still drawing the color line.

It is to meet this situation squarely with direct action that the March on Washington Movement launched its present program of protest mass meetings. Twenty thousand were in attendance at Madison Square Garden, June 16; sixteen thousand in the Coliseum in Chicago, June 26; nine thousand in the City Auditorium of St. Louis, August 14. Meetings of such magnitude were unprecedented among Negroes. The vast throngs were drawn from all walks and levels of Negro life—businessmen, teachers, laundry workers, Pullman porters, waiters, and red caps; preachers, crapshooters, and social workers; jitterbugs and PhDs. They came and sat in silence, thinking, applauding only when they considered the truth was told, when they felt strongly that something was going to be done about it.

The March on Washington Movement is essentially a movement of the people. It is all Negro and pro-Negro, but not for that reason anti-white or anti-Semitic, or anti-Catholic, or anti-foreign, or anti-labor. Its major weapon is the non-violent demonstration of Negro mass power. Negro leadership has united back of its drive for jobs and justice. "Whether Negroes should march on Washington, and if so, when?" will be the focus of a forthcoming national conference. For the plan of a protest march has not been abandoned. Its purpose would be to demonstrate that American Negroes are in deadly earnest, and all out for their full rights. No power on earth can cause them today to abandon their fight to wipe out every vestige of second class citizenship and the dual standards that plague them.

A community is democratic only when the humblest and weakest person can enjoy the highest civil, economic, and social rights that the biggest and most powerful possess. To trample on these rights of both Negroes and poor whites is such a commonplace in the South that it takes readily to anti-social, anti-labor, anti-Semitic and anti-Catholic propaganda. It was because of laxness in enforcing the Weimar constitution in republican Germany that Nazism made headway. Oppression of the Negroes in the United States, like suppression of the Jews in Germany, may open the way for a fascist dictatorship.

By fighting for their rights now, American Negroes are helping to make America a moral and spiritual arsenal of democracy. Their fight against the poll tax, against lynch law, segregation, and Jim Crow, their fight for economic, political, and social equality, thus becomes part of the global war for freedom.

Source: Survey Graphic (November 1942): 488–89.

⌒

The "Double V Campaign"

While the MOWM declined in influence, the campaign for civil rights for African Americans continued during the war. A letter from a young African American facing military service in the segregated armed forces prompted a powerful campaign launched by the Pittsburgh Courier *linking the struggle for civil rights at home with the war against Nazism and Fascism abroad.*

James G. Thompson, "Should I Sacrifice to Live"

Dear Editor:

Like all true Americans, my greatest desire at this time, this crucial point of our history; is a desire for a complete victory over the forces of evil, which threaten our existence today. Behind that desire is also a desire to serve, this, my country, in the most advantageous way. Most of our leaders are suggesting that we sacrifice every other ambition to the paramount one, victory. With this I agree; but I also wonder if another victory could not be achieved at the same time.

After all, the things that beset the world now are basically the same things which upset the equilibrium of nations internally, states, counties, cities, homes and even the individual.

Being an American of dark complexion and some 26 years, these questions flash through my mind: "Should I sacrifice my life to live half American?" "Will things be better for the next generation in the peace to follow?" "Would it be demanding too much to demand full citizenship rights in exchange for the sacrificing of my life?" "Is the kind of America I know worth defending?" "Will America be a true and pure democracy after this war?" "Will colored Americans suffer still the indignities that have been heaped upon them in the past?" These and other questions need answering; I want to know, and I believe every colored American, who is thinking, wants to know.

This may be the wrong time to broach such subjects, but haven't all good things obtained by men been secured through sacrifice during just such times of strife?

I suggest that while we keep defense and victory in the forefront that we don't loose [sic] sight of our fight for true democracy at home.

The "V for Victory" sign is being displayed prominently in all so-called democratic countries which are fighting for victory over aggression, slavery and tyranny. If this V sign means that to those now engaged in this great conflict, then let colored Americans adopt the double VV for a double vic-

tory. . . . The first V for victory over our enemies from without, the second V for victory over our enemies within. For surely those who perpetrate these ugly prejudices here are seeking to destroy our democratic form of government just as surely as the Axis forces.

This should not and would not lessen our efforts to bring this conflict to a successful conclusion; but should and would make us stronger to resist these evil forces which threaten us. America could become united as never before and become truly the home of democracy.

In way of an answer to the foregoing questions in a preceding paragraph, I might say that there is no doubt that this country is worth defending; things will be different for the next generation; colored Americans will come into their own, and America will eventually become the true democracy it was designed to be. These things will become a reality in time; but not through any relaxation of the efforts to secure them.

In conclusion let me say that though these questions often permeate my mind, I love America and am willing to die for the America I know will someday become a reality.

James G. Thompson

Source: Letter to the *Pittsburgh Courier*, January 31, 1942, 3. Printed by permission from the *Pittsburgh Courier Archives*, Pittsburgh, PA 15219.

⌒

Official War Department Policy
Regarding Use of African Americans (1940)

On September 27, 1940, President Roosevelt and his military advisors met with black leaders Walter White, A. Philip Randolph, T. Arnold Hill, and Mary McLeod Bethune to discuss black demands for officer training for African Americans and their assignment to duty according to ability, the full use of African Americans in the Army Air Corps (later Army Air Force), their use in the Selective Service System, and the use of black women as nurses in the army and navy as well as Red Cross. The leaders also asked that officers and men be accepted without regard to race in the army. On October 9 the War Department released a statement of policy that, although it made some concessions, did not grant all that the black representatives had requested. It generated an angry response from the black leaders and much criticism in the black press.

War Department Policy in Regard to Negroes

It is the policy of the War Department that the services of Negroes will be utilized on a fair and equitable basis. In line with this policy provision will be made as follows:

1. The strength of the Negro personnel of the Army of the United States will be maintained on the general basis of proportion of the Negro population of the country.
2. Negro organizations will be established in each major branch of the service, combatant as well as noncombatant.
3. Negro reserve officers eligible for active duty will be assigned to Negro units officered by colored personnel.
4. When officer candidate schools are established, opportunity will be given to Negroes to qualify for reserve commissions.
5. Negroes are being given aviation training as pilots, mechanics, and technical specialists. This training will be accelerated. Negro aviation units will be formed as soon as the necessary personnel has [have] been trained.
6. At arsenals and army posts Negro civilians are accorded equal opportunity for employment at work for which they are qualified by ability, education and experience.
7. The policy of the War Department is not to intermingle colored and white enlisted personnel in the same regimental organizations. This policy has been proven satisfactory over a long period of years and to make changes would produce situations destructive to morale and detrimental to the preparations for national defense. For similar reasons the department does not contemplate assigning colored reserve officers other than those of the Medical Corps and chaplains to existing Negro combat units of the regular army. These regular units are going concerns, accustomed through many years to the present system. Their morale is splendid, their rate of reenlistment is exceptionally high, and their field training is well advanced. It is the opinion of the War Department that no experiments should be tried with the organizational setup of these units at this critical time.

Source: Memorandum to the president, from Robert P. Paterson, assistant secretary of war to the president, October 8, 1940, in File 93, Box 4, Presidential Papers, Franklin Delano Roosevelt Library.

ᴖ

William H. Hastie Outlines the Extent of Discrimination in the Armed Forces in the Black Press

William Hastie followed up his resignation in January 1943 by writing a series of articles for the black newspapers. As he had indicated in his letter of resignation, he now felt free to make critical observations and provided a much fuller account of events than he had in his official letter. The publication of these articles in wartime was quite remarkable and suggests that the black newspapers still provided an important outlet for protest.

Statement of William H. Hastie, Recently Civilian Aide to the Secretary of War

Reactionary policies and discriminatory practices of the Army Air Forces in matters affecting colored men were the immediate cause of my resignation as Civilian Aid[e] to The Secretary of War.

The Army Air Forces are growing in importance and independence. In the post-war period they may become the greatest single component of the armed services. Biased policies and harmful practices established in this branch of the army can all too easily infect other branches as well. The situation had become critical.

Yet, the whole course of my dealings with the Army Air Forces convinced me that further expression of my views in the form of recommendations within the department would be futile. I, therefore, took the only course which can, I believe, bring results. Public opinion is still the strongest force in American life.

To the colored soldier and those who influence his thinking, I say with all the force and sincerity at my command that the man in uniform must grit his teeth, square his shoulders and do his best as a soldier, confident that there are millions of Americans outside of the armed services, and more persons than he knows in high places within the military establishment, who will never cease fighting to remove every racial barrier and every humiliating practice which now confronts him. But only by being at all times a first class soldier can the man in uniform help in this battle which shall be fought and won.

When I took office, the Secretary of War directed that all questions of policy and important proposals relating to colored men should be referred to my office for comment or approval before final action. In December, 1940, the Air Forces referred to me a plan for a segregated training center for colored pursuit pilots at Tuskegee. I expressed my entire disagreement with the plan, giving my reasons in detail. My views were disregarded. Since then, the

Air Command has never on its own initiative submitted any plan or project to me for comment or recommendation. What information I obtained, I had to seek out. Where I made proposals or recommendations I volunteered them.

The situation reached its climax in late December, 1942, when I learned through army press releases sent out from St. Louis and from the War Department in Washington that the Air Command was about to establish a segregated officer candidate school at Jefferson Barracks, Mo., to train colored officers for ground duty with the Army Air Forces.

Here was a proposal for a radical departure from present army practice, since the officer candidate training program is the one large field where the army is eliminating racial segregation.

Moreover, I had actually written to the Air Command several weeks earlier in an attempt to find out what was brewing at Jefferson Barracks.

The Air Command replied as late as December 17, 1942, giving not even the slightest hint of any plan for a segregated officer candidate school. It is inconceivable to me that consideration of such a project had not then advanced far enough for my office to have been consulted, even if I had not made specific inquiry. The conclusion is inescapable that the Air Command does not propose to inform, much less counsel with, this office about its plans for colored soldiers.

But the reactionary policies and discriminatory practices of the Air Forces are much more serious than the matter of ignoring my office. It should be understood that from the beginning the Air Command did not want colored personnel. Resistance bred of that attitude has been met ever since. Moreover, even now the Air Command views the use of the colored man as an "experiment" designed to determine whether he can do this or that in the field of aviation. This attitude is the result of wholly unscientific notions that race somehow controls a man's capacity and aptitudes. The tragedy is that by not wanting the colored man in the first place and by doubting his capacity, the Air Command has committed itself psychologically to courses of action which themselves become major obstacles to the success of colored men in the Air Forces.

The colored program of the Air Forces began some two years ago with the organization of several so-called "Aviation Squadrons (Separate)." These units, now greatly increased in number, were organized to serve no specific military need. They have never had a defined function.

Except as individual commanders on their own initiative have found some military function for particular small groups of men, the characteristic assignment of the "Aviation Squadrons (Separate)" has been the performance of

odd jobs of common labor which arise from time to time at air fields. There are no equivalent white organizations.

"Aviation Squadrons (Separate)" would never have come into existence except for the necessity of making some provision for colored enlisted men in the Air Forces. Reluctant to use colored men at all, the Air Command started off on the wrong foot by organizing some colored labor units, while every effort was being made to recruit white volunteers with mechanical ability for skilled service.

Somewhat later, in order to provide enlisted technicians for the new air base at Tuskegee, a few colored soldiers were accepted for technical training at Chanute Field where a large school is maintained. The men were well received and did excellent work.

I urged the importance of continuing such training of colored men in this existing unsegregated school. But the program stopped with the first group. The Air Forces then made efforts to set up segregated technical training at Tuskegee or elsewhere. Difficulties were encountered. Meanwhile, successive classes of colored pilots were being trained, but no technical schooling of supporting ground crew members was in progress.

Thus, even the segregated program got badly out of balance in the effort to effect its extension. The prospect is that in 1943, even with a tardy resumption of technical ground training, colored pilots will be ready before adequate numbers of trained ground crews are available.

The Air Forces also are rejecting colored applicants who wish to become weather officers or officers in other highly specialized technical fields. A few such men were trained for Tuskegee. But for a period of more than six months, all qualified colored candidates have had their completed applications returned to them with the information that the Air Forces need no more colored weather officers.

The Air Forces, however, do need large numbers of additional weather officers so badly that white volunteers are being solicited and accepted, despite a general policy against voluntary enlistments in the army. Yet, it is unthinkable to those in authority that a colored officer can fill such a position except at Tuskegee.

The same situation exists in armament and engineering, both ground specialities for which the Air Forces have been accepting cadets generally, but refusing colored men.

To date, all colored applicants, a number of them well and fully qualified for appointment as army service pilots, have been rejected. Two applicants were actually instructed to report for training. They did so but were sent home as soon as it was discovered that they were colored men. I am advised that this matter is receiving further study.

The simple fact is that the Air Command does not want colored pilots flying in and out of various fields, eating, sleeping and mingling with other personnel, as a service pilot must do in carrying out his various missions.

Colored medical officers in the Air Forces are getting only part of the special training in aviation medicine which is available. They are not admitted to the principal school of aviation medicine at Randolph Field. Even the branch school program in which it is represented that colored officers share without discrimination is in fact discriminatory.

Many white officers enrolled at branch schools of aviation medicine have the opportunity of full time resident study. The colored officer is permitted to commute periodically from his home station at Tuskegee for work at the Maxwell Field branch school. Such grudging partial tender of makeshift schemes may be expected to continue unless a genuine change of racial attitude and policy occurs in the Air Command.

While colored trainees and cadets at the Tuskegee Air Base have done well from a strictly technical point of view, they have suffered such demoralizing discrimination and segregation that, in my judgment, the entire future of the colored man in combat aviation is in danger. Men cannot be humiliated over a long period of time without a loss of combat efficiency.

Specifically, colored and white officers serving at Tuskegee in the common enterprise of training colored men for air combat have separate messes. They are not permitted to have quarters in the same building. Separate toilet facilities have been provided. If the group of white officers at Tuskegee insist upon this—and I have no evidence that they do—they are psychologically unsuited to train colored men for combat. If they do not so insist, the racial attitude of the local commander or of higher authority is all the more apparent.

Despite original design to advance colored officers and to place them in posts of administrative responsibility at Tuskegee as rapidly as they should qualify, that design is not being carried out in the post administration except in the station hospital.

Early in the history of the Tuskegee project, a colored soldier guarding a warehouse was disarmed and arrested by civilian authorities because he had challenged a white civilian.

From then on friction continued. A new commander was appointed. He disarmed colored military policemen assigned to patrol duty in the town of Tuskegee.

A recent member of the Alabama state police force was assigned to Tuskegee as an army officer with duties related to his civilian experience. The colored soldier was embittered but the prejudiced community was somewhat mollified.

Fundamentally, it seems to me the Air Command has either failed to comprehend or failed to care that its policies and practices are tending to tear down rather than build up the pride, dignity and self-respect which colored soldiers, like all other soldiers, must possess if they are to achieve maximum combat efficiency.

Military men agree that a soldier should be made to feel that he is the best man, in the best unit in the best army in the world. When the Air Command shall direct its policies and practices so as to help rather than hinder the development of such spirit among its colored soldiers, it will be on the right road.

Source: Baltimore Afro-American, February 2, 1943. Printed with permission from the Afro-American Newspapers Archives and Research Center, Baltimore, Maryland.

⁓

A Black Soldier's Point of View on the War and The African American Experience

Many African American soldiers wrote to the black newspapers, politicians, the civilian aide to the secretary of war, and even the president about the conditions they faced in military service and about the situation of African Americans generally in relation to the war. The extract from a letter here, from the files of then civilian aide Truman Gibson, gives some indication both of the conditions black soldiers faced in training camps and of the way the war reflected on the racial situation in the United States and the paradox of fighting racism abroad while it still existed at home. Pvt. Bert B. Babero wrote several times to Gibson, who on this occasion replied that steps were being taken to address the conditions Babero described. Nonetheless, prior to his embarkation to go overseas, Babero wrote on May 13, 1944, "When inducted I honestly believed that as a Negroe [sic], I comprised an important part of this nation and it was my patriotic duty to avail myself when my country was in peril. My attitude now is really changed. I'm indifferent to the whole affair." He must have been expressing the view of many black soldiers.

Atty. Truman K. Gibson   Co. A 66th Med. Trg. Bn.
Civilian Aide to Secy. of War   M. R. T. C.
White House   Camp Barkeley, Texas
Washington, D.C.   Feb. 13th, 1944
Dear Mr. Gibson:

Your letter of the 20th was received and I must say it was received most cordially. It proved evident that you are interested in acquiring equality in army camps.

Camp Barkeley is one of the largest army camps in Texas and the only Medical Replacement Training Center in the south. We, approximately two hundred of us, were the first Colored to be stationed here, now however, there are roughly over five hundred of us. The latter of which will replace us since our training is nearing completion. None of our commissioned officers are Colored despite the fact that located here are Officer Candidate and Medical Administration schools. There are relatively few of our boys who attend these schools and those who are fortunate to finish are immediately shipped to Ft. Huachuca or elsewhere. Up until a few weeks ago, we could attend only one theater out of five on the post. This theater was an open air theater which we could only attend when the weather was favorable. By protest, we acquired the right to attend any theater of our choice but are forced to contend with being segregated. We have buses which are local and those that run to and from camp, on the local buses we are compelled to sit in the back, threaten by the drivers if we refuse. Despite the fact that buses run all day back and forth to camp at regular one half hour entervals, we have only three which we may ride. Our buses are crowded to the extent that it is practically impossible to close the doors and yet extra buses has been refused us. The camp provides army buses that carry soldiers to town but we aren't allowed to ride them. Our sector is completely ostrasized from the camp proper so we rarely see the other group. Our living quarters are terrible being formerly C.C.C. barracks, located just in from of the camp cess pool. When I first arrived, our sector actually looked like a garbage dump in comparison with the rest of the camp. We spent three weeks cleaning the place before we could begin training. There is also a quarter master outfit stationed near us, this outfit was here at least six months before we arrived. It consist of no lest than nine companies. These nine companies, including our two, are forced to use a small post-exchange capable of convienely servicing no lest than three companies the most. The nearest post-office is the other side of the camp; approximately 2 1/2 miles away. We have one service club shared by both divisions. It is poorly equipped having nothing but writting tables, a pingpong table and a piano. We don't have a library, a chapel or a chaplain. We conduct our own services in one of the poorly constructed class rooms. We have had Joe Louis to give a boxing exhibition and two dances in the three months I've been here. We were told that if we wanted entertainment we would have to provide it ourselves.

It was to my amazement, a short time ago, when I had the opportunity of visiting the German concentration camp here at Barkeley to observe a sign in the latrine, actually segregating a section of the latrine for Negro soldiers, the other being used by the German prisoners and the white soldiers. Seeing

this was honestly disheartening. It made me feel, here, the tyrant is actually placed over the liberator.

Many of the existing conditions we discussed with our company commander but to no avail. Being himself a Texan and probably accoustomed to the maltreatment of Negroes, we find it extremely difficult to obtain his assistance. I was severly repremanded by the company commander, one afternoon, after a class on court martial, for asking "To who could we, as Colored soldiers turn to if we were innocently maltreated." He asked me to be specific. I spoke of the treatments we received in town, on camp buses and theaters. My question was very diplomatically ignored and after class, in his office, he called me a trouble maker and gave me an order not to even discuss the subject with the other fellows, who were aware of the existing conditions as myself. There are many reasons in my estimation which makes our company commander, Lt. Schuessle unfit for leadership.

I realize that as a soldier there is very little I can do in remedying the conditions that exist in the outside world. I am of the opinion, the undemocratic conditions that is in army camps are caused by prejudice officials and if the right sources were informed, immediate steps would be taken for correction. I sincerely hope that from the meagre information I have given you that it might prove advantageous in your ultimate objective, of course, in writting, I couldn't tell every thing for fear of boring you or perhaps making you think of my possible exaggeration but I assure you, I have written only the concised facts.

Sincerely yours,

Pvt. Bert B. Babero

Source: Civilian assistant to secretary of war, Office of Assistant Secretary of War, National Archives Record Group 107.

⌢

The Impact of War on Black Women

The reminiscences of African American women provide valuable insights into some of the ways the war affected women, particularly black women, in terms of personal relations and work on the home front. Sarah Killingsworth had moved from Tennessee to California in 1935 and held a number of jobs, mainly in domestic service, before the war began. Sybil Lewis moved from Oklahoma to Los Angeles during the war and, after working in a restaurant, trained to work in the aircraft industry. She progressed from riveting to welding in the shipyards and enjoyed the new opportunities the war offered.

Sarah Killingsworth

The war started and jobs kinda opened up for women that the men had. I took a job at a shoe-repair place on Wilshire Boulevard. Cleanin' shoes and dyin' shoes, the same thing that men did. They started takin' applications at Douglas, to work in a defense plant. I was hired.

I didn't want a job on the production line. I heard so many things about accidents, that some girls got their fingers cut off or their hair caught in the machines. I was frightened. All I wanted to do was get in the factory, because they were payin' more than what I'd been makin'. Which was forty dollars a week, which was pretty good considering I'd been makin' about twenty dollars a week. When I left Tennessee I was only makin' twofifty a week, so that was quite a jump.

I got the job workin' nights in the ladies' rest room, which wasn't hard. We had about six rest rooms to do. They would stay up all night and they would be sleeping. I had bought some of those No-Doz tablets, and I would give them a No-Doz so they could stay awake all night. This was the graveyard shift. Some of 'em had been out drinkin', and we would let them take a nap for about fifteen minutes. We would watch out for them, so their supervisor wouldn't miss 'em. We'd put the sign out: Closed. We'd wake 'em up, and sometimes they'd give us tips. They would give me fifty cents for a tablet or a cup of coffee, so they could stay awake. Especially on weekends.

They weren't interested in the war. Most of them were only interested in the money. Most of us was young and we really didn't know. All we were after was that buck. I didn't care about the money. That was a big salary for me, I was satisfied with that.

My husband was in the service. He had been drafted. While he was there, he got promoted to chaplain. He wasn't a minister, just always a religious man. He tried everything to keep from goin' out on that battlefield. He didn't see much action. He just devoted most of his time around the kitchen. Right after he got out, I divorced him. You weren't in love in the first place, I call your first marriage a trial marriage. Most of the girls married soldiers at that time because that was a sure income. You knew you were gonna get a check. They had a song about fifty dollars a month once a day. Fifty dollars a month was a lot of money, you could live offa that. I was payin' twenty-five dollars a month rent, so I could live off the other twenty-five dollars. And then I did a little sewin'. I've always been the type of person could always find work to do, so I never suffered too much. I didn't marry my husband because he was a soldier. We were married before the war. I stayed single for about five years and then I married again.

I do know one thing, this place was very segregated when I first come here. Oh, Los Angeles, you just couldn't go and sit down like you do now. You had certain places you went. You had to more or less stick to the restaurants and hotels where black people were. It wasn't until the war that it really opened up. 'Cause when I come out here it was awful, just like bein' in the South.

I was relating this to my daughter last night. What am I gonna relate to my children? "You young people are makin' money and you're doin' well," I says. "You would never struggle and go through the hardships that I went through to get where I am today." So she said, "In other words, from rags to riches." I said, "That's just the way you would probably explain my life: from rags to riches."

For a person that grew up and knew nothin' but hard times to get out on my own at eighteen years old and make a decent livin' and still make a decent person outa myself, I really am proud of me.

I had so many opportunities to go wrong. I was waitin' on the bus on Wilshire, girls were there. Prostitutes would come up and tell you, "What kind of work do you do?" I'd tell 'em I'm doin' domestic work. They'd say, "We got good jobs. You could make as much money in one day as you do in a month." They'd go out and date these white fellas and spend the night with 'em. I was never interested in that kind of life, because I wasn't raised that way.

Some of the people I worked with saved money. Some of 'em, they were just out havin' a good time. They were just makin' this big money and they were spendin' it as fast as they were makin' it.

I also had a restaurant, which we opened when my husband got out of the army. The prostitutes used to come in. I had good, good business. They had a red-light district in San Bernardino, where the soldiers would all go. Some of the girls were married, very attractive women. Their husbands would take them down there and they would pick 'em up on weekends. They called 'em pimps in those days. The girls were high-class, they didn't work on the streets. But I was always a strong person. I could never be tempted. I was never interested in selling my body for a few dollars.

I really didn't know what the war was about. I was in the house one day and all of a sudden they started yellin' about the war, war, war. Roosevelt had declared war. Well, they know that when there's a war, somebody's gonna get a job. This was during the Depression, so I think people were kinda glad the war had started. So right away they started hirin'. I think the war had kind of a pleasure. People didn't realize the seriousness of the war. All they were thinkin' about is they had lived in these Depression days. It was so hard to come by a dollar.

Those who had to go, that was the sad part. I had a brother that went to war, my youngest. He come back. The war helped some people because they come back, they took trades, learned to do things. My brother come back and now he is very successful. I think the army really made a man out of him. He works at Rockwell in the missile department and he's a supervisor. He wouldn't have known what to do if he hadn't gone in the army.

I have a friend tells us different things he experienced in the war. We sit up and listen to him. He was really in the battle zone. He was injured. Right now he's losing his hearing, he's losing his eyesight. He was so proud he really didn't tell them how he had got the hand grenade. He couldn't even get a pension and he didn't get a medical discharge. Yet he was in the hospital there for a long time, you know. He injured his spine 'cause he had to grab a rope and swing over a branch. Well, he missed the rope and fell and struck his back. He had to have surgery on his spine. They told him it was a fifty-fifty chance whether he'd ever walk again. He's walkin', but he's been affected a lot, uh-huh.

They didn't mix the white and black in the war. But now it gives you a kind of independence because they felt that we gone off and fought, we should be equal. Everything started openin' up for us. We got a chance to go places we had never been able to go before.

In ways it was too bad that so many lives were lost. But I think it was for a worthy cause, because it did make a way for us. And we were able to really get out.

Source: Studs Terkel, "The Good War": An Oral History of World War II (London: Hamish Hamilton, 1985), 113–16. Printed by permission of Penguin Books UK Ltd and Donadio & Olson, Inc. Copyright 1985 Studs Terkel.

Sybil Lewis Comments on the Home Front
Had it not been for the war I don't think blacks would be in the position they are now. The war and defense work gave black people opportunities to work on jobs they never had before, it gave them opportunity to do things they had never experienced before. They made more money and began to experience a different lifestyle. Their expectations changed. Money will do that. You could sense that they would no longer be satisfied with the way they had lived before.

When I got my first paycheck, I'd never seen that much money before, not even in the bank, because I'd never been in a bank too much. I don't recall exactly what it was in the aircraft plant, but it was more than three hundred

dollars a month, and later, in the shipyard, it was even more. To be able to buy what you wanted, your clothing and shoes, all this was just a different way of life.

When I first got my paycheck I bought everything that I thought I had ever wanted, but in particular I bought shoes. I wore a large size as a child and I could never be fitted properly for shoes. The woman I worked for in Oklahoma wore beautiful shoes, and I remember thinking then that when I got a chance to make some money I was going to buy shoes first. So my first paycheck I bought mostly shoes. And it felt very good. To be honest, today I still buy more shoes than anything else.

Other experiences I had during the war were important, too, like having to rivet with a white farm girl from Arkansas and both of us having to relate to each other in ways that we had never experienced before. Although we had our differences we both learned to work together and talk together. We learned that despite our hostilities and resentments we could open up to each other and get along. As I look back now I feel that experience was meaningful to me and meaningful to her. She learned that Negroes were people, too, and I saw her as a person also, and we both gained from it,

I also saw in California that black women were working in many jobs that I had never seen in the South, not only defense work but working in nice hotels as waitresses, working in the post office, doing clerical work. So I realized there were a lot of things women could do besides housework. I saw black people accepted in the school system and accepted in other kinds of jobs that they had not been accepted in before. It's too bad it took a war to motivate people to move here to want to make more of their lives, but if it had not been for the war offering better jobs and opportunities, some people would have never left the South. They would have had nothing to move for.

After I graduated from college I returned to California and started applying for civil-service jobs. Had it not been for the war I probably would have ended up a schoolteacher in rural Oklahoma, but the impact of the war changed my life, gave me an opportunity to leave my small town and discover there was another way of life. It financed my college education and opened my eyes to opportunities I could take advantage of when the war was over.

Source: Mark Jonathan Harris, Franklin Mitchell, and Steven Schecter, eds., *The Homefront: America during World War II* (New York: G. P. Putnam's Sons, 1984), 251–52. Printed by kind permission of Mark Jonathan Harris, Distinguished Professor, University of Southern California.

~

Langston Hughes, "Beaumont to Detroit: 1943"

The black poet Langston Hughes here reflects on the wave of riots that affected the United States in 1943 in the context of the war.

Looky here, America
What you done done—
Let things drift
Until the riots come.

Now your policemen
Let the mobs run free;
I reckon you don't care
Nothing about me.

You tell me that hitler
Is a mighty bad man.
I guess he took lessons
From the ku klu klan.

You tell me mussolini's
Got an evil heart.
Well, it mus-a been in Beaumont
That he had his start—

Cause everything that hitler
And mussolini do,
Negroes get the same
Treatment from you.

You jim crowed me
Before hitler rose to power
And you're STILL jim crowing me
Right now, this very hour.

Yet you say we're fighting
For democracy.
Then why don't democracy
Include me?

I ask this question
Cause I want to know
How long I got to fight
BOTH HITLER —AND JIM CROW.

Source: People's Voice, July 3, 1943.

～

The Emergence of New Civil Rights
Protest and the Formation of CORE

Early in 1942 members of a pacifist Christian group, the Fellowship of Recon-
ciliation, including African Americans Bayard Rustin and James Farmer, met in
Chicago to establish a new civil rights organization based on new approaches. Here
Rustin outlines what African Americans face during the war and also how they
might respond. In drawing upon the Gandhian techniques of nonviolent protest, he
articulates the methods already proposed by A. Philip Randolph in the MOWM,
but he also spells out the approach that proved central to the civil rights movements
in the mid-1950s and 1960s.

Since the United States entered the war white-Negro tension has increased steadily. Even in normal times changes in the social and economic
patterns cause fear and frustration, which in turn lead to aggression. In time
of war the general social condition is fertile soil for the development of hate
and fear, and transference of these to minority groups is quite simple.

These and other humiliations have had a very marked effect on great
masses of Negroes, who are being told by the press "that equality of opportunity and social and political recognition will come now or never, violently
or nonviolently." The *Pittsburgh Courier* and the *People's Voice*, typical of
the general Negro press, initiators of the double victory campaign (victory
at home and victory abroad), constantly remind the masses that greater economic and political democracy were supposed to have followed the last war.
Instead, they pointed out, the Negro found himself the scapegoat, "last hired
and first fired," in a period of economic and social maladjustment that has
lasted until the present time. Thus the average Negro is told "there can be
no delay. What achievement there will be, must come now."

An increasingly militant group has in mind to demand now, with violence
if necessary, the rights it has long been denied. "If we must die abroad for
democracy we can't have," I heard a friend of mine say, "then we might as
well die right here fighting for our rights."

This is a tragic statement. It is tragic also how isolated the average Negro
feels in his struggle. The average Negro has largely lost faith in middle-class
whites. In his hour of need he seeks not "talk" but dynamic action. He looks
upon the middle-class idea of long-term educational and cultural changes
with fear and mistrust. He is interested only in what can be achieved immediately by political pressure to get jobs, decent housing, and education
for his children. He describes with disgust the efforts on his behalf by most
middle-class Negro and white intellectuals as "pink tea methods—sometimes
well-meanin' but gettin' us nowhere." It is for this reason, in part, that the

March on Washington Movement, aiming to become a mass movement, has tended to "black nationalism." Its leadership, originally well-motivated, now rejects the idea of including whites in constituency or leadership. One local official said: "These are Negroes' problems and Negroes will have to work them out."

The March on Washington Movement is growing, but at best is only a partial answer to the present need. While the movement already exerts some real political pressure (President Roosevelt set up the F.E.P.C. at its request), it has no program, educational or otherwise, for meeting immediate conflict. To demand rights but not to see the potential danger in such a course, or the responsibility to develop a means of meeting that danger, seems tragic.

There are many Negroes who see mass violence coming. Having lived in a society in which church, school, and home problems have been handled in a violent way, the majority at this point are unable to conceive of a solution by reconciliation and non-violence. Thus, I have seen school boys in Arkansas laying away rusty guns for the time "when." I have heard many young men in the armed forces hope for a machine gun assignment "so I can turn it on the white folks." I have seen a white sailor beaten in Harlem because three Negroes had been "wantin' to get just one white . . ." before they died. I have heard hundreds of Negroes hope for a Japanese military victory since "it don't matter who you're a slave for."

These statements come not only from bitterness but from frustration and fear as well. In many parts of America the Negro, in his despair, is willing to follow any leadership seemingly sincerely identified with his struggle if he is convinced that such leadership offers a workable method. Those of us who believe in the non-violent solution of conflict have in this crisis a duty and an opportunity. In all those places where we have a voice it is our high responsibility to indicate that the Negro can attain progress only if he uses, in his struggle, nonviolent direct action—a technique consistent with the ends he desires. Especially in this time of tension we must point out the practical necessity of such a course.

Non-violence as a method has within it the demand for terrible sacrifice and long suffering, but, as Gandhi has said, "freedom does not drop from the sky." One has to struggle and be willing to die for it. J. Holmes Smith has indicated that he looks to the American Negro to assist in developing, along with the people of India, a new dynamic force for the solution of conflict that will not merely free these oppressed people, but will set an example that may be the first step in freeing the world.

Certainly the Negro possesses those qualities essential for non-violent direct action. He has long since learned to endure suffering. He can admit his own share of guilt and has to be pushed hard to become bitter. He has produced, and still sings, such songs as "It's Me, Oh Lord, Standin' in the Need of Prayer" and "Nobody Knows the Trouble I've Seen." He follows this last tragic phrase by a salute to God—"Oh! Glory, Hallelujah." He is creative and has learned to adjust himself to conditions easily. But, above all, he possesses a rich religious heritage and today finds the Church the center of his life.

Yet there are those who question the use of non-violent direct action by Negroes in protesting discrimination on the grounds that this method will kindle hitherto dormant racial feeling. But we must remember that too often conflict is already at hand, and that there is hence a greater danger: the inevitable use of force by persons embittered by injustice and unprepared for non-violence. It is a cause for shame that millions of people continue to live under conditions of injustice while we make no effective effort to remedy the situation.

Those who argue for an extended educational plan are not wrong, but there also must be a plan for facing immediate conflicts. Those of us who believe in non-violent resistance can do the greatest possible good for the Negro, for those who exploit him, for America, and for the world, by becoming a real part of the Negro community, thus being in a position to suggest methods and to offer leadership when troubles come.

Identification with the Negro community demands considerable sacrifices, for the Negro is not to be won by words alone, but by an obvious consistency in words and deeds. The identified person is the one who fights side by side with him for justice. This demands being so integral a part of the Negro community in its day-to-day struggle, so close to it in similarity of work and so near its standard of living, that when problems arise, he who stands forth to judge, to plan, to suggest, or to lead is really one with the Negro masses.

Our war resistance is justified only if we are going to see to it that an adequate alternative to violence is developed. Today, as the Gandhian forces in India face their critical test, we can add to world justice by placing in the hands of thirteen million black Americans a workable and Christian technique for the righting of injustice and the solution of conflict.

Source: Bayard Rustin, "The Negro and Non-Violence," *Fellowship* 8 (October 1942): 166–67. Printed by permission of the Fellowship of Reconciliation, Box 271, Nyack, NY 10960, USA, www.forusa.org.

⌐

President Harry Truman's Committee on Civil Rights Issues Its Report To Secure These Rights

Following reports of murders and violent attacks suffered by African Americans in the immediate aftermath of the war, President Harry Truman established a committee "to study, report and recommend effective means and procedures for the protection of the civil rights of the people of the United States." The committee issued its report the following year, and in spelling out proposals to ensure that four basic rights—safety and security of person; citizenship privileges, including armed service and voting; freedom of conscience and expression; and equality of opportunity—were available to all Americans regardless of race, color, creed, or national origin, the committee laid down the agenda for the civil rights movement for the next twenty years. These extracts demonstrate the influence of the war years and the United States' new international role, as well as the impact of writing such as Gunnar Myrdal's An American Dilemma.

Chapter 4: A Program of Action: The Committee's Recommendations
THE TIME IS NOW

TWICE BEFORE in American history the nation has found it necessary to review the state of its civil rights. The first time was during the 15 years between 1776 and 1791, from the drafting of the Declaration of Independence through the Articles of Confederation experiment to the writing of the Constitution and the Bill of Rights. It was then that the distinctively American heritage was finally distilled from earlier views of liberty. The second time was when the Union was temporarily sundered over the question of whether it could exist "half-slave" and "half-free."

It is our profound conviction that we have come to a time for a third re-examination of the situation, and a sustained drive ahead. Our reasons for believing this are those of conscience, of self-interest, and of survival in a threatening world. Or to put it another way, we have a moral reason, an economic reason, and an international reason for believing that the time for action is now.

The Moral Reason

We have considered the American heritage of freedom at some length. We need no further justification for a broad and immediate program than the need to reaffirm our faith in the traditional American morality. The pervasive gap between our aims and what we actually do is creating a kind of moral dry rot which eats away at the emotional and rational bases of democratic beliefs. There are times when the difference between what we preach

about civil rights and what we practice is shockingly illustrated by individual outrages. There are times when the whole structure of our ideology is made ridiculous by individual instances. And there are certain continuing, quiet, omnipresent practices which do irreparable damage to our beliefs.

As examples of "moral erosion" there are the consequences of suffrage limitations in the South. The fact that Negroes and many whites have not been allowed to vote in some states has actually sapped the morality underlying universal suffrage. Many men in public and private life do not believe that those who have been kept from voting are capable of self rule. They finally convince themselves that disfranchised people do not really have the right to vote.

Wartime segregation in the armed forces is another instance of how a social pattern may wreak moral havoc. Practically all white officers and enlisted men in all branches of service saw Negro military personnel performing only the most menial functions. They saw Negroes recruited for the common defense treated as men apart and distinct from themselves. As a result, men who might otherwise have maintained the equalitarian morality of their forebears were given reason to look down on their fellow citizens. This has been sharply illustrated by the Army study discussed previously, in which white servicemen expressed great surprise at the excellent performance of Negroes who joined them in the firing line. Even now, very few people know of the successful experiment with integrated combat units. Yet it is important in explaining why some Negro troops did not do well; it is proof that equal treatment can produce equal performance.

Thousands upon thousands of small, unseen incidents reinforce the impact of headlined violations like lynchings, and broad social patterns like segregation and inequality of treatment. There is, for example, the matter of "fair play." As part of its training for democratic life, our youth is constantly told to "play fair," to abide by "the rules of the game," and to be "good sports." Yet, how many boys and girls in our country experience such things as Washington's annual marble tournament? Because of the prevailing pattern of segregation, established as a model for youth in the schools and recreation systems, separate tournaments are held for Negro and white boys. Parallel elimination contests are sponsored until only two victors remain.

Without a contest between them, the white boy is automatically designated as the local champion and sent to the national tournament, while the Negro lad is relegated to the position of runner-up. What child can achieve any real understanding of fair play, or sportsmanship, of the rules of the game, after he has personally experienced such an example of inequality?

It is impossible to decide who suffers the greatest moral damage from our civil rights transgressions, because all of us are hurt. That is certainly true of those who are victimized. Their belief in the basic truth of the American promise is undermined. But they do have the realization, galling as it sometimes is, of being morally in the right. The damage to those who are responsible for these violations of our moral standards may well be greater. They, too, have been reared to honor the command of "free and equal." And all of us must share in the shame at the growth of hypocrisies like the "automatic" marble champion. All of us must endure the cynicism about democratic values which our failures breed.

The United States can no longer countenance these burdens on its common conscience, these inroads on its moral fiber.

The Economic Reason

One of the principal economic problems facing us and the rest of the world is achieving maximum production and continued prosperity. The loss of a huge, potential market for goods is a direct result of the economic discrimination which is practiced against many of our minority groups. A sort of vicious circle is produced. Discrimination depresses the wages and income of minority groups. As a result, their purchasing power is curtailed and markets are reduced. Reduced markets result in reduced production. This cuts down employment, which of course means lower wages and still fewer job opportunities. Rising fear, prejudice, and insecurity aggravate the very discrimination in employment which sets the vicious circle in motion. Minority groups are not the sole victims of this economic waste; its impact is inevitably felt by the entire population. Eric Johnston, when President of the United States Chamber of Commerce, made this point with vividness and clarity:

> The withholding of jobs and business opportunities from some people does not make more jobs and business opportunities for others. Such a policy merely tends to drag down the whole economic level. You can't sell an electric refrigerator to a family that can't afford electricity. Perpetuating poverty for some merely guarantees stagnation for all. True economic progress demands that the whole nation move forward at the same time. It demands that all artificial barriers erected by ignorance and intolerance be removed. To put it in the simplest terms, we are all in business together. Intolerance is a species of boycott and any business or job boycott is a cancer in the economic body of the nation. I repeat, intolerance is destructive; prejudice produces no wealth; discrimination is a fool's economy.

Economic discrimination prevents full use of all our resources. During the war, when we were called upon to make an all-out productive effort, we found that we lacked skilled laborers. This shortage might not have been so serious if minorities had not frequently been denied opportunities for training and experience. In the end, it cost large amounts of money and precious time to provide ourselves with trained persons.

Discrimination imposes a direct cost upon our economy through the wasteful duplication of many facilities and services required by the "separate but equal" policy. That the resources of the South are sorely strained by the burden of a double system of schools and other public services has already been indicated. Segregation is also economically wasteful for private business. Public transportation companies must often provide duplicate facilities to serve majority and minority groups separately. Places of public accommodation and recreation reject business when it comes in the form of unwanted persons. Stores reduce their sales by turning away minority customers. Factories must provide separate locker rooms, pay windows, drinking fountains, and wash-rooms for the different groups.

To the costs of discrimination must be added the expensive investigations, trials, and property losses which result from civil rights violations. In the aggregate, these attain huge proportions. The 1943 Detroit riot alone resulted in the destruction of two million dollars in property.

Finally, the cost of prejudice cannot be computed in terms of markets, production, and expenditures. Perhaps the most expensive results are the least tangible ones. No nation can afford to have its component groups hostile toward one another without feeling the stress. People who live in a state of tension and suspicion cannot use their energy constructively. The frustrations of their restricted existence are translated into aggression against the dominant group. Myrdal says:

> Not only occasional acts of violence, but most laziness, carelessness, unreliability, petty stealing and lying are undoubtedly to be explained as concealed aggression. . . . *The truth is that Negroes generally do not feel they have unqualified moral obligations to white people.* . . . The voluntary withdrawal which has intensified the isolation between the two castes is also an expression of Negro protest under cover.

It is not at all surprising that a people relegated to second-class citizenship should behave as second-class citizens. This is true, in varying degrees, of all of our minorities. What we have lost in money, production, invention,

citizenship, and leadership as the price for damaged, thwarted personalities—these are beyond estimate.

The United States can no longer afford this heavy drain upon its human wealth, its national competence.

The International Reason

Our position in the postwar world is so vital to the future that our smallest actions have far-reaching effects. We have come to know that our own security in a highly interdependent world is inextricably tied to the security and well-being of all people and all countries. Our foreign policy is designed to make the United States an enormous, positive influence for peace and progress throughout the world. We have tried to let nothing, not even extreme political differences between ourselves and foreign nations, stand in the way of this goal. But our domestic civil rights shortcomings are a serious obstacle.

In a letter to the Fair Employment Practice Committee on May 8, 1946, the Honorable Dean Acheson, then Acting Secretary of State, stated that:

> the existence of discrimination against minority groups in this country has an adverse effect upon our relations with other countries. We are reminded over and over by some foreign newspapers and spokesmen, that our treatment of various minorities leaves much to be desired. While sometimes these pronouncements are exaggerated and unjustified, they all too frequently point with accuracy to some form of discrimination because of race, creed, color, or national origin. Frequently we find it next to impossible to formulate a satisfactory answer to our critics in other countries; the gap between the things we stand for in principle and the facts of a particular situation may be too wide to be bridged. An atmosphere of suspicion and resentment in a country over the way a minority is being treated in the United States is a formidable obstacle to the development of mutual understanding and trust between the two countries. We will have better international relations when these reasons for suspicion and resentment have been removed.
>
> I think it is quite obvious . . . that the existence of discriminations against minority groups in the United States is a handicap in our relations with other countries. The Department of State, therefore, has good reason to hope for the continued and increased effectiveness of public and private efforts to do away with these discriminations.

The people of the United States stem from many lands. Other nations and their citizens are naturally intrigued by what has happened to their American "relatives." Discrimination against, or mistreatment of, any racial, religious

or national group in the United States is not only seen as our internal problem. The dignity of a country, a continent, or even a major portion of the world's population, may be outraged by it. A relatively few individuals here may be identified with millions of people elsewhere, and the way in which they are treated may have world-wide repercussions. We have fewer than half a million American Indians; there are 30 million more in the Western Hemisphere. Our Mexican American and Hispano groups are not large; millions in Central and South America consider them kin. We number our citizens of Oriental descent in the hundreds of thousands; their counterparts overseas are numbered in hundreds of millions. Throughout the Pacific, Latin America, Africa, the Near, Middle, and Far East, the treatment which our Negroes receive is taken as a reflection of our attitudes toward all dark-skinned peoples.

In the recent war, citizens of a dozen European nations were happy to meet Smiths, Cartiers, O'Haras, Schultzes, di Salvos, Cohens, and Sklodowskas and all the others in our armies. Each nation could share in our victories because its "sons" had helped win them. How much of this good feeling was dissipated when they found virulent prejudice among some of our troops is impossible to say.

We cannot escape the fact that our civil rights record has been an issue in world politics. The world's press and radio are full of it. This Committee has seen a multitude of samples. We and our friends have been, and are, stressing our achievements. Those with competing philosophies have stressed—and are shamelessly distorting—our shortcomings. They have not only tried to create hostility toward us among specific nations, races, and religious groups. They have tried to prove our democracy an empty fraud, and our nation a consistent oppressor of underprivileged people. This may seem ludicrous to Americans, but it is sufficiently important to worry our friends. The following United Press dispatch from London proves that (*Washington Post*, May 25, 1947):

> Although the Foreign Office reserved comment on recent lynch activities in the Carolinas, British diplomatic circles said privately today that they have played into the hands of Communist propagandists in Europe. . . .
>
> Diplomatic circles said the two incidents of mob violence would provide excellent propaganda ammunition for Communist agents who have been decrying America's brand of "freedom" and "democracy."

The international reason for acting to secure our civil rights now is not to win the approval of our totalitarian critics. We would not expect it if our

record were spotless; to them our civil rights record is only a convenient weapon with which to attack us. Certainly we would like to deprive them of that weapon. But we are more concerned with the good opinion of the peoples of the world. Our achievements in building and maintaining a state dedicated to the fundamentals of freedom have already served as a guide for those seeking the best road from chaos to liberty and prosperity. But it is not indelibly written that democracy will encompass the world. We are convinced that our way of life—the free way of life—holds a promise of hope for all people. We have what is perhaps the greatest responsibility ever placed upon a people to keep this promise alive. Only still greater achievements will do it.

The United States is not so strong, the final triumph of the democratic ideal is not so inevitable that we can ignore what the world thinks of us or our record.

Mr. President:

Your Committee has reviewed the American heritage and we have found in it again the great goals of human freedom and equality under just laws. We have surveyed the flaws in the nation's record and have found them to be serious. We have considered what government's appropriate role should be in the securing of our rights, and have concluded that it must assume greater leadership.

We believe that the time for action is now. Our recommendations for bringing the United States closer to its historic goal follow.

Source: *To Secure These Rights: The Report of the President's Committee on Civil Rights* (Washington, DC: Printing Office, 1947), 139–50.

~

A. Philip Randolph Urges Civil Disobedience against a Jim Crow Army

The move toward reintroducing the draft in 1948 as the Cold War developed raised once again the issue of segregation in the U.S. armed forces. A. Philip Randolph and Grant Reynolds organized a Committee against Jim Crow in Military Service and Training and took up the issue that had been part of the program of the March on Washington Movement since 1941. In meetings with President Truman and statements to the Senate Armed Services Committee, they warned that they would lead a massive civil disobedience campaign and urge African Americans not to register for a draft while segregation persisted. In this extract Randolph spells out their position and makes interesting references both to the protest methods of Gandhi in India and to the Cold War situation.

Today I should like to make clear to the Senate Armed Services Committee and through you, to Congress and the American people that passage now of a jimcrow draft may only result in a mass civil disobedience movement along the lines of the magnificent struggles of the people of India against British imperialism. I must emphasize that the current agitation for civil rights is no longer a mere expression of hope on the part of Negroes. On the one hand, it is a positive, resolute outreaching for full manhood. On the other hand, it is an equally determined will to stop acquiescing in anything less. Negroes demand full, unqualified first-class citizenship.

In resorting to the principles of direct-action techniques of Gandhi, whose death was publicly mourned by many members of Congress and President Truman, Negroes will be serving a higher law than any passed by a national legislature in an era when racism spells our doom. They will be serving a law higher than any decree of the Supreme Court which in the famous Winfred Lynn case evaded ruling on the flagrantly illegal segregation practiced under the wartime Selective Service Act. In refusing to accept compulsory military segregation, Negro youth will be serving their fellow men throughout the world.

I feel qualified to make this claim because of a recent survey of American psychologists, sociologists and anthropologists. The survey revealed an overwhelming belief among these experts that enforced segregation on racial or religious lines has serious and detrimental psychological effects both on the segregated groups and on those enforcing segregation. Experts from the South, I should like to point out, gentlemen, were as positive as those from other sections of the country as to the harmful effects of segregation. The views of these social scientists were based on scientific research and on their own professional experience.

So long as the Armed Services propose to enforce such universally harmful segregation not only here at home but also overseas, Negro youth have a moral obligation not to lend themselves as world-wide carriers of an evil and hellish doctrine. Secretary of the Army Kenneth C. Royall clearly indicated in the New Jersey National Guard situation that the Armed Services do have every intention of prolonging their anthropologically hoary and untenable policies.

For 25 years now the myth has been carefully cultivated that Soviet Russia has ended all discrimination and intolerance, while here at home the American Communists have skillfully posed as champions of minority groups. To the rank-and-file Negro in World War II, Hitler's racism posed a sufficient threat for him to submit to the jimcrow Army abuses. But this factor of

minority group persecution in Russia is not present, as a popular issue, in the power struggle between Stalin and the United States. I can only repeat that this time Negroes will not take a jimcrow draft lying down. The conscience of the world will be shaken as by nothing else when thousands and thousands of us second-class Americans choose imprisonment in preference to permanent military slavery.

While I cannot with absolute certainty claim results at this hour, I personally will advise Negroes to refuse to fight as slaves for a democracy they cannot possess and cannot enjoy. Let me add that I am speaking only for myself, not even for the Committee Against Jimcrow in Military Service and Training, since I am not sure that all its members would follow my position. But Negro leaders in close touch with GI grievances would feel derelict in their duty if they did not support such a justified civil disobedience movement—especially those of us whose age would protect us from being drafted. Any other course would be a betrayal of those who place their trust in us. I personally pledge myself to openly counsel, aid and abet youth, both white and Negro, to quarantine any jimcrow conscription system, whether it bear the label of UMT or Selective Service.

I shall tell youth of all races not to be tricked by any euphonious election-year registration for a draft. This evasion, which the newspapers increasingly discuss as a convenient way out for Congress, would merely presage a synthetic "crisis" immediately after November 2nd when all talk of equality and civil rights would be branded unpatriotic while the induction machinery would move into high gear. On previous occasions I have seen the "national emergency" psychology mow down legitimate Negro demands.

From coast to coast in my travels I shall call upon all Negro veterans to join this civil disobedience movement and to recruit their younger brothers in an organized refusal to register and be drafted. Many veterans, bitter over Army jimcrow, have indicated that they will act spontaneously in this fashion, regardless of any organized movement. "Never again," they say with finality.

I shall appeal to the thousands of white youth in schools and colleges who are today vigorously shedding the prejudices of their parents and professors. I shall urge them to demonstrate their solidarity with Negro youth by ignoring the entire registration and induction machinery. And finally I shall appeal to Negro parents to lend their moral support to their sons—to stand behind them as they march with heads high to federal prisons as a telling demonstration to the world that Negroes have reached the limit of human endurance—that is, in the words of the spiritual, we'll be buried in our graves before we will be slaves.

May I, in conclusion, Mr. Chairman, point out that political maneuvers have made this drastic program our last resort. Your party, the party of Lincoln, solemnly pledged in its 1944 platform a full-fledged Congressional investigation of injustices to Negro soldiers. Instead of that long overdue probe, the Senate Armed Services Committee on this very day is finally hearing testimony from two or three Negro veterans for a period of 20 minutes each. The House Armed Services Committee and Chairman Andrews went one step further and arrogantly refused to hear any at all! Since we cannot obtain an adequate Congressional forum for our grievances, we have no other recourse but to tell our story to the peoples of the world by organized direct action. I don't believe that even a wartime censorship wall could be high enough to conceal news of a civil disobedience program. If we cannot win your support for your own Party commitments, if we cannot ring a bell in you by appealing to human decency, we shall command your respect and the respect of the world by our united refusal to cooperate with tyrannical injustice.

Since the military, with their Southern biases, intend to take over America and institute total encampment of the populace along jimcrow lines, Negroes will resist with the power of non-violence, with the weapons of moral principles, with the good-will weapons of the spirit, yes with the weapons that brought freedom to India. I feel morally obligated to disturb and keep disturbed the conscience of jimcrow America. In resisting the insult of jimcrowism to the soul of black America, we are helping to save the soul of America. And let me add that I am opposed to Russian totalitarian communism and all its works. I consider it a menace to freedom. I stand by democracy as expressing the Judean-Christian ethic. But democracy and Christianity must be boldly and courageously applied for all men regardless of race, color, creed or country.

We shall wage a relentless warfare against jimcrow without hate or revenge for the moral and spiritual progress and safety of our country, world peace and freedom.

Finally let me say that Negroes are just sick and tired of being pushed around and we just don't propose to take it, and we do not care what happens.

Source: "Testimony of A. Philip Randolph, National Treasurer of the Committee against Jim Crow in Military Service and Training and President of the Brotherhood of Sleeping Car Porters, AFL, Prepared for Delivery before the Senate Armed Services Committee Wednesday, March 31, 1948," mimeograph, copy in CORE Archives, State Historical Society of Wisconsin. Printed by permission of the Wisconsin Historical Society.

⌣

Executive Order 9981:
Desegregation of the Armed Forces (1948)

In response to Randolph's campaign against segregation in the armed forces, and following the report of the President's Committee on Civil Rights, President Truman issued an executive order confirming that the policy of equality of treatment would be enforced in the U.S. armed forces. Although not specifically excluding segregation, this order began the process of integration in the military, confirming developments already under way in some branches of the services. Undoubtedly also crucial to the president's decision was the fact that this was an election year.

Establishing the President's Committee on Equality of Treatment and Opportunity in the Armed Forces

WHEREAS it is essential that there be maintained in the armed services of the United States the highest standards of democracy, with equality of treatment and opportunity for all those who serve in our country's defense:

NOW THEREFORE, by virtue of the authority vested in me as President of the United States, by the Constitution and the statutes of the United States, and as Commander in Chief of the armed services, it is hereby ordered as follows:

1. It is hereby declared to be the policy of the President that there shall be equality of treatment and opportunity for all persons in the armed services without regard to race, color, religion or national origin. This policy shall be put into effect as rapidly as possible, having due regard to the time required to effectuate any necessary changes without impairing efficiency or morale.
2. There shall be created in the National Military Establishment an advisory committee to be known as the President's Committee on Equality of Treatment and Opportunity in the Armed Services, which shall be composed of seven members to be designated by the President.
3. The Committee is authorized on behalf of the President to examine into the rules, procedures and practices of the Armed Services in order to determine in what respect such rules, procedures and practices may be altered or improved with a view to carrying out the policy of this order. The Committee shall confer and advise the Secretary of Defense, the Secretary of the Army, the Secretary of the Navy, and the Secretary of the Air Force, and shall make such recommendations to the President and to said Secretaries as in the judgment of the Committee will effectuate the policy hereof.

4. All executive departments and agencies of the Federal Government are authorized and directed to cooperate with the Committee in its work, and to furnish the Committee such information or the services of such persons as the Committee may require in the performance of its duties.

5. When requested by the Committee to do so, persons in the armed services or in any of the executive departments and agencies of the Federal Government shall testify before the Committee and shall make available for use of the Committee such documents and other information as the Committee may require.

6. The Committee shall continue to exist until such time as the President shall terminate its existence by Executive order.

Harry Truman
The White House
July 26, 1948
Source: "Executive Order 9981," Truman Library, www.trumanlibrary.org/9981a.htm.

⟳

Walter White Offers a Retrospective View of the War and Postwar Years

Walter White played a major role in the early civil rights movement as assistant secretary, field secretary, and finally executive secretary of the NAACP through the 1920s to the 1940s. His autobiography provides a not always full account of developments before and during the war years. In this extract from the final chapter, he offers a view of the advances made.

All Shadows Are Dark
As my father lay dying in a jimcrow hospital in Atlanta he put into words for my brother and me the faith which had sustained him throughout his life. "Human kindness, decency, love, whatever you wish to call it," he said, "is the only real thing in the world. It is a dynamic, not a passive, emotion. It's up to you two, and others like you, to use your education and talents in an effort to make love as positive an emotion in the world as are prejudice and hate. That's the only way the world can save itself. Don't forget that. No matter what happens, you must love, not hate."

I have remembered that. I have remembered that when, sitting in the gallery of the House or the Senate, I have heard members of our Congress rise and spill diatribe and vilification on the Negroes. I have remembered it when the Negroes were condemned as utter failures in soldiering.

I remembered it when I talked with my nephew for the last time, as he lay in a bitterly cold, rain-drenched tent on the edge of the Capodichina airfield near Naples. He was a Georgia boy, the youngest of four children. His father, like mine, was a mail carrier. He, like me, could have passed for a white man. By sacrifice and labor his parents provided him with a college education. He won a master's degree in economics, and the next day enlisted in the Army Air Forces, as a Negro. He went to the segregated field at Tuskegee, Alabama.

He hated war, he loathed killing. But he believed that Hitler and Mussolini represented the kind of hate he had seen exhibited in Georgia by the Ku Klux Klan and the degenerate political demagogues. He believed that the war would bring all of that hate to an end. He was a fighter pilot. He fought well. Over the Anzio beachhead he was shot down, bailing out and escaping with his right leg broken in two places. He was offered an opportunity to return home but he refused it. "I'll stick it out until the war is finished or I am," he told a friend. Later, returning from a bomber escort mission to Germany, his plane lost altitude over Hungary, was fired upon by antiaircraft batteries, and was seen striking a tree and bursting into flames. That was the end of one of the men Senator Eastland of Mississippi described as "utter and dismal failures in combat in Europe."

It would be easy to grow bitter over such things, but in remembering my nephew and our last conversation, in which he asked me whether the war would really bring an end to prejudice and race hatred, I remember also the Negro corporal of an engineers unit, who said to me, "This is the only work they would give me, but I don't mind. We learn a trade; we do constructive work. The combat soldiers are taught how to kill. It will bother them. It will stick with them. It will have no effect on us. We will not have to unlearn it."

There have been times when I have felt with a sweep of fear that the patience of the colored man is close to its end. I remember the clamoring stillness and the blood heat of a day in Georgia. I remember how I felt when I stood beside my father and feared that the whites would not let me live, that I must kill them first and then be killed.

Yet I know, I know, I know that there is no reason for this killing, this hatred, this demarcation. There is no difference between the killer and the

killed. Black is white and white is black. When one shoots the other he kills his reflection. Only hate, the negative force, can separate them; only love, the positive force, can bind them together.

I am one of the two in the color of my skin; I am the other in my spirit and my heart. It is only a love of both which binds the two together in me, and it is only love for each other which will join them in the common aims of civilization that lie before us. I love one for the sins she has committed and the fight she has made to conquer them—and conquer them, in great degree, she has. I love the other for her patience and her sorrows, for the soft sound of her singing, and for the great dawn which is coming upon her, in which her vigor and her faith will serve the world.

I am white and I am black, and know that there is no difference. Each casts a shadow, and all shadows are dark.
Source: "All Shadows Are Dark," in A Man Called White (New York: The Viking Press 1948), 365–66. Printed by kind permission of Mrs Jane White Viazzi.

⌢

Alexander J. Allen Looks Back at the Legacy of World War II

Alexander Allen went to work in Baltimore in 1942 as industrial relations director for the Baltimore Urban League, working to open up job opportunities for African Americans. Due to the demands of war, employment of blacks in manufacturing industries in Baltimore rose from nine thousand to thirty-six thousand between 1942 and 1944. Allen looks back at the war's overall impact on African Americans and race relations.

I'd say World War II was a watershed for blacks. Up to that point the doors to industrial and economic opportunity were largely closed. Under the pressures of the war, the pressures of governmental policy, the pressures of world opinion, the pressures of blacks themselves and their allies, all of this began to change. You get a new beginning in a sense. After World War II people began to relate to each other in a different way.

Prior to the war it was believed, particularly by whites, that it was impossible for blacks and whites to work together, or to live in the same neighborhoods, or to use the same public facilities. We used to have an expression during that period—"You learn what you live." Preaching, teaching, is not too effective, but if you actually live it, then you learn. So, our objective was not to get a chance to preach at people so much as it was to influence policy—policy decisions that resulted in people being thrown together on a

peer basis, so that out of that experience their attitudes would change, and they usually did.

After the war was over, then some of the earlier divisions in our society began to be felt again. The old rules for minorities began to apply: last hired, first fired. That meant a disproportionate loss for blacks. But there certainly were some lasting benefits that came out of the experience. The war forced the federal government to take a stronger position with reference to discrimination, and things began to change as a result. There was also a tremendous attitudinal change that grew out of the war. There had been a new experience for blacks, and many weren't willing to go back to the way it was before. That laid the basis for change later on. I think that *Brown v. Board of Education*, the 1954 Supreme Court case that began the dismantling of the segregated school system in this country, was a logical and perhaps predictable outgrowth of the trends started during the war.

Source: Mark Jonathan Harris, Franklin Mitchell, and Steven Schecter, eds., *The Homefront: America during World War II* (New York: G. P. Putnam's Sons, 1984), 252–53. Printed by kind permission of Mark Jonathan Harris, Distinguished Professor, University of Southern California.

Notes

Overview

1. www.whitehouse.gov/the_press_office/Remarks-by-the-President-at-D-Day-65th-Anniversary-Ceremony/.

Introduction

1. Published in *Douglass' Monthly*, August 1863, and available at "Should the Negro Enlist in the Union Army? [July 6, 1863]," Marxists Internet Archive, www.marxists.org/history/etol/newspape/fi/vol07/no09/freddoug.htm#s2 (accessed October 2, 2009).

2. Walter White, "The Right to Fight for Democracy," *Survey Graphic* 21, no. 11 (November 1942): 473.

Chapter 1

1. Studs Terkel, *Hard Times* (New York: Avon Books, 1971), 60. Printed by permission Donadio & Olson Inc. Copyright 1970 Studs Terkel.

2. Michelle A. Palmer, *Radicalism and Sedition among Negroes as Reflected in Their Publications*, Exhibit no. 10, Senate Documents, vol. 12, 66th Congress, 1st Session, 1919, included in *New York Times*, November 23, 1919, 21.

3. Maya Angelou, *I Know Why the Caged Bird Sings* (London: Virago, 1991), 48.

Chapter 2

1. In *Opportunity* 22, no. 3 (July–September 1944): 114.

2. *Pittsburgh Courier*, December 14, 1940.

3. Selective Service System, *Special Groups: Special Monograph No. 10* (Washington, DC: Government Printing Office, 1953), 41–44.

4. Press release, October 9, 1940, 93:4, Franklin D. Roosevelt Library, Hyde Park, New York.

5. Walter White, *A Man Called White* (New York: Viking Press, 1948), 187.

6. *Baltimore Afro-American*, October 10, 1942.

7. Press release, National Committee for Winfred Lynn, Lynn file, Schomburg Collection, New York.

8. This account of the meeting with Roosevelt is based on White, *A Man Called White*, 191–92.

9. White, *A Man Called White*, 191–92.

10. Herbert Garfinkle, *When Negroes March: The March on Washington Movement in the Organizational Politics for FEPC* (New York: Atheneum, 1969), 63.

11. *Chicago Defender*, July 3, 1943.

12. Col. E. R. Householder at the Conference of Negro Newspaper Representatives, Munitions Building, Washington, D.C., December 8, 1941, in Office of Assistant Secretary of War (OASW) 273, National Archives Record Group (NARG), 107.

13. C. L. R. James quoted in Maggi M. Morehouse, *Fighting in the Jim Crow Army: Black Men and Women Remember World War II* (Lanham, MD: Rowman & Littlefield Publishers, 2000), 18.

Chapter 3

1. In *Opportunity* 22, no. 3 (July–September 1944): 114.

2. Witter Bynner, "Defeat," in *Take Away the Darkness* (New York: Alfred Knopf, 1947), 12.

3. Ulysses G. Lee, *The Employment of Negro Troops, U.S. Army in World War II, Special Studies 8* (Washington, DC: Office of the Chief of Military History, United States Army, 1966), 348–79 (chapter 12).

4. Gunnar Myrdal, *An American Dilemma: The Negro Problem and Modern Democracy* (New York: Harper, 1944), 1006–7.

5. "On God's Side," *New York Times*, May 16, 1942, 14.

6. Mary Penick Motley, ed. *The Invisible Soldier: The Experience of the Black Soldier in World War II* (Detroit, MI: Wayne State University Press, 1975), 266.

7. Charity Adams Earley, *One Woman's Army: A Black Officer Remembers the WAC* (College Station: Texas A&M University, 1989), 154.

8. Quoted in Earley, *One Woman's Army*, 151.

9. Manfred Berg, *"Ticket to Freedom"*: *The NAACP and the Struggle for Black Political Integration* (Gainesville: University Press of Florida, 2005), 95.

Chapter 4

1. Mark Jonathan Harris, Franklin Mitchell, and Steven Schecter, eds. *The Homefront: America during World War II* (New York: G. P. Putnam's Sons, 1984), 98.

2. Gunnar Myrdal, *An American Dilemma: The Negro Problem and Modern Democracy* (New York: Harper, 1944), 997.

3. Robert C. Weaver, *Negro Labor: A National Problem* (New York: Harcourt Brace, 1946), 78.

4. Sybil Lewis, in Harris, Mitchell, and Schecter, *The Homefront*, 251.

5. Karen T. Anderson, "Last Hired, First Fired: Black Women Workers during World War II," *Journal of American History* 69, no. 1 (June 1982): 24.

6. William Barber in Harris, Mitchell, and Schecter, *The Homefront*, 101–4.

7. Chester Himes, *If He Hollers, Let Him Go* (1945), (Serpent's Tail, 1999), 4.

8. Langston Hughes, "Roland Hayes Beaten" in *One Way Ticket* (New York: Alfred Knopf, 1949), 86; published as "Warning" in *The Collected Poems of Langston Hughes*, edited by Arnold Rampersad and David Roessel, copyright 1994 by the Estate of Langston Hughes. Used by permission of Alfred A. Knopf, a division of Random House, Inc.

9. Robin Kelley, "Congested Terrain: Resistance on Public Transportation," chapter 3 in *Race Rebels: Culture, Politics, and the Black Working Class* (New York: The Free Press, 1996), 55–77.

10. Malcolm X with the assistance of Alex Haley, *The Autobiography of Malcolm X* (Harmondsworth, Middlesex: Penguin Books, 1968), 156, 193–96.

11. Kenneth B. Clark and James Barker, "The Zoot Effect in Personality: A Race Riot Participant," *Journal of Abnormal and Social Psychology* 40, no. 2 (April 1945): 145.

12. Flora Bryant Brown, "NAACP Sponsored Sit-in by Howard University Students in Washington, D.C., 1943–1944," *Journal of Negro History* 85, no. 4 (2000): 279–80.

Chapter 5

1. William Faulkner in Joseph Blotner, ed., *Selected Letters* (New York: Random House, 1977), 175–76.

2. Robert Cooper Howard in Jay MacLeod, *Minds Stayed on Freedom: The Civil Rights Struggle in the Rural South, An Oral History* (Boulder, CO: Westview Press, 1991), 94.

3. Neil R. McMillen, "How Mississippi's Black Veterans Remember World War II," in *Remaking Dixie: The Impact of World War II on the American South*, ed. Neil R. McMillen (Jackson: University Press of Mississippi, 1997), 103.

4. John Egerton, *Speak Now against the Day: The Generation before the Civil Rights Movement in the South* (Chapel Hill: University of North Carolina Press, 1994), 365.

5. *Baltimore Afro-American*, May 26, 1945.

6. Myrlie Evers-Williams and Manning Marable, eds., *The Autobiography of Medgar Evers* (New York: Civitas Books, 2005), 7.

7. Quoted in Egerton, *Speak Now against the Day*, 327.

8. Lyndon Johnson quoted in Nicholas Lemann, *The Promised Land: The Great Black Migration and How It Changed America* (New York: Alfred Knopf, 1991), 136.

9. Michael R. Gardner, *Harry Truman and Civil Rights: Moral Courage and Political Risks* (Carbondale: Southern Illinois University Press, 2002), 71–87.

~

Annotated Bibliography

The now enormous amount of primary and secondary source material dealing with the African American experience in World War II is leading to a great deal of new scholarship. Probably the most important archive collection is the Papers of the National Association for the Advancement of Colored People (NAACP) in the Library of Congress. This also includes the papers of William H. Hastie, the NAACP legal counsel and civilian aide to the secretary of war from 1941 to 1943. The papers of the NAACP executive secretary, Walter White, are in the Beinecke Library at Yale University. The Library of Congress also holds the papers of the National Urban League (NUL) and Lester B. Granger, as well as of A. Philip Randolph and Bayard Rustin. Unfortunately most of the papers relating to the March on Washington Movement (MOWM) appear to have been destroyed. However, relevant material can be found in the records of government agencies in the National Archives, particularly the records of the Fair Employment Practice Committee (FEPC). FBI records also contain material relating to Randolph as well as to many other smaller organizations and lesser-known individuals—some of this is published in Robert A. Hill, ed., *The FBI's RACON: Racial Conditions in the United States during World War II* (Boston: Northeastern University Press, 1995).

Many aspects of wartime life relating to African Americans can be found in the National Archives records of the War Manpower Commission, Office of the Assistant Secretary of War, Selective Service System, and War Department. The records of the various branches of the armed services can also be found in the National Archives at College Park, Maryland. A useful published collection is by Bernard C. Nalty and Morris J. MacGregor, eds., *Blacks in the Military: Essential Documents* (Wilmington, DE: Scholarly Resources, 1981). The presidential papers of Franklin D. Roosevelt and Harry S. Truman and the papers of Eleanor Roosevelt also contain

a great deal of relevant correspondence, records of meetings, newspaper clippings, and other materials.

Relevant biographical and other information is often provided in John A. Garraty and Mark Carnes, eds., *The American National Biography* (New York: Oxford University Press, 1999), available online at www.anb.org. The Columbia Oral History Center in New York has a great deal of relevant material, and published oral histories—such as Mark Jonathan Harris et al. eds., *The Homefront: America during World War II* (New York: G. P. Putnam's Sons, 1984), William H. Chafe, *Remembering Jim Crow: African Americans Tell about Life in the Segregated South* (New York: New Press, 2001), and Studs Terkel's classic *"The Good War": An Oral History of World War II* (New York: Pantheon Books, 1984)—include a number of black contributors. Autobiographies by key figures from the period are few, but Walter White, *A Man Called White* (New York: Viking Press, 1948), is useful, if not always as full and frank as one might hope. Similarly, Truman K. Gibson Jr., *Knocking Down Barriers: My Fight for Black America, a Memoir* (Evanston, IL: Northwestern University Press, 2005), gives a more positive view of Gibson's role as Hastie's successor as civilian aide than was commonly held at the time.

The black press provides an invaluable source, and newspapers like the *Baltimore Afro-American*, *Chicago Defender*, and *Pittsburgh Courier*, major sources of influence during the war, have become subjects of historical study themselves in Lee Finkle, *Forum for Protest: The Black Press during World War II* (London: Associated University Presses, 1975), and "The Conservative Aims of Militant Rhetoric: Black Protest during World War II," *Journal of American History* 60, no. 3 (December 1973): 692–713, as well as in Patrick S. Washburn, *A Question of Sedition: The Federal Government's Investigation of the Black Press during World War II* (New York: Oxford University Press, 1986). The NAACP's *The Crisis* magazine, the NUL's *Opportunity: A Journal of Negro Life*, *Black Worker*, and other journals such as *Journal of Negro Education* all contained a great deal of war-related material.

Among the many historical encyclopedias, Nina Mjagkij, ed., *Organizing Black America: An Encyclopedia of African American Associations* (New York: Garland Publishing, 2001), John Phillips Resch and Walter Sargent, eds., *Americans at War: Society, Culture, and the Home Front*, vol. 3 (New York: Macmillan Reference, 2005), James Climent and Thaddeus Russell, eds., *The Home Front Encyclopedia: United States, Britain and Canada in World Wars I and II*, vol. 2, *World War II* (Santa Barbara, CA: ABC-Clio, 2007), and Jonathan D. Sutherland, ed., *African Americans at War. An Encyclopedia* (Santa Barbara, CA: ABC-Clio, 2003), provide useful basic information on a variety of individuals, organizations, and subjects.

A number of general surveys of the American home front offer useful chapters on the subject of the African American experience in World War II. Richard D. Polenberg's *War and Society: The United States, 1941–1945* (Philadelphia: J. B. Lippincott & Co., 1972), was one of the first detailed analyses, followed by John Morton Blum, *V Was for Victory: Politics and American Culture during World War II* (New York: Harcourt Brace Jovanovich, 1976), John W. Jeffries, *Wartime America: The World*

War II Home Front (Chicago: Ivan R. Dee, 1996), Robert J. Norrell, *Dixie's War: The South and World War II* (Tuscaloosa: University of Alabama Press, 1992), William L. O'Neill, *A Democracy at War: American's Fight at Home and Abroad in World War II* (New York: Free Press, 1993), and Alan M. Winkler, *Homefront, U.S.A.: America during World War II* (Arlington Heights, IL: Harlan Davidson, 2000). Alan Clive, *State of War: Michigan in World War II* (Ann Arbor: University of Michigan Press, 1979), focuses on a state in which African Americans played a significant wartime role.

Specific writing on the black experience in World War II has grown considerably over the last thirty years as more archive material has become available. Initially, the key texts were Richard M. Dalfiume's detailed study *Fighting on Two Fronts: Desegregation of the U.S. Armed Forces, 1939–1953* (Columbia: University of Missouri Press, 1969) and his ground-breaking article "The Forgotten Years of the Negro Revolution," *Journal of American History*, 55, no. 1 (June 1968): 90–106. Like Dalfiume, Neil A. Wynn, in *The Afro-American and the Second World War* (New York: Holmes & Meier, 1976, 1993) and "The Impact of the Second World War on the American Negro," *Journal of Contemporary History* 6, no. 2 (1971): 42–53, tend to emphasize the positive impact of the war and its links with the later civil rights movement. While Dalfiume concentrates on the military aspect, Wynn looks at economic, social, and cultural aspects. A. Russell Buchanan, *Black Americans in World War II* (Santa Barbara, CA: Clio Books, 1977), covers similar ground in a survey of African Americans in the military, the judicial system, the status of black women, organized labor, and race violence. Later studies pointing up the less positive aspects of the black war experience and also more critical black voices include Nat Brandt, *Harlem at War: The Black Experience in WWII* (Syracuse, NY: Syracuse University Press, 1997), Dominic Capeci Jr., *Race Relations in Wartime Detroit: The Sojourner Truth Housing Controversy of 1942* (Philadelphia: Temple University Press, 1984), Charles D. Chamberlain, *Victory at Home: Manpower and Race in the American South during World War II* (Athens: University of Georgia Press, 2003), and Neil McMillen, ed., *Remaking Dixie: The Impact of World War II on the American South* (Jackson: University of Mississippi Press, 1997). The essay in this last volume by Harvard Sitkoff, "African American Militancy in the World War Two South: Another Perspective," does much to question the idea of the war as a watershed in civil rights and stresses continuities with earlier years. Sitkoff's study of the 1930s, *A New Deal for Blacks: The Emergence of Civil Rights as a National Issue*, vol. 1, *The Depression Decade* (New York: Oxford University Press, 1978), provides a strong case for this. Nonetheless, the argument in favor of the war as formative in a new emerging movement is made in local studies like Adam Fairclough, *Race and Democracy: The Civil Rights Struggle in Louisiana, 1915–1972* (Athens: University of Georgia Press, 1995), as well as John Egerton, *Speak Now against the Day: The Generation before the Civil Rights Movement in the South* (Chapel Hill: University of North Carolina Press, 1994).

The role of A. Philip Randolph and the MOWM is the focus of Andrew E. Kersten, *A. Philip Randolph: A Life in the Vanguard* (Lanham, MD: Rowman & Littlefield

Publishers, 2007), Jervis Anderson, *A. Philip Randolph: A Biographical Portrait* (New York: Harcourt Brace Jovanovich, 1973), and Paula P. Pfeffer, *A. Philip Randolph: Pioneer of the Civil Rights Movement* (Baton Rouge: Louisiana State University Press, 1990), as well as Beth Tompkins Bates, *Pullman Porters and the Rise of Protest Politics in Black America, 1925–1945* (Chapel Hill: University of North Carolina Press, 2001). The MOWM and FEPC are discussed in detail in Herbert Garfinkel, *When Negroes March: The March on Washington and the Organizational Politics for FEPC* (Glencoe, IL: Free Press, 1959), Andrew E. Kersten, *Race, Jobs and the War: The FEPC in the Midwest, 1941–46* (Urbana: University of Illinois Press, 2000), Daniel Kryder, *Divided Arsenal: Race and the American State during World War II* (Cambridge: Cambridge University Press, 2000), Merl E. Reed, *Seedtime for the Modern Civil Rights Movement: The President's Committee on Fair Employment Practice, 1941–1946* (Baton Rouge: University of Louisiana Press, 1991), and Louis Ruchames, *Race, Jobs and Politics* (New York: Columbia University Press, 1953).

The NAACP is now the subject of a growing number of works, including Manfred Berg, *"Ticket to Freedom": The NAACP and the Struggle for Black Political Integration* (Gainesville: University Press of Florida, 2005), and Gilbert Jonas, *Freedom's Sword: The NAACP and the Struggle against Racism in America, 1909–1969* (New York: Routledge, 2007), and of biographical studies like Kenneth Robert Janken, *White: The Biography of Walter White, Mr. NAACP* (New York: New Press, 2003). Phillip McGuire's short study of William H. Hastie, *He, Too, Spoke for Democracy: Judge Hastie, World War II and the Black Soldier* (Westport, CT: Greenwood Press, 1988), is also of some value. The early history of the Congress on Racial Equality is dealt with briefly in August Meier and Elliott M. Rudwick, *CORE: A Study in the Civil Rights Movement, 1942–1968* (New York: Oxford University Press, 1973). A radical perspective of the black experience is provided in the material collected in C. L. R. James et al., *Fighting Racism in World War II* (New York: Monad Press, 1980). More indirect and individual forms of protest are the subject of Robin D. G. Kelley's thought-provoking article "'We Are Not What We Seem': Rethinking Black Working-Class Opposition in the Jim Crow South," *Journal of American History* 80, no. 1 (December 1993): 75–112.

The African American military experience during the war is now extensively covered in books ranging from general historical surveys and unit histories through to those based on oral histories, personal accounts, and memory. The starting point is the "official" history by Ulysses Lee, *U.S. Army in World War II: Special Studies: The Employment of Negro Troops* (Washington, DC: U.S. Army, Center of Military History, Office of the Chief of Military History, 1966). Jean Byers, *A Study of the Negro in Military Service* (Washington, DC: U.S. Department of Defense, 1950), is also based on official records, as is Morris J. MacGregor, *Integration of the Armed Forces, 1940–1965* (Washington, DC: U.S. Army, Center of Military History, Office of the Chief of Military History, 1981).

General surveys of black military history include Gail L. Buckley, *American Patriots: The Story of Blacks in the Military from the Revolution to Desert Storm* (New

York: Random House, 2001), and Bernard C. Nalty, *Strength for the Fight: A History of Black Americans in the Military* (New York: Free Press, 1986). Among the best studies of African American service in World War II are Bryan D. Booker, *African Americans in the United States Army in World War II* (Jefferson, NC: McFarland, 2008), Charles E. Francis, *The Men Who Changed a Nation: The Tuskegee Airmen* (Boston: Branden Publishing Co., 1988), Phillip McGuire, ed., *Taps for a Jim Crow Army: Letters from Black Soldiers in World War II* (Lexington: University Press of Kentucky, 1993), Sherie Mershon and Steven Schlossman, *Foxholes and Color Lines: Desegregating the U.S. Armed Forces* (Baltimore: Johns Hopkins University Press, 1998), Christopher P. Moore, *Fighting for America: Black Soldiers, the Unsung Heroes of World War II* (New York: One World, 2004), Maggi M. Morehouse, *Fighting in the Jim Crow Army: Black Men and Women Remember World War II* (Lanham, MD: Rowman & Littlefield Publishers, 2000), Mary Penick Motley, ed. *The Invisible Soldier: The Experience of the Black Soldier in World War II* (Detroit, MI: Wayne State University Press, 1975), Lou Potter, William Miles, and Nina Rosenblum, *Liberators: Fighting on Two Fronts in World War II* (New York: Harcourt Brace Jovanovich, 1992), Alan M. Osur, *Blacks in the Army Air Force during World War II: The Problem of Race Relations* (Washington, DC: Government Printing Office, 1977), Stanley Sandler, *Segregated Skies: All-Black Combat Squadrons of WWII* (Washington, DC: Smithsonian Institution Press, 1992), Charles W. Sasser, *The African-American 761st Tank Battalion in World War II: Patton's Panthers* (New York: Pocket Books, 2005), and Lawrence P. Scott and William M. Womack Sr., *Double V: The Civil Rights Struggle of the Tuskegee Airmen* (East Lansing: Michigan State University Press, 1998).

Some narrower studies also provide insight into specific aspects of black military service, such as Phillip McGuire, "Desegregation of the Armed Forces: Black Leadership, Protest and World War II," *Journal of Negro History* 68, no. 2 (spring 1983): 147–58, John Modell, Marc Goulden, and Sigurder Magnusson, "World War II in the Lives of Black Americans: Some Findings and Interpretations," *Journal of American History* 76, no. 3 (December 1989): 830–48, and George Q. Flynn, "Selective Service and American Blacks during World War II," *Journal of Negro History* 69, no. 1 (winter 1984): 14–25. The experience of black service personnel in Britain is the subject of Graham Smith, *When Jim Crow Met John Bull: Black American Soldiers in World War II Britain* (London: Tauris, 1987), and Hondon B. Hargrove looks at experiences of the Ninety-second Infantry in Italy in *Buffalo Soldiers in Italy: Black Americans in World War II* (Jefferson, NC: McFarland & Co., 1985).

Women's service in the military is now also increasingly recognized in Maureen Honey, ed., *Bitter Fruit: African American Women during World War II* (Columbia: University of Missouri Press, 1999), and Martha S. Putney, *When the Nation Was in Need: Blacks in the Women's Army Corps during World War II* (Metuchen, NH: Scarecrow Press, 1992). The autobiographies by Charity Adams Earley, *One Woman's Army: A Black Officer Remembers the WAC* (College Station: Texas A&M University Press, 1996), and Brenda L. Moore, *To Serve My Country, to Serve My Race:*

The Story of the Only African American WACs Stationed Overseas during World War II (New York: New York University Press, 1996), provide stimulating insights.

The impact of the war at home on African Americans has not received quite as much attention as the military aspect, but a number of the general studies and those related to the MOWM, employment, and the FEPC do touch on this. The impact on employment and economic opportunity is examined in Herbert C. Northrup, *Negro Employment in Basic Industry: A Study of Racial Policies in Six Industries* (Philadelphia: University of Pennsylvania, 1970), and in a summary chapter of William H. Harris, *The Harder We Run: Black Workers since the Civil War* (New York: Oxford University Press, 1982).

General and economic trends, including the migration of African Americans during the war, are the subject of Nicholas Lemann, *The Promised Land: The Great Black Migration and How It Changed America* (New York: Alfred Knopf, 1991). Bernard Sternsher, ed., *The Negro in Depression and War: Prelude to Revolution, 1930–1945* (Chicago: Quadrangle Books, 1969), also offers some perspective on related issues. Robert C. Weaver's contemporary studies, *Negro Labor: A National Problem* (New York: Harcourt Brace, 1946) and *The Negro Ghetto* (New York: Harcourt Brace, 1948), are enormously well informed and offer a great deal of insight. A more recent interpretation of the effects of migration and population growth in a northern city can be found in Arnold R. Hirsch, *Making the Second Ghetto: Race and Housing in Chicago, 1940–1960* (Cambridge: Cambridge University, 1983).

Maureen Honey, ed., *Bitter Fruit: African American Women during World War II* (Columbia: University of Missouri Press, 1999), contains a great deal of documentary material on aspects of black women's work experience, and Karen T. Anderson provides a detailed critical view in "Last Hired, First Fired: Black Women Workers during World War II," *Journal of American History* 69, no. 1 (June 1982): 82–93, as does Shirley Ann Wilson Moore in "'Not in Somebody's Kitchen:' African American Women Workers in Richmond, California, and the Impact of World War II," in *Writing the Range: Race, Class, and Culture in the Women's West*, ed. Elizabeth Jameson and Susan Armitage (Norman: University of Oklahoma Press, 1997). Lisa K. Boehm, *Making a Way Out of No Way: African American Women and the Second Great Migration* (Jackson: University of Mississippi Press, 2009), also includes much relevant material.

Labor unions and African Americans during the war are dealt with in Nelson Lichtenstein, *Labor's War at Home: The CIO in World War II* (Cambridge: Cambridge University Press, 1982), Bruce Nelson, "Organized Labor and the Struggle for Black Equality in Mobile during World War II," *Journal of American History* 80 (December 1993): 952–88, Robert J. Norrell, "Caste in Steel: Jim Crow Careers in Birmingham, Alabama," *Journal of American History* 73, no. 3 (December 1986): 669–94, and Allan Winkler, "The Philadelphia Transit Strike of 1944," *Journal of American History* 59, no. 2 (June 1972): 73–89.

Race riots are the subject of Robert M. Fogelson, *Violence as Protest: A Study of Riots and Ghettos* (Garden City, NY: Doubleday & Co., 1971), and Arthur I. Waskow's

broad comparative study, *From Race Riot to Sit-in: 1919 and the 1960s* (Garden City, NY: Doubleday & Co., 1967). More specific focus is provided in Dominic J. Capeci Jr., *The Harlem Riot of 1943* (Philadelphia: Temple University Press, 1977), Dominic J. Capeci and Martha Wilkerson, *Layered Violence: The Detroit Rioters of 1943* (Jackson: University of Mississippi Press, 1991), and Robert Shogan and Tom Craig, *The Detroit Race Riot: A Study in Violence* (New York: Chilton Books, 1964). More recently attention was turned to the Los Angeles "zoot suit riots" in Luis Alvarez, *The Power of the Zoot: Youth Culture and Resistance during World War II* (Berkeley: University of California Press, 2008), and Kevin Allen Leonard, *The Battle for Los Angeles: Racial Ideology and World War II* (Albuquerque: University of New Mexico Press, 2006).

Race relations in the postwar period and Truman years are examined in William C. Berman, *The Politics of Civil Rights in the Truman Administration* (Columbus: Ohio State University Press, 1970), Michael R. Gardner, *Harry Truman and Civil Rights: Moral Courage and Political Risks* (Carbondale: Southern Illinois University Press, 2002), Donald R. McCoy and Richard T. Ruetten, *Quest and Response: Minority Rights and the Truman Administration* (Lawrence: University Press of Kansas, 1973), Mary L. Dudziak, *Cold War Civil Rights: Race and the Image of American Democracy* (Princeton, NJ: Princeton University Press, 2000), and Brenda Gayle Plummer, *Rising Wind: Black Americans and U.S. Foreign Affairs, 1935–1960* (Chapel Hill: University of North Carolina Press, 1996). Gunnar Myrdal's *An American Dilemma: The Negro Problem and Modern Democracy* (New York: Harper, 1944), was enormously influential during and after the war and is a useful source of detailed information on the situation of the African American population in the 1930s and 1940s. Walter A. Jackson, *Gunnar Myrdal and America's Conscience* (Chapel Hill: University of North Carolina Press, 1994), offers a useful interpretation of this influential author.

Index

~

About the Author

Neil A. Wynn is professor of twentieth-century American history at the University of Gloucestershire. He previously taught for many years at the University of Glamorgan, Wales, and on international programs at Central Missouri State University and at the Maastricht (now Middleburg) Center for Transatlantic Studies in The Netherlands. He is the author of *Historical Dictionary of the Roosevelt-Truman Era* (2008), *Historical Dictionary from the Great War to the Great Depression* (2003), *The Afro American and the Second World War* (1976, 1993), *From Progressivism to Prosperity: World War I and American Society* (1986), and various articles on African American and American history and culture, and chapters on "The 1940s" and "The 1960s" in Willi Paul Adams, ed., *Die Vereinigten Staaten von Amerika* (*The United States of America*) (1977). He also coedited *America's Century: Perspectives on U.S. History since 1900* (1993), and edited *"Cross the Water Blues": African American Music in Europe* (2007).